TAX EVASION
AND THE
RULE OF LAW
IN
LATIN AMERICA

MARCELO BERGMAN

TAX EVASION
AND THE
RULE OF LAW
IN
LATIN AMERICA

THE POLITICAL CULTURE
OF
CHEATING AND COMPLIANCE
IN ARGENTINA AND CHILE

THE PENNSYLVANIA STATE UNIVERSITY PRESS
UNIVERSITY PARK, PENNSYLVANIA

Library of Congress Cataloging-in-Publication Data

Bergman, Marcelo.
Tax evasion and the rule of law in Latin America :
the political culture of cheating and compliance in
Argentina and Chile / Marcelo Bergman.
p.   cm.
Includes bibliographical references and index.
Summary: "Compares the tax systems in Argentina
and Chile. Examines differences in law abidance between
the two countries and the effectiveness of legal
enforcement"—Provided by publisher.
ISBN 978-0-271-03562-8 (cloth : alk. paper)
1. Tax evasion—Argentina.
2. Tax evasion—Chile.
3. Taxpayer compliance—Argentina.
4. Taxpayer compliance—Chile.
5. Tax administration and procedure—Argentina.
6. Tax administration and procedure—Chile.
7. Taxation—Law and legislation—Argentina.
8. Taxation—Law and legislation—Chile.
I. Title.

KH917.B47   2009
345.82'02338—dc22
2009010761

The Pennsylvania State University Press is a member of
the Association of American University Presses.

It is the policy of The Pennsylvania State University Press
to use acid-free paper. Publications on uncoated stock
satisfy the minimum requirements of American National
Standard for Information Sciences—Permanence of
Paper for Printed Library Material, ANSI Z39.48—1992.

This book is printed on Natures Natural, which
contains 50% post-consumer waste.

CONTENTS

FIGURES AND TABLES

Figures

Tables

PREFACE AND ACKNOWLEDGMENTS

When Benjamin Disraeli, the distinguished British prime minister, pronounced his maxim that there are two inevitabilities in life, death and taxation, he surely did not have the Argentines in mind. Indeed, the inhabitants of the pampas have yet to find a way to avoid death, but they have certainly mastered the art of avoiding taxes. On the other side of the Andes Mountains, the human genome of the Chileans is no different from that of the Argentines. And although for some Chileans taxes are as evitable as for the Argentines, for most of them taxes are much more serious and unavoidable. Human behavior, and not genetics, explains tax evasion.

Tax compliance is one of the central political and social behaviors in modern states. The willingness of citizens to comply with tax laws reflects several features of social and political life: the ability of central governments to enforce laws, the level of a government's legitimacy, and the extent of social solidarity, among others. Yet compliance with tax laws depends on many personal and elusive decisions, which are embedded in a wide range of social processes. Culture, perceptions of law enforcement, and self-interest constrain an individual's decision to comply with tax laws. In *Tax Evasion and the Rule of Law in Latin America*, I argue that tax compliance should be understood as an outcome of individual decisions based on socially determined self-interests. This has crucial implications for public policies and governance.

By systematically studying taxation as law, this book contributes to the understanding of a much broader problem, the rule of law. I empirically show how enforcement operates under favorable or adverse conditions, and how culture preconditions and limits the success of state measures. In this study, I provide answers to two important concerns of social scientists studying the developing world: Why are rules consistently violated? And what are the conditions that make norms and policies viable?

I have studied and lived in four very different countries for extended periods, speaking several languages and engaging with different cultures.

One of the most challenging questions that I pondered over the years is how social orders come to embrace norms, to cooperate and undertake difficult social endeavors for the welfare of the people. Conversely, I was puzzled that certain societies fail to develop the tools for distributive justice. This book is a response to years of observation and personal engagement. Combining strong empirical research and sound methods, I invite readers to rethink models of social cooperation and to envision intellectual reflection and novel practices that will enhance fairness and welfare.

I began this journey more than ten years ago with a desire to uncover the paradoxical, split paths of many developing and developed nations regarding their ability to foster cooperative behavior and adherence to norms. From the early stages of this research I had, and still have, a strong conviction that the riddle of compliance and legal behavior has to be tested empirically. I firmly believe that data must be produced if it is not available. A large part of this project has been the relentless pursuit of the best available data to study these problems.

I would like first to acknowledge my mentor, professor Carlos Waisman from UC San Diego, who guided me through the many phases of my dissertation. Carlos's unflagging perfectionism, coupled with his trust in me and in this project, was essential to the definition of my dissertation and all my ensuing research. A special recognition goes to professor Joseph Gusfield, who introduced me to the novel world of sociology of law. My teachers and colleagues at the Hebrew University of Jerusalem, the University of California at San Diego, and the University of Oregon have contributed directly or indirectly to the refinement of my arguments.

The collection of data took five years and many twists. I am indebted to the hundreds of officers at the Chilean and Argentine tax agencies who helped me throughout the process. Special thanks go to current or past officers at both agencies, especially to Carlos Silvani, Horacio Castagnola, and Mario Roselló in Argentina, and to Michel Jorrat and Juan Toro in Chile. Many thanks to Estela Calello, Jaime Etcheberry, Juan Carlos Gomez Sabaini, Alejandro Otero, Antonio Ostornol, Javier Portal, Pablo Serra, and Jorge Trujillo.

Six surveys, laboratory experiments, and extensive tax return data processing required generous financial support. I am indebted first to the tax administrations that embraced part of the project as their own. At different phases, I participated in and directed some of these studies in exchange for the data. Other data collections were financed by generous support from the Ford Foundation, the United Nations Program for Development, and the William and Flora Hewlett Foundation.

Many people have helped me define, revise, sharpen, and fine-tune this book. I want to thank Kent Eaton and an anonymous reviewer at Penn State University Press for very detailed and insightful readings of my book. My appreciation goes to Sandy Thatcher for his very professional and diligent attention to this project, and for the care that he took to make this book the best it could be.

I would not have been able to find a more encouraging institution to house my work than the Centro de Investigación y Docencia Económica (CIDE) in Mexico City. I thank Carlos Elizondo and Blanca Heredia for their professional encouragement from the inception of this project and for sharing my passion for taxes and the rule of law. Enrique Cabrero and Ana Laura Magaloni fully endorsed my work and provided me with extraordinary encouragement. A long list of colleagues and friends have read or discussed chapters and ideas of this book. Sergio Berensztein, Fabrice Lehoucq, James Mahon, Jaime Malamud, Gabriel Negretto, Guillermo O'Donnell, Carlos Rosencrantz, Silvio Waisbord, and Laurence Whitehead stimulated new questions and offered helpful comments. For hours and hours of stimulating debates on taxes, compliances, and the challenges of the rule of law in developing countries, I thank my colleagues at CIDE: Javier Aparicio, David Arellano, Victor Carreon, Gustavo Fondevila, Juan Pablo Guerrero, Fausto Hernandez, Benito Nacif, Rodolfo Sarsfield, Andreas Schedler, John Scott, and Juan Manuel Torres. A special acknowledgment goes to my assistant, Adriana Villalon, for her exceptional support, to Ruth Homrighaus for her professional editing work, to Ruth Halvey for her support with revisions, and to Armando Nevarez for helping me with the data.

My parents deserve special recognition. My mother, Rosa, who passed long before I began this project, gave me her dedication, love, and faith to follow my dreams and pursue this path until the very end. My father, Abraham, has always encouraged me to undertake complex projects. Although neither of them had the privilege of achieving more than a grade-school education, they both taught me perseverance and discipline, and gave me the strength and support to pursue an academic career.

I began this research when my oldest son, Eyal, was cheerfully finishing elementary school, my middle son, Martín, was beginning to be a passionate reader, and my youngest, Adriel, had barely and enthusiastically begun to walk. They have seen me through my highs and lows, and have given me the strength and optimism to complete this work. I want to thank these once-small and now-big creatures for being my genuine inspiration and source of joy.

My special thanks go to Monica, my true love, partner, and friend. She trusted me when no one else did. She supported and guided me through dark and bright days. I thank her for reading, discussing, and helping to edit many versions of this manuscript. Without Monica this book would never have come to life. But, more important, without her I would not have been so happy. That is why, Monica, I dedicate this work to you.

Portions of chapters 2, 4, and 5 were previously published in the *Journal of Social Policy*, the *Journal of Latin American Studies*, the *National Tax Journal*, and the *International Journal of the Sociology of Law*, and are reprinted with permission.

INTRODUCTION

Why do states with similar tax systems have different rates of tax compliance? Why do the citizens of countries with equivalent levels of development, similar macroeconomic policies, and a shared cultural heritage show remarkable differences in their abidance by the law and prescribed rules? This book explains why Chile has been more successful than Argentina in achieving compliance with taxes, and it presents a conceptual framework to account for disparities in law abidance and conformity to rules. In *Tax Evasion and the Rule of Law in Latin America*, I argue that countries with established rule of law traditions, where norms and rules are widely embraced, have better levels of tax compliance and are capable of developing sound fiscal policies. Conversely, countries whose citizens live on the margins of the law face great difficulties in reversing tax evasion, because they are unable to resolve basic collective-action problems. Countries that reach virtuous equilibria between government enforcement and social adherence to norms are better suited to enter a path of development.

Scholars in legal studies, political science, and sociology have studied the role of law in modern states, as well as the social and political benefits of the rule of law. This literature, however, has largely ignored the questions of how law becomes effective, under what conditions stable equilibria are reached, and what mechanisms enable optimal legal behavior. I contend that the effectiveness of law relies heavily on self-enforcement and voluntary compliance, and that citizens comply to the extent that they believe adherence to law represents the best alternative among different possible outcomes. By analyzing the institutionalization of tax behavior, I contribute to an explanation of how voluntary compliance emerges, survives, or fails. Approaching tax compliance from this perspective allows me to uncover many blind spots in traditional theories of voluntary compliance.

Tax evasion is just one of many individual acts that defy the ability of states to enforce enacted laws, and it is found everywhere. What distinguishes most developed countries from developing nations is the magnitude of noncompliance. For example, the value-added tax (VAT) compliance rate for OECD (Organization for Economic Cooperation and Development) countries is in the 70–85 percent range, compared to 45–77 percent for Latin America. But even in countries with similar levels of development, we find vast differences in tax compliance levels. Chile and Argentina have similar tax structures and comparable tax rates and enforcement mechanisms, yet compliance has been far superior in Chile.

Taxpayers in Chile conform better to tax laws in part because they perceive their own tax authorities as more effective and legitimate than Argentines perceive theirs to be. Compliance, however, depends on more than an effective tax administration (TA). Tax evasion has cultural roots in social norms and institutional arrangements. I argue that deterrence is more effective in societies with better norm abidance, because government threats of law enforcement become more credible, thereby nurturing cooperative "compliance equilibria." In countries where norms are not widely upheld and where laws are consistently violated, on the other hand, citizens develop attitudes and beliefs that inhibit their compliance with rules, contributing to the formation of "noncompliance equilibria." The failure to develop a culture of conformity to norms biases individual perceptions and limits the effectiveness of government deterrence, leading taxpayers in noncompliant environments to defy government authorities; these taxpayers believe that noncooperation is rational behavior. In other words, where only suckers get taxed, *it pays to cheat.*

Because nobody likes to pay taxes, there is a need to study the social mechanisms that compel taxpayers to comply in certain environments and to cheat in others; there is also a need to inquire about why similar enforcement yields differences in rule conformance. These questions also have important implications beyond fiscal policies. Tax evasion inhibits the creation of healthy economies and sound paths for development. It is harder for states that fail to elicit high tax compliance to gain wide approval, because the quality of public goods in such states diminishes. Conversely, higher compliance is self-sustaining because it enables sound fiscal policies that promote improved consent.

This book is about cheaters, about suckers, and about legalists. Depending on the interplay of different variables, cheaters will predominate in one society and legalists in others. In the following pages I examine the motivations that lead people to cheat, comply with, or challenge the government in the field of taxes. It presents an in-depth analysis of a large set of data collected exclusively for this project over many years. It includes six new surveys on tax compliance, individual tax-return and tax-enforcement records on more than thirty thousand taxpayers, and an experimental laboratory study with college students in both Chile and Argentina. In order to study how social equilibria operate, the data-driven research on which this study is based evaluates, among other topics, the effect of government enforcement of tax law, the legitimacy of authorities, the scope of deterrence, and the role of culture.

This has larger implications that transcend the field of taxation. At stake is the study of states and societies that seek a clear path for development, for consolidation of democratic regimes, and for pacific resolutions of income distributions and social conflicts. The in-depth investigation of why similar policies and enforcement yield very different outcomes reveals the complexities of developing paths to stability and growth, or to unrest and stagnation.

This book sheds light on at least three central questions debated in the literature. First, how does path dependency operate to enhance or constrain the ability of governments to raise revenues? This is crucial for middle- and low-income nations to enter a development path. In this study, I provide the data and the quantitative approach to explain how culture and social learning affect compliance with laws, and why citizens' compliance is crucial for sustainable growth. Second, this book provides additional insights regarding the nature of the relationship between democracy and taxation. Over the last decades many countries have proceeded on a different track compared to early modern nations such as Britain and the United States, where democracy and taxation developed hand in hand. Re-democratization in countries such as Argentina did not have a meaningful impact on citizens' acquaintance with taxation, and social and political instability is tied to these broader processes. This book investigates the peculiar nature of taxation, which is not firmly grounded in representation and citizenship. Third, by going through the painstaking intricacies of citizens' tax behavior, this study answers broader questions: how laws and institutional arrangements can effectively produce social and political change, under what set of conditions can change be brought about, and what are the limitations of legal entrepreneurship in social change. Although an all-encompassing answer to these questions is outside the scope of this book, I hope to provide a conceptual framework that articulates a preliminary answer to this puzzle.

COMPLIANCE AND EVASION IN CHILE AND ARGENTINA

The Scope of the Problem

Although Argentina and Chile have similar levels of development, tax evasion differs markedly in the two nations. More than 85 percent of taxpayers in Argentina acknowledge that they cheated on their taxes during the previous year, and more than 50 percent admit to failing to pay more than 20 percent of their legally owed taxes. In Chile, on the other hand, fewer than 20 percent of taxpayers admit to cheating on their taxes, and very rarely do they fail to pay less than 80 percent of their true tax dues. Income-tax noncompliance in Argentina exceeds 50 percent of legally expected revenues, and 30 to 50 percent of the expected revenue from the compliance-friendly VAT remains uncollected each year.[1] Social security and payroll taxes fare even worse. In Chile, total noncompliance is estimated at less than 35 percent (Barra and Jorrat 1999), whereas the VAT-evasion rate averaged 22 percent in the 1990s.

Worldwide tax-evasion rates differ markedly. For most developed countries, VAT evasion averages 25 percent, whereas for developing nations it averages 48 percent. Data on the income tax, though incomplete, suggests that differences between developed and developing countries are even larger. For OECD nations, income tax–evasion rates range from 15 to 30 percent, whereas for Latin America income tax–noncompliance rates range from 29 to 75 percent. In this respect, Chile is considerably closer to the OECD standard, and the pattern in Argentina is more similar to that of the rest of Latin America.

Tax evasion in Argentina is a well-entrenched phenomenon. In contrast to Chile or the United States, where many taxpayers report cheating in small amounts, taxpayers in Argentina participate in bold, large-scale evasion schemes. In Argentina, evading taxes is not a peripheral activity or a way to make a quick extra buck but rather an institutionalized behavior and a source of revenue deemed legitimate by Argentine society. Chileans also try to maximize benefits and reduce their taxes, yet most taxpayers do so within the margins of the law. Some participate in tax evasion, but the majority of taxpayers who cheat do so marginally.

The magnitude of tax evasion affects national prosperity. Whereas the lost revenues in Argentina exceed US$45 billion per year (15 percent of

---

1. The value-added tax is among the easiest taxes to collect in terms of compliance rates. A detailed explanation of the compliance aspects of this tax is found in chapters 4 and 6.

GDP), in Chile the estimated lost revenues are US$4.7 billion a year (less than 7 percent of GDP).[2] In recent years, the Argentine government has spent more on controlling tax evasion than on programs for fighting poverty and unemployment. In order to collect taxes, Argentina spends three times as much as Chile and over four times as much as the United States. The budget of the tax administration is twice as large as that of the federal education department and almost three times larger than that of the social-welfare department.

Legal and Political Context

Political instability and social conflict have dominated Argentina for many decades. From the 1930s to the 1980s, Argentina faced several institutional and social crises that generated a deep but subtle breach of trust in the political system; despite re-democratization in 1983, Argentines' profound lack of faith in the government remains very much alive. The disenchantment with the country's social, political, and economic institutions is a symptom of a broader social unrest. The inability of social institutions to manage the disastrous fiscal crisis of 2001 is intrinsically tied to this public disenchantment with government.

Chile has also been mired in political and social upheaval. A bloody 1973 coup ushered in a sixteen-year military dictatorship that disrupted more stable and pacific mechanisms for the resolution of social and political conflict. Setting aside this interval and a single episode of military rule in the 1920s, however, civilian rule and a proud legal tradition since the mid-nineteenth century have fostered political and judicial traditions in which law abidance and obedience to authority are predominant. As some scholars argue (Angell 2006; Valenzuela 1998), the military dictatorship was an aberration that did not entirely disrupt this pattern. The civilian legalist tradition has been easily recaptured and has yielded strong institutional performance. In fact, Chilean tax compliance was much higher during the 1990s than under the Pinochet dictatorship.[3]

Compliance is a symptom of the strength of a country's institutional legitimacy. Chile is one of the few Latin American countries where obedience to rules is widely upheld, authorities enjoy high levels of approval, and the rule of law is deeply rooted. On the other hand, the evasion

2. These estimates are for 1997. For Chile, they are based on Barra and Jorrat 1999, and for Argentina, on AFIP 1998.
3. VAT compliance during the 1990s averaged 23 percent (Barra and Jorrat 1999), whereas between 1975 and 1985 it averaged 35 percent (Marcel 1986).

of taxes is just one of many rule-breaking behaviors of the Argentines.[4] Argentine noncompliance with many other laws clearly points to a state of anomie and social disintegration (Nino 1992). Subtly, and sometimes openly, the rule of law is challenged in everyday behaviors in Argentina (O'Donnell 1999). As we shall see, the difference in tax compliance between Chile and Argentina is tied to these broader differences of social and political context.

Case Selection

The study of compliance with law in general, and taxation in particular, requires a comparative perspective. There is little doubt that a deep understanding of the variables that affect compliance must take into consideration the social ecologies in which these laws operate. A central claim of this book—that the unit of analysis for tax behavior is not the individual's self-motivation but the environment in which this individual operates—certainly calls for a comparative perspective.

Chile and Argentina are ideal cases for this study. The two countries have more in common with each other than either of them has with any other country in the world. That alone would make them very good comparative cases; a more important reason, however, is that through this research it is possible to identify the divergent effect that rules and institutions have on social and political outcomes in both countries.

Argentina is a representative example of a country that has fallen into the "noncompliance trap." Over the last century this country's reversal of development (Waisman 1987) has puzzled social scientists, who have struggled to explain how such benign social and economic conditions (skilled workforce, homogeneous population, fertile farming land, abundant natural resources) were dilapidated. This country's noncompliance is not of mere academic interest: it has a direct effect on the country's inability to put its finances in order, and it partially accounts for the economic crisis (including devaluations, huge resource transferring, and freezing of bank deposits) that led to social violence, the resignation of presidents, and large waves of out-migration.

A comparative and empirical approach allows us to identify the legal institutions and cultural attributes that effect compliance, as well as social and political stability. This is why a successful case such as Chile is compared to a social trap such as Argentina. Chile has managed to avoid

4. I provide evidence to support this claim in surveys throughout the book, especially in chapter 6.

the noncompliance equilibria that are so common and devastating in the region. For Chile, the compliance equilibrium helps to explain why it has one of the most dynamic and stable economies in the area, and why a higher level of consensus and compromise (for the most part absent in the region) characterizes its democratic institutions.

The divergent trend of Argentina and Chile illuminates processes and features that transcend both taxation and Latin America. This study tests hypotheses crucial for the socioeconomic and political outcomes in many countries around the world. Comparative research on these case studies is important because: (1) individual choices are greatly influenced by the environment, and therefore a systematic comparison of equilibria sheds light on individual outcomes; (2) Chile and Argentina are great representative examples of compliance and noncompliance equilibria; (3) these outcomes cause some of the most important differences between these countries; and (4) such a comparison sheds light on structural characteristics that affect development and social and political stability.

PERSPECTIVES ON TAX COMPLIANCE

Scholars have approached tax compliance from a number of different perspectives and disciplines over the past four decades. Microeconomic theories of tax evasion claim that people pay taxes if their subjective perception of the likelihood of detection and punishment is higher than the cost of full compliance; such theories maintain that taxpayers' calculations about the utility of taxation are only very rarely related to the actual provision of goods and services (Becker 1968; Cowell 1990).[5] Numerous studies, however, have demonstrated that such an invariant assumption about taxpayers' rationality does not fully capture the range of human motivations and aspirations (Tversky and Kahneman 1982; Elster 1989; Frey 1997).[6] Deterrence theory has emerged as a valuable approach to

5. Taxpayers are conceived as free riders who will take advantage of opportunities to cheat irrespective of moral and normative constraints. Over the last twenty years, an expanding body of research has examined these general propositions; see excellent reviews by Andreoni, Erard, and Feinstein (1998) and Alm (2000). Researchers have based the forecasting of taxpayer decision making on variations of cost-benefit analysis, and have often modeled costs and benefits in monetary terms (Allingham and Sandmo 1972; Clotfelter 1983; Dubin, Graetz, and Wilde 1990).

6. Individuals do not attach the same weight to pecuniary gains and losses, and the perceived costs of detection and the conceptualization of punishment are socially constructed categories. As such, they are subject to cultural and social understandings.

account for differences in individual decision making.[7] Its advocates point out that costs, benefits, and opportunities are subjectively perceived and should be evaluated accordingly.[8] In particular, the actual effectiveness of the range of government enforcement tools is secondary to the way that this effectiveness is individually perceived; therefore, differences in compliance are tied both to culture and to actual enforcement of the law.

Sociologists and social psychologists have examined the effects of norms and culture on individuals' tax behavior (Grasmick and Bursik 1990; Cialdini 1989; Lederman 2003) but have failed to show how these macro-structures produce micro-behaviors; these studies have ignored the interesting question of how individuals adopt or reject cultural norms in specific taxation situations.[9]

Political scientists have addressed taxation and compliance in two dimensions. A sociopolitical perspective ties the capacity of governments to raise taxes to the "warrior state."[10] A few studies use this perspective within the Latin American context (Centeno 2002; Lopez-Alvez 2000), and they help to successfully explain the emergence of a stronger state in Chile than in Argentina in the nineteenth century. More research is needed, however, to explain how nineteenth-century formations and institutions linger in the present. A second tradition has emphasized that modern states must develop strong political capacities to convey one of the central principles of taxation: equity. According to this perspective, people comply with taxation law to the extent that they receive tangible

7. There is a large literature on this subject as it relates to taxes (see, e.g., Roth, Scholz, and Witte 1989; Klepper and Nagin 1989a, 1989b; Martinez-Vazquez and Alm 2003).

8. This introduces a contextual variable that affects the way that people come to perceive the costs and benefits of taxation. Although this implies a latent cultural and sociological dimension to the problem, deterrence does not provide a full causal explanation of how environmental and cultural dimensions affect individual rational decision making.

9. Conformity to norms and rules has been a major concern for sociologists, who argue that human behavior is largely governed by social dictates (Merton 1957; Gouldner 1960; Eisenstadt 1966; Parsons 1977; Elster 1989; Bourdieu 1990). Deviance from established conventions has been explained with structural, cultural, and socialization models. According to standard sociological interpretations, the cohesiveness of the social fabric, the impact of rule violation in a given social structure, and the way that people elaborate their choices has a much greater impact on individual decisions than does the search for a large monetary profit.

10. According to theories of state formation, kingdoms and modern states were largely shaped around the structures of their tax systems (see, in particular, Tilly 1975, 1990; Bendix 1978; Levi 1988; Skocpol 1979). Governments have risen and fallen depending on their capacity to foster a balance between the extraction of revenues and the provision of services (especially defense). Taxpayers rebel against or cooperate with central governments to the extent that they feel at least some involvement or membership in the community, making tax compliance contingent on some measure of citizenship.

benefits from their contributions, fostering a working contract between citizens and rulers.[11] If true, however, it is unclear how the free-riding paradigm was overcome in Chile. Even under a brutal dictatorship from 1973 to 1990, in which Chileans had no meaningful representation, no voice, and minimal provision of goods and services, Chile still enjoyed high levels of tax compliance compared to other countries of the region.

Without an interdisciplinary dialogue, the riddle of tax compliance will remain difficult to solve. In this book, I provide an institutional and interdisciplinary analysis of tax evasion. I follow Nobel laureate Douglas North's general understanding of individual behavior in conceptualizing how taxpayers make compliance decisions. North writes: "Human behavior appears to be more complex than that embodied in the individual utility function of economists' models. . . . People decipher the environment by processing information through preexisting mental constructs through which they understand the environment and solve the problems they confront. Both the computational abilities of the players and the complexity of the problems to be solved must be taken into account in understanding the issues" (1990, 20). Regarding the importance of the environment in shaping choices, North adds: "Uncertainties arise from incomplete information with respect to the behavior of other individuals in the process of human interaction. The computational limitations of the individual are determined by the capacity of the mind to process, organize, and utilize information. From this capacity taken in conjunction with the uncertainties involved in deciphering the environment, rules and procedures evolve to simplify the process. The consequent institutional framework, by structuring human interaction, limits the choice set of the actors" (25).

Using North's understanding of individual behavior to extend the pure microeconomic perspective, I argue throughout *Tax Evasion and the Rule of Law in Latin America* that taxpayers' decisions transcend the realm of profit maximization. Taxpayers do not purely optimize but rather mostly satisfy personal expectations (Simon 1999). Their decisions, however, are heavily determined by an evolutionary conceptualization of compliance and responsiveness to rules. Following sociological traditions, I argue that

---

11. Because taxation has been the basis for representation and has provided legitimacy for republican political participation, the success of a tax system lies in arriving at an equilibrium between the natural desire of citizens to pay less in taxes and their wish to participate in the political process (Steinmo 1993; Heredia 2006; Scholz 2003). The central feature in the study of taxation is the threat of the Leviathan, which can create the right incentives for people to comply with taxes and benefit from public goods (Levi 1988; Tilly 1990).

the way individuals perceive costs, obligations, duties, and social sanctions is critical for each compliance decision. Those perceptions evolve from a set of social interactions and structure individual strategic decisions (Coleman 1990). People maximize utilities inasmuch as they pay as little in taxes as they can. But the environment in which people operate fundamentally shapes how they frame the maximization of their benefits. In that sense, *tax evasion depends more on the ecology of taxation than on the optimality of enforcement.* Yet institutions do matter a great deal in this context, because they account for the formation of tastes and preferences. Political perspectives are instrumental to showing how states become effective in both generating an equity contract with taxpayers and producing enforcement to deter free riders from undermining the compliance game. Tax evasion, then, should be understood as highly sensitive to social, political, and cultural processes; any attempt to understand variation in tax evasion across cases must incorporate social, political, cultural, and economic perspectives on the problem.

ASSUMPTIONS AND A GENERAL INITIAL HYPOTHESIS

I begin my analysis of tax noncompliance with three basic assumptions. First, I assume that *nobody likes to pay taxes.* Given the choice to free ride without being punished, most people would avoid paying taxes yet still benefit from public goods. This assumption, however, does not imply that most people cheat. Some do, and some do not. An analysis of tax compliance must consider the factors that enhance or constrain people's decisions about whether to cheat.

My second assumption is that the distribution of risk-averse individuals and risk takers is similar across nations, except where a causal factor accounts for differences in the distribution.[12] Thus, the starting unit of analysis ought to be the "tax environment." Tax compliance is exogenous, in the sense that external factors make taxpayers react to their perceptions of social and economic conditions in particular ways. Thus, analysis of the contextual world in which taxpayers operate, rather than of individual differences, better explains variance in tax compliance across countries. Variation within a country's population does exist, of course; however, this within-country variance is random among different

---

12. Personal history and personality traits vary randomly within countries at a constant rate, and where such randomness does not hold, we must search for an external factor that accounts for the difference.

societies.[13] The majority of research on tax evasion has been conducted from a within-country perspective. Such studies lack enough across-country variation to isolate causal explanations. A comparative approach illuminates an under-examined aspect of tax compliance behavior: *the way that taxpayers come to perceive their tax environment successfully explains variation in tax compliance.*

This leads to a third assumption, related to the self-sustaining nature of compliance. Tax decisions are tied to personal and ecological features, such as the routine of making tax decisions, the role of accountants as informants, and the makeup of the tax system.[14] Within the constraints imposed by the tax structure and the filing system, *taxpayer decisions become self-sustaining, resulting in an equilibrium that explains the stability of aggregate compliance rates.* Nations rarely witness sudden shifts in overall compliance, because taxpayers rarely change their tax decisions from one year to the next. Rather, improvements in compliance are modest even when enforcement is stringent, because taxpayers are reluctant to alter tax practices unless they have substantial (generally firsthand) information that affects the prior equilibrium.

Most taxpayers are not sophisticated rationalizers who evaluate options and estimate risk levels thoroughly, then multiply these by the cost of punishment to arrive at optimal decisions. Rather, they decide using different value scales. Because taxpayers have access to only selective and limited information, they maximize benefits to themselves by relying on a complex set of variables that they can trust as good predictors of "safe" decisions. In a country whose citizens perceive that evasion goes unpunished, where the opportunities to cheat are large, and where the moral inhibitors against tax cheating are very low, we find higher levels of tax evasion. Therefore, I hypothesize that *when there is room for individual tax decisions (i.e., controlling for the nature of tax system), taxpayers arrive at their best choices based on social learning, in which the perceived standardized behavior of peers and the previous levels of enforcement contribute to shape rules and norms that routinize most tax decisions.* This is a path-dependent explanation of compliance based on culture,

13. Individual attributes of one population do not explain the aggregate levels of risk; they depend on exogenous factors, such as the legal culture and the social construction of enforcement.

14. Taxpayers whose taxes are withheld at the source make their tax decisions within a limited range, although in some cases they can claim refunds. In the case of the VAT, taxpayers have more leverage because the tax-filing system requires a balance of sales and purchases, which can be manipulated. Property taxes are levied as fixed amounts determined by a central office, thus offering taxpayers limited opportunities to cheat.

enforcement, and tax structures, all of which combine and operate in different scenarios to produce different outcomes. It is based on two general propositions: First, *the higher the internalized level of enforcement of norms and rules, the more citizens will tend to comply with rules (including tax laws)*. Second, *after these conditions are met, the friendlier the tax system is to compliance, the lower the level of tax evasion will be*.

KEY ANALYTICAL TOOLS FOR EXPLAINING DIFFERENCES IN TAX COMPLIANCE AND LAW ABIDANCE

My approach to understanding tax compliance behavior relies on a particular understanding of voluntary compliance, the role of enforcement, and social mechanisms of decision making in taxation, which I briefly outline here. Chapter 1 will revisit and expand on the discussion introduced in this section.

Voluntary Compliance

Over the last few decades, economists, political scientists, and sociologists have demonstrated the virtues of cooperation to solve collective-action problems. In the realm of taxes, it has been stated that cooperation is attained through voluntary compliance. This does not imply that the threat of sanctions is absent but rather that enforcement is secondary to the free decision of taxpayers to report and pay their taxes without the threat of punishment. Margaret Levi has called this behavior "quasi-voluntary compliance": "It is voluntary because taxpayers *choose* to pay. It is *quasi*-voluntary because the noncompliant are subject to coercion—if they are caught" (1988, 52).

A central element of Levi's argument is that voluntary compliance is a rational choice tied to individuals' perceptions of fellow taxpayers' behavior and to the responsiveness of government. Levi explains: "Taxpayers have confidence that (1) rulers will keep their bargains and (2) the other constituents will keep theirs. Taxpayers are strategic actors who will cooperate only when they can expect others to cooperate as well. The compliance of each depends on the compliance of others. No one prefers to be a *sucker*" (53). Levi's analysis privileges the extracting capacities of authorities: "To minimize the costs of enforcement and to maximize the output that can be taxed, rulers have to create quasi-voluntary compliance. Quasi-voluntary compliance rests on reciprocity. It is a contingent strategy in which individual taxpayers are more likely to cooperate if they have reasonable expectation that both the rulers and other taxpayers are also cooperating. The key lies in what rulers and other government officials do to create mutual expectations of tax payments" (69).

In this argument, compliance is an assurance game wherein taxpayers end up believing that rulers will punish free riders and deliver goods and services.[15] Taxpaying is tied to the equity or fairness of the system: rulers must convince taxpayers that the system is fair, that there is equity in taxation, and that the burden of taxpaying is shared. Levi's pathbreaking perspective assumes that tax compliance is a cooperation game scheme in which taxpayers opt to engage in mutually advantageous exchanges to maximize utility. According to Scholz and Lubell (1998, 411), "Citizens will meet obligations to the collective despite the temptations to free-ride as long as they trust other citizens and political leaders to keep up their side of the social contract." Bo Rothstein (2005, 4) puts it plainly: "First . . . people [have to] believe that most others probably pay what they are supposed to, and second that most of the money is used for purposes people consider legitimate."

Will people always line up happily to pay their taxes if these two conditions are met? Probably not. In the United States, for example, although 99.1 percent of wages and salaries are reported to the IRS, sole proprietors report only 67.7 percent, and informal suppliers report only 18.6 percent (Bakija and Slemrod 2004). Free-riding temptations are apparently still strong within certain groups in a country where, according to many scholars, quasi-voluntary compliance works.

Economists and tax administrators have always claimed that compliance lies in the power of the stick. On the other hand, voluntary-compliance scholars like Levi and Scholz focus on fairness but overlook the social conditions that make enforcement effective. I propose to bridge the two perspectives by extending the voluntary-compliance approach, with some caveats. Compliance can be conceived as a cooperation game if we distinguish between two types of cooperators: *active cooperators* and *passive cooperators*. Conditional cooperators in the tax game belong to the second category, but they will actively seek the exit door if they become

---

15. One of these strategies is to pre-commit in order to gain credibility. Levi (1988) also identifies the virtuous effect of enforcement under voluntary compliance: "Quasi-Voluntary compliance rests on the effectiveness of sanctions when enough constituents are already cooperating. . . . The importance of deterrence is that it persuades taxpayers that others are being compelled to pay their shares" (54). But she never really extends the implications of these ideas.

suckers, thereby becoming *active defectors*.[16] This take on compliance has important implications for enforcement strategies. Passive cooperators are more concerned with the horizontal fairness of the system (that everybody pays their share and that there is no cheating) than with the equity of their payments.[17] More important, enforcement is easier in compliance equilibria, where strategies are geared to convince passive cooperators that everybody else is playing the game fairly; in noncompliance equilibria, similar enforcement yields poorer results because suckers see cheaters everywhere, and therefore become active defectors.

Conditional (passive) cooperators expect the ruler first and foremost to punish free riders. But how do taxpayers know that the contract is being honored?[18] More important, why are rulers able to coordinate conditional cooperation in one social setting while other rulers using the same repertoire of strategies in other contexts cannot attain similar results? In this book, I build on Levi's argument about fairness and equity and apply it to the Latin American context. The chapters that follow will present additional proof of the validity of voluntary-compliance and contingent-consent propositions. States are indeed better off when they generate voluntary compliance, and good governance enables the extraction of revenues. More important, people are willing to pay their share of taxes, but this willingness is contingent on other taxpayers' compliance, as well as on the rulers' ability to deliver public goods as promised.

I depart from Levi, however, in several important ways. First, I propose that compliance and noncompliance equilibria are the most significant constraints on the ability of rulers to extract revenues and on the willingness of citizens to pay taxes. Second, I argue that such equilibria determine the type and viability of different enforcement strategies, which ultimately yield different outcomes.[19] Third, I show by what mechanisms culture affects tax compliance behavior by demonstrating the coevolution

16. There are no active cooperators in the sense that taxpayers accept the burden but are not eager to comply. If they observe others failing to meet their obligation, however, they will actively look for ways to escape the game.

17. Levi (1988), Scholz (2003), and particularly Rothstein (2005) have put more emphasis on the virtues of good governance (in the sense of providing decent returns for the values of taxes) than on the role of government as guarantor of free riders; they believe that equity is what enhances cooperation.

18. It is much easier to know whether a good or service is being delivered by the state than to know if other taxpayers are cheating on their taxes and getting away with it.

19. Levi (1988) states that rulers can reduce costs of compliance by the use of coercion, by the maintenance of norms, or by quasi-voluntary compliance. I claim that these are not mutually exclusive strategies. The mild coercion needed in quasi-voluntary compliance is only viable under these particular equilibria.

of enforcement and compliance culture. Finally, whereas for Levi and her followers the central unit of analysis is the ruler's ability to raise revenues, I analyze the social and political arrangements that precondition citizens' decisions to enter the quasi-automatic paths of either obeying or defying the laws. These arrangements have profound implications for both the creation of the rule of law and the spiraling declines of failing states.

The Role of Enforcement

Tax compliance rests on two principles: exchange (vertical) equity and horizontal fairness. Most studies of the subject have been devoted to considering how rulers can create the right institutions to enhance vertical equity and trust, but, surprisingly, much less energy has been directed toward understanding how rules can guarantee that cooperators are not being exploited (horizontal fairness). Better compliance can be ensured if states succeed in deterring passive cooperators from defecting in the tax game.

Taxpayers are more concerned to avoid being exploited by others than to secure the diffuse public goods that taxes produce. They will, for the most part, forego the benefits of exchange equity if they can successfully free ride. They will accept fate and passively cooperate, on the other hand, if compliance is the dominant social strategy. Understanding this should refocus our attention on states' function from their role as institutions that deliver universal rights (Levi 1997; Scholz 2003; Steinmo 1993; Rothstein 2005) to their role as guarantors of cooperation. I do not underestimate the importance of exchange equity, but I believe that taxpayers are guided by fairness and impartiality first and foremost as they relate to not being exploited. Nothing unravels trust more quickly than the feeling of being a sucker, which creates a strong motive to defect. Thus, any tax compliance analysis must consider whether a tax environment allows free riders to escape social and political sanction—that is, whether it is an environment of widespread impunity.

Scholars have largely overlooked enforcement because they have perceived it as a technical aspect of taxation. As I will demonstrate, however, enforcement is a key aspect of tax compliance, and it merits serious, in-depth research. Authors such as North (1990) and Fukuyama (2004) have shown that enforcement transcends the consolidation of bureaucratic capacities. Moreover, the assumption that tax evasion in some countries is high because tax-enforcement agencies' are not technically skilled, or because these agencies are corrupt, is simply misguided. Argentina, for example, has invested more resources in combating tax evasion than has Chile; the Argentine tax-agency staff, management, and auditors are as capable as their Chilean and U.S. counterparts—and still tax evasion persists. Clearly, cheaters in Argentina thrive because tax evasion goes unpunished, but why has a good tax administration been unable to reverse cheating? Why is there greater horizontal fairness in Chile than in Argentina? Answers to these questions are to be found in the interplay among enforcement strategies and the type of social equilibrium found in a particular country. Enforcement is at the heart of the tax compliance game because it elicits—or inhibits—the conditions for cooperation.

It is the subjectively perceived credibility of effective enforcement that compels citizens to abide by the rules. The threat of credible sanctions creates a virtuous circle because it both develops social and human capital and economizes on individual cost-driven decisions. Taxpayers who do not have to look for ways to evade taxes to be competitive in the marketplace can save in transaction costs and invest these resources in productive endeavors. The perception that rules are being enforced effectively reduces free riding and optimizes resource allocation, and more widespread tax compliance raises revenues and improves the quality of public goods.

In order to understand tax compliance, then, it is necessary to consider how taxpayers perceive enforcement, how their perceptions of the fairness and legitimacy of the tax system are formed, and how they process information. We need to proceed in redressing what North (2005) has identified as a lack of theory on learning, standards, and beliefs. This book theorizes about how the ecologies of taxation and the social environment affect individual learning and legal behavior in the tax field.

At the center of this book is a debate about how enforcement enhances compliance with laws. This question is relevant for thinking about how to deal with a wide range of social outcomes, such as informal economies and black markets, hiring practices, illegal immigration, environmental pollution, traffic violations, and trade in illegal substances. Enforcement needs to be studied by taking into account the distribution of compliance within a population, and the best strategies of enforcement should be formulated with the compliance (or noncompliance) culture of the affected population in mind. It is easier to ensure that rules will be widely obeyed in a law-abiding society; enforcement agencies have a strategic advantage in such societies because they target a comparatively small pool of cheaters. Hence, their enforcement measures cannot be successfully replicated in social settings where the scale of the problem is much larger and where cheaters have a strong incentive to imitate successful free riders. The split potential effect of enforcement calls for differentiated policy strategies: it may be feasible to expand tax laws and make them more complex in law-abiding societies, whereas minimal law should be pursued in non-compliant contexts.

The makeup of the equilibria explains why culture matters. "Culture" is defined here in very practical terms as the range of standard procedures, common beliefs, and shared values rooted and widely accepted within a community. A legalist culture is one in which the mandate of the law is usually embraced by the community, and in which people adopt strategic decisions with the functioning of legal institutions in mind (Friedman 1975, 1985). In a culture of compliance, most people adopt a disposition to comply with the law before undertaking any cost-benefit analysis. Of course, individuals can deviate from compliance if they realize that the costs vastly exceed the benefits. More important, not all members of a compliance culture behave in the same way. At times, existing subcultures are important to individuals, and these may be at odds with the larger culture. For our purposes, culture matters because people rely on it to help them guess their optimal strategies, thereby creating average behavior in equilibrium. In compliance climates, enforcement assures conditional cooperators that cheaters are being punished; therefore, a culture of compliance thrives. In noncompliance environments, by contrast, there are no conditions for cooperation. Enforcement is effective in compliance equilibria because it reproduces legal culture; it is usually ineffective in noncompliance equilibria because it can rarely reverse a nonlegal culture. Enforcement, therefore, is to some extent endogenous to the prevailing legal culture.

In failing states, laws and regulations are perceived as unenforceable, and they mostly do not deter disobedience. Under compliance equilibria, conversely, enforcement enhances general deterrence and contributes to the image of an efficient administration. Whether such a situation lasts depends, of course, on continuous improvement and the strategic decisions of state agencies. There are three initial elements that account for the effectiveness of enforcement.

First, successful enforcement depends on the scale or size of the problem. To the extent that norms and rules in the polity are largely upheld, the effect of enforcement is greater. When more people abide by norms, there is less need for monitoring and large watchdog organizations. Here, an additional marginal unit of enforcement yields bigger marginal units of compliance. Conversely, the larger the number of cheaters, the more difficult it is for regulators or enforcement agencies to achieve comparable results. Thus, a similar level, depth, and scope of enforcement measures might yield completely different results in different environments: in the first environment, moderate enforcement achieves reasonable compliance, whereas in the second, similar or even more extensive enforcement is inadequate for achieving greater law abidance.

Second, in compliance environments, enforcement is geared to limit free riding. In this sense, the role of the enforcer in compliant orders is to signal to passive cooperators that conditions for cooperation are being met. Here, to be a legalist pays off, because cheaters are more likely to be detected and punished; greater resources are allocated to generate more and better public goods, thereby enhancing a stronger sense of fairness. Moreover, when most people conform to costly laws, they have an incentive to ensure that other people are complying as well, fostering an environment in which horizontal enforcement (among peers) supports the vertical enforcement of the legal order.

Third, in noncompliance ecologies, enforcement must first generate the basic conditions of cooperation. Because there are so many free riders, the enforcer is always playing catch-up. In compliance equilibria, the role of the enforcer is containment; in noncompliance equilibria, the enforcer must wage an all-out war to transform the status quo. Comparable enforcement measures achieve better compliance results when the enforcer can select targets more efficiently.

Mechanisms of Taxation Decision Making

This book offers a set of sensible explanations to solve the riddle of tax-law noncompliance in many developing countries. I do not offer a comprehensive theory of enforcement and compliance, nor do I suggest a set of laws to predict outcomes. Rather, I present an empirically driven account of a two-country comparison that can shed light on many other cases. I contend that the appropriate approach to the study of tax compliance focuses on social mechanisms—that is, the set of causal patterns that enable explanations for how similar conditions produce disparate outcomes.[20] Given that tax evasion has a strong cultural or ecological component that evolves from social, political, and economic conditions,

---

20. Social scientists will be better served by focusing on the *how* rather than the *why* in their studies of conformance to rules. Motive-based explanations are difficult to prove; mechanism-based propositions can be better tested empirically (Hedstrom and Swedberg 1998; Elster 1999; Reskin 2003).

there is a need to identify the processes that explain how people arrive at decisions that maximize their utilities in a context of bounded rationality. I focus on three such mechanisms: contagion effects, reciprocity for public goods, and the lasting endowment of effective enforcement.[21]

Contagion—that is, the way that taxpayers rationally imitate the behavior of peers and other players—is the crucial first mechanism, because it explains how a critical mass of cheaters or legalists is formed and why changes in enforcement very rarely neutralize the powerful effects of imitation. When taxpayers learn that others cheat, they will be inclined to cheat; if they perceive that most taxpayers comply, they will be inclined to be legalists.

The second mechanism derives from the norm of reciprocity for the provision of public goods, which states that people tend to reciprocate for the allowances that they receive. Reciprocity in taxes, however, has not been well specified or convincingly tested. My results suggest that, far from being free riders, most individuals tend to cooperate when they receive allowances in return for their contributions. Whether the political system fairly redistributes tax revenues affects tax behavior, because when people receive public goods, they reciprocate with better compliance. Underlying this mechanism is a sense of vertical fairness. In addition, reciprocity operates horizontally: temptations to free ride can be overcome when individuals believe that other taxpayers are overcoming them.

The third mechanism is the lasting effect of enforcement. Individuals make choices based on default rules, which are heavily dictated by perceptions regarding the effect of sanctions, and they are strongly influenced by what they experience or learn from others regarding the effectiveness of tax-law enforcement. Both positive and negative experiences with enforcement have a lasting effect. Taxpayers caught cheating at an early stage assign higher detection capacity to their tax administrations than do those who are never caught. Effective enforcement has a strong evolutionary component, and it is particularly crucial that enforcement be strong at the outset or enactment of any law (I call this "norm-emerging enforcement"). To the extent that citizens perceive that the state is effective in curtailing free riders, they tend to obey the law. This has an enduring effect that allows the tax agency to concentrate its resources on fewer tax evaders, get good results from its enforcement, and reproduce its efficient image (I call this "norm-maintenance enforcement"). Whereas good, norm-emerging enforcement enhances a self-sustaining equilibrium

---

21. For a good review of the literature of mechanisms in the social sciences, see Hedstrom and Swedberg 1998.

of compliance, poor enforcement at earlier stages weakens the enforcement capacities of the norm, forging a noncompliance equilibrium.

The State and the Rule of Law

The erosion of the state's enforcement capacities is a sign of its weakness. My analysis of tax behavior and of the ruler's inability to curtail free riding sheds light on a broader problem: the weakness of the state and of the rule of law in Latin America. I do not attempt in this book to present a complete theory on this important topic.[22] I do contribute to the understanding of state weakness, however, by providing a conceptual approach to ascertain the nature of certain institutional deficiencies. In appendix D, I provide some reflections that transcend the realm of taxes and consider legal failure in general, a key issue in contemporary Latin America.[23]

The recent growing interest in the rule of law has centered on why rulers decide to abide by laws and not transgress the rules established between them and their subjects (Maravall and Przeworski 2003; Shapiro 1994; Weingast 1997). This is, however, an incomplete line of inquiry, because why rulers rule is no more important than why the ruled consent (Barzel 2002).[24] There is no rule of law if people do not abide by the norms, and there is a latent trade-off between the legitimacy of the norm and the perceived sanctioning capacity of the enforcer. Both the carrot and the stick are needed, but the relative inverse importance of each will dictate the type of policy needed to ensure compliance.

As I will argue, the rule of law fosters environments of compliance where rational individuals have a predisposition to comply, because under these equilibria the payoffs of cooperation are perceived as higher from the inception. Compliance environments enable the promotion of fairness and citizenship, which are crucial for reproducing initial compliance equilibria. Therefore, under the rule of law, people perceive that they are more likely to maximize their benefits than they would be otherwise.

22. See, for example, Centeno 2003, chap. 1, for a good description of the problem.

23. Legal failure is noticeable beyond Latin America; it is well entrenched in eastern Europe, central Asia, Africa, and the Middle East (Galligan and Kurkchiyan 2003; Murrell 2001).

24. Levitzky and Murillo (2005) have called for a similar approach in their general conclusions about the weakness of Argentina's political institutions. According to the authors, institutional strength is contingent on the actor's willingness to abide by the rules, as it represents the best possible alternative for action. For Levitzky and Murillo, durability (or stability) and enforcement of rules are key to the strength of institutions. In this book, I treat enforcement as endogenous to stability, as they both coevolve in a virtuous compliance equilibrium.

Countries able to establish the rule of law are more successful in promoting passive cooperation than those that are not. I maintain that the establishment of the rule of law is a precondition for reducing tax evasion.

Given the limited effect of enforcement under noncompliance equilibria, I also argue that governments are better off when they enact a few enforceable taxes than when they enact a variety of taxes that are difficult to collect. Simplicity serves the tax administration. When tax evasion is high, the goal of government should be to reverse the equilibrium, because only a compliant environment produces steady, high revenues. The actions of governments in many underdeveloped countries have been precisely the opposite: to address mounting deficits, most Latin American states levy taxes that quickly became widely evaded, fostering a higher perception of noncompliance. Because populist governments incur larger social expenditures in noncompliance environments, it is more difficult for them to enable a compliance equilibrium. This produces a circular crisis of fiscal deficit, thus prompting the passage of more unenforceable laws. Conversely, minimalist states that are capable of enforcing a few important laws that can progressively address social demands under stable equilibria.

The rule of law depends ultimately on the strength of the state. I claim that we must transcend the narrow approach that conceives of states as a set of predatory rulers that successfully extract revenues from individuals in exchange for security and other services. This is more accurately a theory of government. In this book, the state is construed as set of organizations that operate under and are constrained by certain rules or institutions. In this sense, enforcement agencies are much more than a set of organizations with technical capabilities. Given the type of equilibrium in which states operate, enforcement agencies affect the development of rules of law. Rulers in Argentina might want to raise more revenue through taxation and invest heavily in tax administration capacities, but the type of institutions in place constrains their ability to do so. In short, the rule of law depends on strong states, and strong states depend on the type of institutions that gave rise to them and shape them continuously. Successful states are those that, taking into account this path dependency, address enforcement strategies accordingly.

ON DATA AND METHOD

Most studies of compliance in developing countries use aggregate information. Such data cannot successfully test individual behavior, nor can it identify the conditions and mechanisms that lead to decisions about law abidance. This book, by contrast, studies taxpayer behavior using individual data collected systematically for this purpose.

The empirical study of tax compliance is cumbersome because individual-level data is very difficult to collect. Most government agencies are reluctant or legally unable to allow research on individual tax returns. Even when such information becomes available, it is usually impossible to create data sets that also include individual preferences and attitudes, which are needed to explain tax behavior. Therefore, most studies are based on aggregate data and self-reports, which present problems of validity and reliability.

In order to provide satisfactory answers to my research questions, I assembled a completely new database drawn from specially requested tax information and newly designed surveys.[25] This data consists of six different surveys conducted in the late 1990s, four in Argentina and two in Chile. For each country, I conducted one survey among general taxpayers and another among the recently audited.[26] In addition, for Argentina I conducted similar surveys with tax officials and tax auditors. The tax-return data I collected consists of the individual tax reports of fifteen thousand taxpayers from periods before and after enforcement measures were taken against them. These randomly selected cases have matching control groups. I also conducted an experimental study to test hypotheses about the effect of enforcement on both individual consent and the social mechanisms of compliance. I present further explanations of the data in appendix A.

The evidence in the chapters is usually presented very directly and clearly in the form of graphs and tables. I sacrifice in-depth statistical analysis in favor of simplicity, fluidity, and a less technical presentation. Only four simple, multivariate models are included; readers unfamiliar with regression analysis can skip them without missing the core of the argument. The broad evidence is compelling and speaks for itself.

Comparison in taxation is difficult because differences between countries and economies cause problems of interpretation, making multiple-variable models hard to evaluate. This study takes the logic of the most

---

25. I thank the tax administrations of Chile and Argentina for permitting the analysis of individual tax information, for enabling me to draw survey samples from the active registrar of taxpayers, and for providing me with other aggregate enforcement information.

26. I administered five of these surveys. Estudios Mori conducted the sixth general taxpayer survey for Chile, and the Chilean tax authority kindly provided me with the database.

alike cases. As mentioned above, Chile and Argentina are very good candidates for a systematic comparative analysis, in terms of both their tax structure and their political and economic makeup.

OVERVIEW

The first and last chapters encompass broad conceptualizations of law abidance under adverse conditions. Chapter 1 develops the necessary theoretical repertoire for the rest of the book. I explain the merits of the two-equilibria approach, and I systematically discuss the role of enforcement in enhancing compliance through a model that integrates the role of culture, individual costs, and legitimacy. I further examine some of these ideas in appendix B, using simple game situations to explain the logic of my arguments. In appendix C, I use a simulative evolutionary game to explain the joint evolution of enforcement and compliance culture. I demonstrate that enforcement at the emergence stage of the norm, as well as the initial acceptance of the law, matters greatly in later rounds. This evolutionary approach shows that equilibria tend to stabilize under both noncompliance and compliance environments, and that the effect of recent individual enforcement is meager. Enforcement has a cumulative effect.

Chapter 2 presents a comparative empirical assessment of tax compliance in Argentina and Chile, including some glimpses at other countries. This chapter lays the groundwork for subsequent analysis by defining and measuring the dependent variable. I present estimates for the magnitude of tax evasion, and I develop a set of methods to assess voluntary compliance with the VAT for Argentina and Chile.

In chapters 3–7, I develop a detailed, evidence-driven analysis of tax compliance based on surveys, tax returns, and quasi-experimental data. Chapters 3, 4, and 5 examine the successes and limitations of enforcement efforts. I analyze data from surveys, courts, and individual tax returns, and I offer disaggregate and self-reported data on this subject for the first time. In chapter 3, I describe the similarities in the enforcement capacities of Chile and Argentina, and I demonstrate that the certainty of detection in the latter country is perceived as very weak, contributing to greater tax evasion and reinforcing a cycle of the permanent failure of tax reforms. Conversely, Chilean taxpayers believe that the tax administration has larger capabilities to detect significant tax evasion. It should be noted that tax-enforcement capacities are similar, although perceptions in both countries differ.

Chapter 4 examines the role of sanctions and their impact on tax evasion in an entire population—that is, their effectiveness as a form of general deterrence. For Argentina, I analyze the effects of penal-prosecution policies, concluding that the criminalization of tax evasion has had very limited results. In the case of Chile, I analyze administrative sanctions and show that they are much more effective in enhancing voluntary compliance. For both countries, I present self-reported data regarding individual assessments of the perceived severity of punishment for tax fraud, and I address problems of institutional coordination. I conclude that the key for effective sanctions is the high probability of their imposition. Impunity is perceived as very high in Argentina, leading to high tax evasion.

Chapter 5 undertakes an empirical analysis of individual tax-return data to answer the question of how enforcement affects post-enforcement tax decisions—that is, the effectiveness of enforcement as a form of specific deterrence. I examine the effects of three measures: audits, closure of businesses, and invoicing requirements. The effect of individual enforcement in eliciting future individual compliance is meager in Chile and totally ineffective in Argentina. I conclude that deterrence becomes a tautology: reforms fail because detection of evasion is weak, and detection of evasion is weak because enforcement lags behind noncompliance. Taken together, chapters 3, 4, and 5 demonstrate that enforcement yields better results in promoting general deterrence than particular deterrence does, because taxpayers under compliance equilibria believe that cheaters are more likely to be caught—cheaters, rooted in noncompliance practices, very rarely change.

Chapter 6 turns to an investigation of the role of culture and social norms in eliciting compliance behavior. I analyze the role of trust, reciprocity, moral obligation, and duty—as well as the role of inhibitors such as shame and guilt—in the formation of subjective perceptions of the effectiveness of detection and punishment for tax fraud. I pay particular attention to the process of information gathering. I stress the need to provide a culturally contextualized explanation of the way that societies come to recognize the significance of compliance in social cooperative endeavors.

Chapter 7 presents the results of an experiment conducted with students in both countries to evaluate the effect of social and economic variables on compliance. I describe the basic mechanisms that account for differences in individual compliance. This evidence allows me to speculate on how preferences are formed in relation to tax evasion.

The final chapter summarizes the arguments and extends them into guiding principles for policy prescriptions. These concluding remarks have broader implications for the study of law, politics, and the successful emergence of compliance environments. Along those same lines, appendix D examines the conditions for the establishment of the rule of law, represented by the lively image of compliance equilibria.

1

COMPLIANCE AND ENFORCEMENT

Cuando a Roma fueres, haz como vieres.
[When thou art at Rome, do as thou seest.]
— DON QUIXOTE

The introduction presented three essential concepts in my approach to tax compliance behavior: voluntary compliance, the role of enforcement, and the social mechanisms of decision making in taxation. This chapter revisits the first two concepts and uses them to develop the set of theoretical propositions tested by this study of taxation and conformance behavior. In the following pages, I develop a conceptual framework that builds on the merits of the two-equilibria approach to tax compliance. The concept of compliance and noncompliance environments allows us to explain why enforcement succeeds or fails. I show that because these environments are stable, it is rational for citizens to choose a dominant strategy based on the expected choices of others. Any intermediate environment is unstable and will ultimately be pulled toward either compliance or noncompliance. More important, given the stability of equilibria, enforcement becomes effective when most citizens abide by the laws. I also argue that the success of deterrence depends largely on the magnitude of noncompliance. In noncompliance equilibria, the capacity of the state to instill fear is limited.

In order to make up for limited information, taxpayers rely on common knowledge as a good predictor of right choices in a context of uncertainty. I hypothesize that where noncompliance is prevalent, people learn that it is foolish to comply. But when the same people migrate to social orders in which legal obedience is predominant, they quickly adapt to these new environments and begin complying. Aligning citizens' incentives with cooperative endeavors, rather than by means of particular deterrence, encourages law abidance.[1] By punishing free riders, states reward legalists for their obedience.

---

1. Particular deterrence, as opposed to general deterrence, refers to the effect that a legal provision or an enforcement measure has on individual behavior (e.g., how an audit affects this *particular* audited taxpayer's future compliance, as opposed to how audit policies affect the *general* taxpayers' compliance) (Paternoster et al. 1982).

The evolution of enforcement and its relationship to compliance with the norm of taxation is the concept at the heart of the chapter. The first section describes the basic framework of noncompliance and compliance equilibria and analyzes the makeup of compliance with taxes, clarifying concepts such as culture, representation, and deterrence. The second section develops a theory of the relationship between enforcement and compliance. Those wishing for a more detailed and technical discussion might also consult appendix B, which presents simple properties of tax compliance games. Readers might also consult appendix C, in which I develop a tax simulation game to show that enforcement becomes more effective when more people comply.

SOCIAL FOUNDATIONS OF COMPLIANCE

The Two Equilibria

Because I have proposed that compliance is best understood in the context of the dominant equilibria in which taxpayers operate, let us begin with a brief examination of this concept. The idea of stable equilibria has gained strength among scholars in the last few decades. Quoting Hahn (1987, in North 1990, 324), North explains the effect of institutions on the stability of individual behavior in these terms: "The concept of equilibrium is a valuable tool of analysis, but for most of the issues that we are concerned with there is not one but multiple equilibria that arise because 'there is a continuum of theories that agents can hold and act on without ever encountering events which lead them to change their theories'" (1990, 24). Putnam identifies two clearly distinct equilibria: "civic communities," where stocks of social capital such as trust, norms, and networks tend to be self-reinforcing, and "un-civic communities," which are dominated by defection, distrust, shirking, and exploitation. He writes, "This argument suggests that there may be at least *two* broad equilibria toward which all societies that face problems of collective actions (that is, *all* societies) tend to evolve and which, once attained, tend to be self-reinforcing" (1993, 177).

The idea of two equilibria has evolved from the literature of collective action, in which two dominant strategies are understood to be at work: defection and cooperation. Where most people defect, a vicious circle of selfish and deceiving behavior is found. In places where actors are able to solve the "prisoner's dilemma," however, cooperation is attained and payoffs are maximized. Note that multiple equilibria are possible, but societies mostly settle on two equilibria, which roughly correspond to the "mostly defect" or "mostly cooperate" strategies.

Numerous studies have shown that the prisoner's dilemma (or the free-rider dilemma) can be resolved by different strategies when games are repeated (Axelrod 1984), when the cost-benefit ratio of players is favorable (Hardin 1982), or when norms and conventions resolve problems of information (Taylor 1982). Less attention has been paid to what type of enforcement mechanisms elicits cooperation in large-N situations. For example, according to Putnam, "third-party enforcement is an inadequate solution" (1993, 177), and therefore voluntary and spontaneous cooperation is dependent on social capital. Efficient solutions to collective-action problems in large-N situations require individuals to freely choose to cooperate. But it is hard to imagine taxpayers not free riding in countries that lack tax enforcement. I claim that passive cooperators adopt a conditional strategy to cooperate *precisely because* they trust that enforcement agents will punish defectors. Therefore, in the case of taxation, there is no escape from the Hobbesian solution—that is, a strong Leviathan that will punish defectors. Such a solution is contingent, however, on the institutional makeup of the society. The ability of the tax agency to deter taxpayers from free riding is mostly unimpeded in a compliance equilibrium.

A two-equilibria approach provides significant explanatory power to the narrow deterrence perspective. Instead of analyzing the enforcement capacity of the state as exogenous to individual preferences, the makeup of the equilibria explains why similar enforcement capacities and techniques might produce different outcomes. Assuming that sound policies and technical capacities reach a minimal threshold of competence, the effectiveness of state enforcement depends on the "compliance distribution" of citizens. Thus, enforcement becomes endogenous to the type of distribution. Where most people comply (a legalist environment), enforcement is on average more effective, for at least three reasons: First, all things being equal, more resources can be allocated to detect and punish noncompliance. Law enforcement agents who spread their resources among many law violators reduce the stringency of the state's coercion capacity in exchange for wider but more porous enforcement of a given rule. Second, enforcement is effective in legalist environments because, given the reduced pool of defectors, potential conditional cooperators can monitor and watch for cheaters. Where everybody cheats, and in the absence of third-party coercion, self-enforcing agreements are short-lived. (This is the horizontal-enforcement effect.) Third, and perhaps most important, when many people comply, the probability of contagion diminishes, and therefore there are fewer potential defectors to be watched. Thus, the perception of effective enforcement fosters a virtuous equilibrium of compliance.[2]

The idea that different compliance equilibria operate in taxation has gained favor among some scholars. Davis, Hecht, and Perkins (2003) state that tax compliance is dictated by one or two attracting points, as taxpayers become susceptible to either evasion or compliance according to their individual acquaintances and the given social norms within a class of taxpayers. Scholz (2003) has also advanced the idea that people might adjust to the "tax contract" on the basis of the general patterns of behavior surrounding them. In a more implicit approach, Fennell and Fennell (2003) suggest that it is neither fear nor greed, but rather the individual's "fear of the greed" of others, that makes conditional cooperation work, creating environments in which cooperation becomes the dominant strategy. In the same vein, Kahan (2001) refers to "tax climates" wherein the set of individual preferences promotes norms (such as trust and reciprocity) conducive to collective action in taxation, thereby producing high-trust and low-trust equilibria. There are few references in these studies to the relationship between tax compliance environments and broader national legal cultures, however, and little attention is given to the role that enforcement plays in developing high- and low-trust equilibria.

In this book, I also contend that the success of enforcement depends on the scope and depth of a group's attachment to norms.[3] It is a mistake to assume that a nation with a complex set of technical skills, policy prescriptions, and professional cadres will resolve the free-riding problem in taxation. The ability to watch, monitor, and sanction cheaters is tied to at least four variables: the true cost of enforcement vis-à-vis the benefits obtained by means of enforcement, the individual benefits of cheating, the number of cheaters within a group, and the efficacy and sanctioning capacity of a given group. Therefore, any explanation of tax evasion that treats governmental enforcement of tax law as an exogenous variable

---

2. Barzel (2002) signals that the virtuous effect of enforcement depends on the "distribution of compliance." Although he attributes such effects to the power gathered by the enforcer, he contends that such enforcement has a "snowballing effect" that allows the enforcer to use it less and remain in "standby" mode. Here, very much in line with Hardin's argument (1995) about the source of power in coordination games, I claim that such power is precisely endogenous to such "distribution."

3. The more people uphold a norm, the more power is conferred to the authority and, paradoxically, the less need there is to use such power. Hardin (1995) makes a similar argument for all coordination games.

falls short. The institutional analysis of tax compliance must take into consideration the complex set of conditions that yield disparate outcomes and multiple equilibria.

The Tragic Outcome of Noncompliance Equilibria: An Example

Enforcement under noncompliance equilibria is limited because taxpayers' incentives are strongly aligned with defection. In this sense, tax evasion resembles a particular form of the tragedy of the commons, where the overuse of a practice brings about personal and collective diminished returns.[4] Tax evasion differs, of course, from the basic form of the tragedy of the commons: Garret Hardin's tragedy relates to open access to goods, whereas tax decisions have nothing to do with the overuse of available resources. But the structure of tax incentives can produce similar outcomes. Taxpayers have a basic dilemma: they have to decide whether to comply with the law, and their decisions yield lower or higher levels of common resources. A businessperson who cheats while everybody else complies can use the profits of tax evasion in many ways: for investment, consumption, savings, and so on. The businessperson's situation is similar to that of the single herder who grazes livestock in the common and benefits from that grazing. When cheating is rampant in an industry, however, the businessperson must decide whether to cheat in order to remain competitive, or to comply with the law and risk bankruptcy (Davis, Hecht, and Perkins 2003). In addition, compliers from a single industry usually notice when a competitor cheats because tax evaders use the competitive advantage they gain to capture market share, forcing honest taxpayers to follow similar practices. Like the commoners who graze increasing numbers of cattle to offset the diminishing quality of their livestock, which grow thinner due to rampant overgrazing, taxpayers "overuse" tax evasion to remain competitive.

This dynamic has a perverse outcome because it is very hard to reverse course. Taxpayers who decide to comply with the law might fail to stay in business; single taxpayers are at a structural disadvantage if they decide to comply when everybody else does not. Many taxpayers are forced to remain noncompliant even when enforcement becomes more stringent because full compliance in a noncompliance equilibrium is so strongly

---

4. The standard structure for tax compliance games has been the prisoner's dilemma. I will use this game to explain several tax decisions made by individuals. I believe that for noncompliance equilibria, however, the analogy of the tragedy of the commons provides additional explanatory power that has not been properly captured in the tax literature.

counter to their interests (and even their livelihood). In noncompliance equilibria, then, taxpayers who cheat on their taxes often do so because they feel that they must, and it is unclear how enforcement can achieve meaningful results in such a situation.

Cooperation, Imitation, and Tax Decisions

Tax compliance can still be best conceptualized as a cooperation game. As the simulation in appendix C shows, in iterated games a player decides to cooperate (comply) or defect (evade) according to the other player's (the tax agency, in this case) previous action. The taxpayer's perception of an audit, or the outcome of any other enforcement measure, becomes pivotal for enhancing the other player's credibility with regard to future threats. Therefore, compliance in repetitive games is determined by the payoffs of previous rounds—or, in other words, by the history of the interactions between the players.

The results of the simulation discussed in the appendix indicate that where enforcement has a limited effect, future noncompliance should be expected. The credibility of the tax agency's threats is low because enforcement fails to alter the taxpayer's previous utility function (i.e., bribes or fines do not significantly change the taxpayer's basic cost structure). Therefore, where there is a stable pattern of noncompliance, enforcement must be extremely effective to override natural tendencies to cheat. Alternatively, where people comply, tax compliance resembles the warranty game (Levi 1997). In order to assure full cooperation and escape strategies of general defection, players must trust others to cooperate. For instance, a citizen will refrain from littering if she trusts other citizens to do likewise; if they do not, the most rational strategy is to defect. In other words, cooperation is achieved if certain preconditions exist. To cooperate, a single player must have certain *warranties* that the other players will cooperate as well.

In a perfect assurance game, a taxpayer complies with taxation law and other taxpayers reciprocate. In such a situation, optimal welfare is achieved and society maximizes revenues. But the knowledge of widespread tax evasion erodes individuals' will to comply with taxation law because it provides clues regarding the preferences of other taxpayers. Hence, social knowledge and beliefs about such preferences affect taxpayers' decisions. The differences in the perceptions of taxpayers in Argentina and Chile are remarkable. When people were asked to estimate the compliance behavior of society at large, 83 percent of Argentines said that the majority of taxpayers cheat on their taxes in large amounts, whereas in Chile only 22 percent believed this to be the case (surveys 1 and 6). Thus, the expectation of cheating among taxpayers in Argentina is significantly higher than in Chile. Clearly, taxpayers in Argentina do not trust others to comply, and the basic necessary assumption for a warranty-game solution is lacking.

Beginning with Levi's contingent-consent theory, the assumption that taxpayers' dominant strategy is to comply only to the extent that others are living up to their commitments has been developed in the tax compliance literature.[5] Two important considerations, however, have not yet received enough scholarly attention: the effects of contagion as a learning tool for compliance decisions, and the role of governments as guarantors of cooperation. The scarcity of studies of these two important factors is due, to some extent, to the need for longitudinal studies that capture the dynamic adjustment of taxpayers to different environments across time.

Information and communication strongly influence individual decision making. In 2 × 2 or small-N interactive games, people learn to overcome tragic outcomes by observing the moves of other players. But how do individuals learn and communicate in large-N settings? For example, taxpayers file tax returns periodically and shortly thereafter find out whether the taxation authority has decided to take any enforcement actions against them. But how do they know whether others have been sanctioned for cheating, or how do they measure the extent to which they are being exploited by other taxpayers? Imitation and contagion become two of the best mechanisms to predict compliance in large groups.[6] People tend to conform to median behavior and follow others' decisions if they perceive them as worthy.[7] To make sound decisions, people need valuable information acquired from peers, and they anticipate the consequences of group sanctions, leading to the adoption of herd behavior.

Taxpayers must rely on trustworthy information about the best strategic decisions (Scholz 1995, 1998). Given the very limited information

---

5. For a good article that reviews part of the literature on the subject, see Lederman 2003.

6. There is a long sociological tradition on this topic. Two central contributions in the last decades are Coleman 1990 and Granovetter 1978. See also Cialdini 1984 for the concept of imitation and social validation in the psychology literature, and Sunstein 2001, 15–18, for contributions in the field of law.

7. See, for example, the study of childbearing out of wedlock by Akerloff et al. (1996) and the study of social influence in choosing restaurants by Becker (1991). In relation to legal behavior, see the discussion of the two mechanisms that account for the effect of social influence, information, and reputation in Sunstein 2001.

that they have about the likelihood of audits, as well as about the extent of others' compliance, players adopt a strategy based on learned "success," resulting in an evolutionary process. Rational imitation is a powerful mechanism for compliance decisions because, as Cervantes's Don Quixote knew perfectly well centuries ago, it resolves information problems and minimizes exploitation. Where people think that everybody cheats, tax evasion is perceived as safer and, more important, as fair. Looking at peers and competitors becomes the best way for individuals to make compliance decisions (Hedstrom 1998; see also North 2005 for the dynamic of economic change). In this way, rational imitation is a powerful social-proof validation that partly explains how conditional cooperation operates in large tax environments.

The study of enforcement must shift from the strict individual deterrence perspective. The proper frame for the study of enforcement is its role as a third-party guarantor of conditional cooperation. Tax-policy practitioners and the advocates of deterrence theory have traditionally overlooked this very important dimension because their theoretical perspective considers taxpayers only as rational profit maximizers who interact in 2 × 2 games with tax authorities. But this is only a fraction of the problem, because individual motivations to cheat or comply depend largely on others' behavior. This invites different enforcement strategies depending on the culture and social beliefs of the group in question.

Exchange Equity

As I have already noted, conditional cooperation depends on the equity of taxation as a measure of vertical fairness that convinces people to comply. But I contend that, although important, vertical fairness is secondary to the condition of horizontal fairness.

Discount Rates

Rulers can coordinate cooperation by credibly threatening defectors. As the number of potential defectors increases, however, the credibility of rulers' threats decreases, because the efficacy of governmental enforcement diminishes. Therefore, to achieve cooperation the sovereign cannot rely solely on deterrence to enhance voluntary compliance. Players must be enticed to cooperate by acknowledging some returns for their contributions (Hardin 1982).

Margaret Levi claims that under tax regimes, conditional-cooperation players sacrifice current payoffs if they recognize the potential benefits of cooperation. Therefore, an important incentive for cooperation is the value that individuals assign to the provision of public goods. Cooperators will pay their taxes if the ruler delivers on his promises (Levi 1988, 1997). This is the *exchange-equity proposition*. From the perspective of a strict analysis of individual motivations, I stress that this is an incomplete account of the tax compliance game due to the asymmetry of contributions, which renders differentiated incentives among taxpayers. Because the lion's share of taxes is extracted from a small portion of taxpayers, it pays for small taxpayers to contribute to obtain a large return for their contributions, whereas large taxpayers are worse off if they pay their taxes.

The "possibilities of cooperation" can materialize even in the absence of a third-party (vertical) enforcer (Taylor 1995).[8] In such a case, cooperation in N-person games becomes a function of mutual (horizontal) enforcement and the discount rates—that is, the value that cooperators assign to the benefits of exchange equity. Taxpayers with high discount rates prefer to "take the money and run" instead of delaying the gratification of tax evasion for the rewards of future collective goods. Conversely, a low discount rate enhances individual readiness to cooperate. Cooperation in both cases becomes a function of individual preferences about the future.[9]

One problem with this proposition is that preferences are generally treated as exogenous to games—that is, as part of the individual structure of tastes. I contend, however, that discount rates (the value assigned to the future provision of public goods) are *endogenous* to the tax compliance game. Individual tastes, beliefs, and perceptions are shaped by the structure of the cooperation game. Cheaters have high discount rates, and legalists have low discount rates. The environments in which people live create the incentives and the individual structure of their preferences. In a noncompliance environment, people discount the future not because they have an unbiased predisposition to cheat but because this disposition has been acquired through social mechanisms that make such a preference rational.

The endogenous nature of this collective action is at the heart of the culture of compliance, because the distribution of taxpayers with high

---

8. If two players agree about the benefits of cooperation, they do not need an enforcer to entice them into collective action. The best well-known solution to the prisoner's dilemma is the iterated game (tit for tat), wherein continuous interaction evolves into mutual agreements. But the effectiveness of tit for tat diminishes as the number of players increases (Skyrms 1996).

9. See appendix B for a broader description of this problem.

or low discount rates is not random. This poses significant challenges for the exchange-equity proposition. Given that the type of equilibrium largely accounts for discount rates, predispositions and beliefs are not independent of the definition of the game but, on the contrary, are affected by the structure of the payoffs. Therefore, culture is not an independent exogenous variable to tax compliance but rather a reinforcing predictor of a stable outcome.

Voice or Exit?

Before I begin the more formal analysis of the relationship between enforcement and compliance in taxation, something should be said about a classic issue that affects compliance. One of the principles of modern taxation is voice. The call for the sacrifices of citizens and their contributions to the collective well-being rests on an exchange between the government's extraction institutions and the taxpayer's community participation.

Voice can be defined in multiple ways. The basic requirement of representation in exchange for taxation has become the metaphor, or justification, for the legitimacy of taxpaying, but other types of active participation in a political community can also channel the voices of taxpayers. According to this perspective, people will contribute to the extent that they belong to a community that upholds their values and strengthens their identities. In short, voice in modern taxation requires some measure of active citizenship that not only defines rights but also protects them. Inclusive political communities that enfranchise their members and deliver public goods are better positioned to extract higher revenues, because giving citizens voice elicits their cooperation.[10]

Conversely, the failure of citizenship triggers other individual strategies, most notably exit. Citizens who do not feel that their interests, values, or identities are genuinely represented by their political institutions might take noncooperative steps, including tax evasion, as exit strategies. Of course, there is a wide repertoire of exit options, including rebellion and active defiance of authority, but often tax evasion is an important strategy among citizens who lack strong attachments to their political communities (Bird, Martinez-Vazquez, and Torgler 2006). Immigrants and foreigners, on average, pay less in taxes than locals, minorities less than majorities, and the underprivileged less than the well-to-do (Lederman

10. See Scholz 2003 for a more formal development. According to Scholz, democracies are better equipped to establish a "tax contract" with their citizens, making taxpayers "adaptive contractarians" (people who comply when the conditions for cooperation are met but otherwise defect). Democracies nurture these contracts more effectively.

2003). The level of compliance has some positive correlation with political-community membership.[11] On the other hand, active community participation is not a sufficient condition for full tax compliance. Many taxpayers evade taxes despite having voice. Still, the scope of this evasion and citizens' propensities differ significantly: the stronger a citizen's voice, the smaller the temptation to free ride.

For this reason, the claim that dictatorships can reverse the course of noncompliance equilibria and extract higher revenues is flawed. Although such a reversal might temporarily be effected in some cases, I contend, following Scholz (2003), that stable tax collection depends on an explicit social contract between government and taxpayers, according to which the latter have strong feelings of membership and do not feel exploited. Dictatorship can improve tax collection in the short term due to two effects: the perceived sudden severity of strong enforcement is very high, and the support of a new dictatorship by powerful elites can mobilize stronger commitment to contribute for the success of this government. In the latter case, a restricted and powerful economic elite uses its voice to influence tax compliance; this situation very likely explains the increased revenues that the military dictatorship in Chile initially received after the overthrow of democratically elected president Salvador Allende in 1973.

In sum, voice equity and a low discount rate contribute to higher levels of tax compliance, but they are conditional on horizontal fairness.

Information, Culture, and Path Dependency

Tax Culture

Since the inception of work in the field, research on tax compliance has emphasized the normative and cultural dimension of tax culture (Schwartz and Orleans 1967; Cialdini 1989; Kinsey 1987). This scholarship, however, has not accounted for the causal mechanisms affecting how culture or values emerge as explanatory variables for divergent tax compliance. Rather, culture became a default variable when economic and political variables did not fit (Frey and Feld 2002; Alm, Sanchez, and de Juan 1995).

Culture is more than a set of informal institutional rules but far less than an overwhelming force that predetermines agency. The fact that

---

11. See Lieberman 2003 for an excellent case of restricted citizenship. He argues that the white minority in South Africa bore a heavy tax burden throughout the twentieth century precisely because they usually felt included in the political community and had "voice" through their NPC (national political community).

taxpayers have limited information and computational capabilities does not imply they are irrational. Individuals observe other people's behaviors (such as tricks and shortcuts) to evaluate their best strategies for optimizing utility. In this sense, the living culture of the given equilibrium provides the repertoire that serves them best. In that sense, I agree with Rothstein that culture should be understood as a toolbox: "What people 'think what other agents are going to do' is of course something they learn (or make inferences about) from the culture in which they live" (2005, 37).

Legal cultures evolve out of social interactions that are for the most part effective in providing group members with reasonable solutions to social dilemmas. In this way, culture allows for the relaxation of the rational estimation of costs and benefits, which most people rarely use in daily activities. Indeed, many other "devices" and mechanisms, most notably heuristics and adaptation mechanisms, exist to help people resolve difficult cognitive decisions.[12] Culture, or the way that things are "usually done," becomes a source of information for making safe, strategic decisions.

Tax cultures filter the way that taxpayers construct the complexities of the world they inhabit and shape our understanding of behavior in equilibrium. Tax cultures change very slowly, precisely because taxpayers' behaviors are in equilibrium: if the choices of the majority of taxpayers do not change, there are no incentives for individual taxpayers to change course. Note that single taxpayers might be ideologically opposed to the values promoted by the constraining culture, but they will very likely behave as the equilibrium dictates because of the cost involved in standing up to the dominant culture.

Because the stability of tax cultures is tied to the individual costs of compliance, shifts are possible to the extent that sufficient changes occur in the relative cost of tax compliance. There are at least three sources of costs: normative costs, which arise out of the asymmetry between individuals' values and actual behavior; the direct monetary cost of paying taxes; and enforcement costs, or the individual estimation of how likely it is that noncompliance will trigger costly enforcement action. Leaving the first two constant, a noncompliance culture may be transformed into a compliance culture if the relative cost of enforcement is widespread, neutralizing the epidemic effect of tax evasion. Therefore, relying on enforcement alone to change a noncompliance environment requires very effective enforcement among a very large segment of taxpayers. Most tax

12. For a recent review on prospect theory and the law, see Guthrie 2003 and Scholz 2003 on the adaptive contractarian approach.

administrations in noncompliance environments fail in their attempts to change tax climates.

Coevolution of Culture and Enforcement

It is useful to conceptualize culture and enforcement as coevolving. But how does culture evolve? How do people retrieve cultural patterns in order to make choices? Because it is beyond the scope of this book to solve this puzzle, instead I will present a framework that describes how enforcement shapes a culture of compliance and how such a culture conditions the effectiveness of enforcement. The coevolution of enforcement and compliance supports the concept of two equilibria and allows for a flexible framework to explain the success of enforcement.

Tax-filing practices are remarkably stable, as I have mentioned, because most people make only modest adjustments from one year to the next. Several critical events might significantly change an individual's decisions about tax compliance, including sudden changes in income, the introduction of new enforcement measures, the acquisition of new information about others' strategies, or the reversal of economic conditions. Nonetheless, these critical events occur occasionally, and therefore the most predictable outcome is that taxpayers will adopt stable compliance patterns.

Three interconnected dimensions of the coevolution of culture and enforcement emerge from these assumptions. The first is the trajectory path of new taxes (given the initial success of enforcement). The most critical stage for a new tax is at the enactment stage. Taxes have a higher probability of being widely complied with when they are first being imposed. The propagation of compliance or noncompliance with a new tax stabilizes the initial equilibrium and creates a path-dependent trajectory. Therefore, enforcement is extremely important immediately following the enactment of new taxation laws; once equilibrium is reached, the culture of compliance will develop the repertoire of choices that most individuals will undertake. In the second section of this chapter, I describe the different strategies of governmental enforcement, which are dependent on the norm's phase: norm-emerging enforcement and norm-maintenance enforcement. The widespread evasion of a new tax at its earliest stage is difficult to reverse precisely because a noncompliance culture takes root, which weakens enforcement.[13]

---

13. The shortcomings of populism lie precisely at this juncture, where new taxes are levied to compensate for weak-compliance cultures. Because taxes generate meager revenues, new taxes continue to be enacted, furthering the weakness of the tax environment.

Second, in a compliance equilibrium, enforcement and culture coevolve because the individual relative cost of enforcement is high, inhibiting tax-payers from undertaking the risk of getting caught and sanctioned. Up-holding the norm of paying taxes contributes to compliance climates and stabilizes such an equilibrium.

Third, culture also contributes to the success of enforcement. In compliance equilibria, the government enjoys the reputation of being a swift sanctioner, which enables it to promote new taxes that enjoy taxpayers' initial disposition to comply. More widespread initial compliance helps rulers punish free riders and signal to compliers that their choices were the right ones. Enforcement within compliance environments validates individual choices and further reproduces legal culture. Thus, a virtuous equilibrium in taxation helps enforcement and compliance to coevolve.

Critical Mass and Tipping Points

In compliance environments, some cheaters may still opt to actively pursue "tax aversion" (Fennell and Fennell 2003; Davis, Hecht, and Perkins 2003). As a general rule, however, they will invest less effort in cheating when most of their peers or competitors comply with tax laws. Modest levels of underreported income or overstated deductions, which are typically found in compliance environments, differ greatly from the more aggressive forms of tax evasion found in noncompliance cultures, where taxpayers sometimes underreport their income by 60 or 70 percent and engage in fraudulent transactions, bribes, and other illegal behaviors.

The weak enforcement found in noncompliance equilibria poses an important empirical question: to what extent does tax evasion make a noncompliance equilibrium stable? If tax evasion is not widely extended (beyond the marginal "tax misreports" that individuals undertake), it might not reach the critical mass that triggers contagion. Conversely, as we have seen, beyond a given threshold taxpayers are "forced" to cheat (see the previous analogy to the tragedy of the commons), or are more likely to imitate an already-rooted and widespread tax misconduct.

In this book, I suggest that a tipping-point argument can be very useful in examining the stability of both equilibria. Once the number of cheaters reaches a critical mass, it becomes very difficult for governmental enforcement to reverse the course; conditional cooperation is broken and rational imitation produces greater incentives for cheaters to cheat. What is that tipping point? No existing research attempts to answer this question, but published data suggest that when nations have less than 25 percent tax noncompliance, vertical enforcement appears to deter most taxpayers from engaging in active tax evasion. Conversely, where tax non-compliance exceeds 40 percent, my survey data suggest that taxpayers cannot be deterred from noncompliance. These are aggregate compliance rates that do not account for the structure and opportunities presented by different tax systems, nor do they account for within-country variance, in which certain sectors or trades, as a group, present a different compliance trend than the majority of taxpayers.[14] Although in this book I concentrate on the national level, the basic idea of epidemics holds. In addition to infectious agents, contagion depends on the scale of the environment wherein these agents operate.[15]

Some remarks should be made about the bimodal properties of compliance equilibria.[16] That tax compliance tends to support two equilibria does not, of course, imply that other equilibria are impossible. On the contrary, the evidence indicates that tax-evasion rates range widely. My claim is that intermediate equilibria are usually unstable and are pulled toward one of the two extremes. Enforcement may be somewhat successful in the compliance mode, or imitation and contagion may produce strong incentives for taxpayers to cheat, pulling toward a noncompliance equilibrium. Some evidence supports this assertion. The VAT productivity index (see table 2.7 in chapter 2) shows different levels of compliance for different countries in 1992. If it is assumed that 25 percent or less (seven out of the twenty countries) represents a tax compliance equilibrium, and over 40 percent a noncompliance equilibrium (five countries), the countries in the index can be divided into three groups, with the ones in the 25–40 percent range (eight countries) belonging to the intermediate category. A comparison of compliance rates between 1992 and 2002 shows that all seven cases in the compliance environments, and four out of five in the noncompliance environments, remained in their respective categories—that is, the environments were stable. As for the eight nations in the middle, four slipped into the noncompliance equilibrium,[17]

14. For example, because of the level of business concentration, the compliance rate of financial sectors is relatively high even in noncompliance nations.

15. Given the variability and complexity of taxpayers' activity, there is more tax evasion in certain trades than in others; see Davis, Hecht, and Perkins 2003 for the United States. There is also a noncompliance equilibrium within broader compliance environments. Therefore, the tipping-point approach can potentially be extrapolated to sectors or trades.

16. I thank an anonymous reader for the suggestion to delve further into bimodality in tax compliance.

17. In 2002, Mexico, Argentina, Ecuador, and Honduras became highly noncompliant. Conversely, Uruguay was 1 percent short of becoming highly compliant.

one achieved "compliance status," and the remaining three have stayed in the middle category. In short, in the stable equilibria eleven out of twelve remained in their original compliance or noncompliance groups, whereas only three out of eight remained in the intermediate category.

When a tax equilibrium does shift, it is more likely to move from compliance to noncompliance. States that cannot sufficiently curtail free riding might face tax-collection shortages in the long run because the number of noncompliers can reach critical mass, at which point contagion and weak horizontal enforcement undermine a previously virtuous equilibrium. An unstable equilibrium will most likely deteriorate until defection becomes the dominant strategy. The tipping point must be estimated for each tax according to the structure of opportunities, the scope of incentives, and the distribution of the tax burden, among other variables. For example, when income tax is withheld at the source and most taxpayers work in the formal economy, the incentives to evade the tax are small. Conversely, if a sufficient number of taxpayers are exempted from withholding requirements or the informal sector of the economy is large, a shift into more aggressive noncompliance is to be expected, even by those whose income is withheld at the source. Although it is far from an exact estimation, the Argentina-Chile comparison and the evidence from other countries indicate that once a third of taxpayers manage to successfully evade paying a significant share of their taxes, the compliance equilibrium becomes very unstable. The simulation in appendix C confirms this result. Chapters 3–7 will test this proposition for Argentina and Chile.

ENFORCEMENT AND COMPLIANCE WITH NORMS

Let us now consider the theoretical underpinnings of the enforcement of norms and the role of legitimacy, particularly the relationship among enforcement, the individual cost of compliance, and legitimacy.

Norms and Compliance

Norms are expected behavior regularities backed by force. What distinguishes social norms from legal norms is the type of sanctions that backs them. Social norms are enforced by the threat of informal sanctions, such as shame, guilt, shunning, and so forth, whereas legal norms are backed by the threat of formal sanctions. The enforcers of social norms are the members of a community; the enforcer of legal norms is the state.[18]

Enforcement affects the development of norms. Legal enforcement is based on impersonal relations, with sanctions executed by institutions that command certain levels of legitimacy. On the other hand, informal sanctions are more effective in closer groups, in which social norms mediate interpersonal relations to resolve collective endeavors. The institutionalization of norms entails a public, formal recognition of the mechanisms that activate sanctions, and presupposes a reasonable expectation that those sanctions will be applied. Thus, the institutionalization of norms depends on the predictability of sanctions: the higher the expectation that sanctions will be imposed, the more institutionalized the norm. *Formal sanctions* are effective to the extent that legal institutions are capable of imposing them. *Informal sanctions* are effective to the extent that prestige and close-knit relations are important within a community.

Formal and informal sanctions differ in the predictability and universality of enforcement. Informal sanctions are usually more stringent but less predictable. Formal sanctions are less stringent but more predictable. As sanctions become more institutionalized, they become more predictable, but they also become less severe and more likely to be imposed. Predictability allows for the relaxation of the severity in exchange for expected behavior becoming more regular. Formal rules are abided by to the extent that the probability of sanction imposition increases. Informal-rules abidance improves according to the importance of interpersonal relations.

Legitimacy and Enforcement

There is a need to distinguish between two different phases of norm enforcement: the emergence phase and the maintenance phase. An emerging norm generally requires more stringent enforcement than a norm already rooted in the community. As I have mentioned, I call the type of enforcement for the first phase norm-emerging enforcement, and the second stage norm-maintenance enforcement. At both stages, enforcement is tied to the legitimacy of the norm. For the most part, new taxes require norm-emerging enforcement, whereas established taxes require norm-maintenance enforcement.

---

18. There is a large literature on social norms and their effect on compliance in general and taxes in particular. Some will be alluded to here and in following chapters. For general reviews, see Kahan 2001, Ostrom 2000, Chong 1999, Posner 2000, and Bicchieri 1997.

Fig. 1.1 Legitimacy and Enforcement of Norms

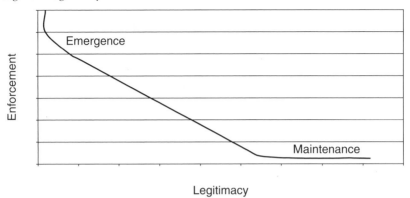

Legitimacy

Legitimacy and the enforcement of norms are inversely associated (see fig. 1.1). The lower the legitimacy of a norm, the more resources the enforcer needs to allocate to ensure that people obey and finally embrace the norm. The goal for every norm is to gain such wide legitimacy that enforcement can be kept to a minimum. That is the nature of tax compliance: the lower the legitimacy of taxes, the more enforcement is needed and the harder it is to attain a good tax compliance rate. Note that even norms with a high level of legitimacy require at least some level of enforcement; otherwise, free riders prevail, and ultimately the norm disappears. On the other hand, even with strong enforcement, good compliance requires some level of legitimacy. Totalitarian states cannot rely solely on brute deterrence to guarantee compliance (which is why the curve in fig. 1.1 is asymptotic).

The individual cost of upholding a norm strongly affects its legitimacy.[19] Conforming to the practice of voting every four years, for example, is less costly than paying taxes every month. There is more need of enforcement of the latter norm than of the former, because legitimacy improves as costs fall. This conclusion is self-evident. What requires a better explanation is why the legitimacy of taxation is higher in some countries than in others, given similar distribution of individual costs. If the assumption that nobody likes to pay taxes holds, then the legitimacy of taxation is exogenous to the norm. Two alternative answers are possible: that the threat of costly sanctions enhances legitimacy, or that norms efficiently resolve

19. For a detailed analysis of this subject, see Bergman 2003. Two factors account for the legitimacy: the value that such a norm embraces for the group to bind it together and resolve collective problems, and the individual cost of abiding. In this chapter, I concentrate on the latter.

collective problems where the perceived benefits of compliance exceed the perceived costs. In these cases, compliance slowly becomes a convention that empowers authorities to curtail free riding.

The association between legitimacy and subjectively perceived cost is also inverted. The higher the subjective individual cost of abiding by a norm (paying taxes, contributing to charities, volunteering, etc.), the lower the perceived individual legitimacy of the norm will be. If all other factors hold constant, the higher the perceived individual cost of adhering to a norm, the less likely a person will be to embrace it. It is important to keep in mind here that costs are not only material but also include normative, emotional, and reputation factors.

In many cases, perceptions of cost are strongly influenced by the way that people perceive the social utility of the norm. Enlisting in the armed forces in time of war is perceived as less socially costly than in peacetime, for example, because the social value placed on volunteering in times of war is very high. Paying taxes when there is an external threat is perceived to be less costly than paying the same amount in taxes when there is no social solidarity among community members.[20] To the extent that people perceive that norms are efficient and are good mechanisms to solve collective-action problems, the social value of these norms increases, as does the level of sanctions for violations.[21]

Enforcement Equilibrium

What level of enforcement is necessary to ensure compliance with a norm? The classic response is that enforcement is effective when its marginal cost does not exceed the marginal utility to be obtained. For the optimal enforcement of taxation norms, every additional dollar invested in audits or other measures should yield at least more than one dollar in additional assessments or fines (Plumley 2002). But this view only considers optimality from the enforcement agency's perspective; it has nothing to do with social welfare.

I claim that optimal enforcement entails the distribution of compliance

---

20. As mentioned in note 11, Lieberman's study (2003) shows that the white minority in South Africa was willing to contribute to fund the state in order to preserve the framework of a new political community, whereas in Brazil the basis for solidarity was fragmented and federalized, creating insurmountable obstacles to the establishment of a widely supported tax system.

21. A highly ranked norm carries stiffer penalties than a low-ranking norm because for high-ranking norms free riding is perceived as a serious threat to the general welfare.

within a society. Research thus far has largely ignored compliance distribution because enforcement has been perceived purely as a deterrence instrument, not as norm-maintenance strategy. Tax administrations, for example, are evaluated primarily by the amount of additional revenues they raise, and therefore they concentrate their resources on monitoring taxpayers in the higher-income brackets. This strategy might be effective when most people comply, but it is far less effective when everybody cheats, because it does not neutralize the imitation and contagion effect in taxation. This is why tax-noncompliance equilibria in developing countries are so resilient.

Optimal enforcement must account for at least four dimensions within the population: (1) the fairness and equality of the tax system, (2) the distribution of compliance, (3) the structures of individual costs (i.e., the relative price of compliance), and (4) the level of individual incentives to cheat. In this chapter, I assume that individual incentives are constant for the purpose of further developing the cultural and compliance argument. In the following chapters, I will integrate individual incentives as a variable that affects optimal enforcement. Let us now consider the first three dimensions in turn.

Fairness and equity of the tax system. Equality and fairness help enforcement. When the tax burden is evenly distributed among the population, everybody shares the costs of upholding the norm, and therefore its legitimacy is higher. Legalists adjust their compliance rate upward, and consequently they invest heavily in horizontal enforcement. The best strategy for the taxation authority is to make sure that nobody becomes a sucker and that compliance becomes self-enforcing. The tax burden is evenly distributed when citizens either make similar tax payments or participate in a perfectly progressive tax system: the fairer the system and the more evenly distributed the burden, the greater the legitimacy of taxation and the more effective the tax administration. State enforcement will benefit from lower taxes, evenly distributed individual costs, and low institutional transaction costs that yield higher welfare.

Compliance distribution. As the variance of individual costs increases, the legitimacy of the norm decreases and the incentives and temptations to free ride dramatically rise. When the tax burden is not evenly divided, compliers feel exploited. In the short run, however, enforcement can still be effective. In a country where 1 percent of the population has a tax burden of 10 percent and 99 percent of taxpayers bear a tax burden of 1 percent, for example, there is no need for stronger enforcement to ensure compliance, because the tax administration can easily monitor the small group of taxpayers who account for the lion's share of this country's revenues. The income tax in many countries started as a tax on large landowners who were easily targeted; decent enforcement ensured wider compliance.[22] As the need for revenue increased, taxation had to be expanded and therefore the number of taxpayers grew. If tax administration was by then not solidly established, the stable compliance equilibrium was threatened; the old enforcement strategies could not prevent the growth of free riding and its epidemic effect. The ensuing fiscal deficit led to the over-taxation of some taxpayers and the under-taxation of others, undermining the legitimacy of the norm (see FIEL 1998 for Argentina, and Arellano and Marfán 1987 for Chile). Under these conditions, some taxpayers carried the burden of funding the state and many others free rode; therefore, governmental enforcement failed and a noncompliance equilibrium thrived. Alternatively, a smaller variance of costs creates higher efficacy of enforcement.

Relative price of compliance. A third factor affecting enforcement is the association between costs and the number of compliers. If the individual cost of taxation is high but everybody pays, a compliance equilibrium is more easily attained than when costs are lower but most people cheat.[23] Legitimacy does not depend solely on the individual cost of taxation but also on the social value of the norm. Conversely, where most people cheat, the value of the norm diminishes and the temptations to free ride increase. The pure high cost of taxation can be mitigated to the extent that the norm is widely shared.[24]

An effective tax administration includes several institutions, formal and informal, legal and nonlegal, that directly frame the way taxation is individually perceived and its costs subjectively processed. Chile, the United States, Germany, and many of the Scandinavian nations enjoy better tax compliance than other nations not only because the perceived costs of punishment are higher but also because the resistance to being taxed is lower. Conversely, countries like Argentina, Indonesia, Mexico, and Russia have higher tax-evasion rates because the legitimacy of taxes

22. There was still vast noncompliance in many countries for an array of reasons. See Levi 1988 and Tilly 1975.

23. Tax rates and the tax burden are very high in northern Europe, whereas tax rates and the tax burden are relatively low in countries such as Argentina and Mexico. Nevertheless, compliance is much higher in the former countries. There are, obviously, other variables that contribute to this puzzle, but I contend that this is an important one.

24. See North 1990 for a theoretical examination of the effect of relative prices on institutional change.

and authorities is lower and the perceived payoffs for cheating are higher, which requires a level of enforcement difficult to attain.

Tax administrations in such countries can still manage to reduce tax evasion. Compliance with the VAT in Argentina during the 1990s, for example, was higher than in Mexico for the same period.[25] The better monitoring capacities and withholding systems of the Argentine tax administration, with respect to Mexico's, helped the former collect more revenues. Although superior tax administrations in adverse social environments cannot dramatically increase compliance, they are capable of somewhat compensating for lower legitimacy. Still, neither of these countries' tax administrations approaches the success of Chile's, which has a tax agency comparable to that of Argentina.[26] In Chile, the legitimacy of taxation is slightly higher that in Argentina. Thus, the penalties for breaking the law are more severe, and, more important, they carry more *credibility* than in Argentina. This is why the similar level of enforcement yields better compliance results in Chile than in Argentina or, to name a comparable case, in Germany than in Italy.

Tax-Enforcement Strategies

Tax administrators face a basic dilemma: they can develop strategies for monitoring and controlling a wide number of taxpayers, or they can concentrate on several exemplary cases, hoping that these will send the right message to the community. The majority of tax-administration policies are determined by this basic predicament. The dilemma is resolved either by a selective, in-depth audit strategy or by widespread but more superficial audit strategies.[27] Usually, the in-depth audit strategy is associated with compliance environments, and the wide-coverage strategy with noncompliance equilibria. Recent evidence in the United States, for example, shows that given the trend of increasing tax evasion, the IRS is slowly shifting from an in-depth audit strategy to a larger number of less stringent audits (Johnston 2007). In addition, other tax policies,

25. Argentina averaged 62 percent compliance during the 1990s and Mexico close to 55 percent for the same period (Bergman 2003).

26. In the simulated game of appendix C, the difference between good and poor tax administration yields a 10 percent difference in total aggregate compliance. Effective administrations generate slightly more compliance than noneffective tax administrations. Of course, the model is far from complete, but it shows the trend.

27. When a TA uses an in-depth audit strategy, it executes a small number of very detailed audits, whereas a wide-coverage audit strategy entails a much larger sample of cases but with less stringency.

such as the criminal punishment of tax evaders, the strategies of taxpayer registration, and the requirements of tax filing, are tied to these strategic goals in tax governance. All seek the optimal mechanism to enhance better compliance.

The success of enforcement measures depends on at least two additional factors that at times transcend tax-administration capacities. First, taxes must be "collection friendly" in order to facilitate the enforcer's job. The fulfillment of this requirement depends on the legislature's capacity to understand compliance constraints, as well as on the political incentives of lawmakers to legislate taxes that allow for better monitoring. Second, effective prosecution and punishment of tax evaders requires institutional coordination of the whole court and prosecutorial system (Bergman 1998). Thus, the institutional capacity of enforcement to achieve optimal results depends on many organizations that very rarely coordinate their actions. This is particularly problematic in countries with poor democratic traditions and weak civil-service administrations.[28] Solid enforcement agencies must first resolve the range of institutional-coordination problems and then design an optimal strategy according to the type of compliance equilibrium that they face.

As derived from the enforcement phase and the legitimacy of the norm shown in figure 1.1, to ensure compliance new taxes have to be simple, compliance-friendly, and not severely costly, enabling norm-emergence enforcement to develop a greater likelihood of success. The enforcement of the complex income tax in a noncompliance environment is challenging, because different tax rates and tax complexities are most easily enforced in already-existing compliance environments. Conversely, where tax evasion is widespread, the best strategy for tax administrators must be to pursue norm-emerging enforcement based on a simple, low-cost, and evenly distributed tax burden. Most countries in Latin America, however, have taken a different course. The fiscal crises of the 1970s, 1980s, and 1990s increased rather than decreased the tax burden of individuals, thereby augmenting the incentives of players to defect from cooperation. As I have shown, the existence of a large number of people with high and unequal tax burdens undermines the social legitimacy of tax norms. Because fostering a strong compliance culture is a painful and piecemeal process, reversal of tax evasion becomes very difficult.

Of course, this conclusion does not imply that tax evasion is static. Change is possible, and indeed there are many examples of nations that

---

28. See Elizondo and Perez de Acha 2006 for an example of the role of constitutional courts and the lack of interagency coordination in undermining tax collection in Mexico.

have been successful in cutting down on tax evasion. In principle, most tax laws in the history of taxation have suffered some degree of resistance, and therefore most taxes require norm-emergence enforcement. The effectiveness of enforcement at the emergence phase dictates the success of enforcement at later stages. In this sense, compliance is path-dependent. The chapter that follows begins to apply some of the theoretical concepts introduced in this chapter to the cases of Argentina and Chile, with a particular focus on defining the dependent variable: the extent of tax compliance in these two countries.

2

MEASURING TAX COMPLIANCE IN
CHILE AND ARGENTINA

> The way in which the authorities have designed the structure of
> taxes in the community will significantly affect not only the amount
> of evasion that is likely to take place but also the means by which
> it takes place.
>
> — COWELL, *Cheating the Government*

This chapter undertakes a historical, political, and institutional comparison of tax compliance in Chile and Argentina. I begin with definitions of tax compliance and an overview of the main aspects of the tax systems in these two countries. After laying the groundwork for my inquiry, I undertake in the second part an in-depth analysis of different measures of noncompliance in historical context and also offer a comparative glance at other countries.

In the next pages, I lay the foundations for the analysis of the following chapters. By describing the fiscal historical trends of these two nations, and by assembling the sort of data necessary to prove the difference in compliance, this chapter presents a detailed description of the dependent variable. The cited data clearly indicates both that Chile has a much lower tax-evasion rate than neighboring Argentina and that these differences have been persistent over time. I show that these countries have a similar tax structure and comparable tax rates, which rules out the tax system as a causal factor for the divergent compliance rates. This difference is partly explained by the legacies of the different equilibria, which have significant implications for the divergent paths of development.

I provide measures of tax collection that demonstrate Argentina's inability to put its finances on stronger footing. This had curtailed the prospects of large-scale economic development, which requires the type of investment in public infrastructure that can only be sustained by more vigorous tax collection. Conversely, I present data on Chile that shows its strong revenue capacity, which at least partly explains why this country has been one of most dynamic and stable economies in the region over the last two decades. In this chapter I start developing the argument that high and sustained revenues can only be attained through solid tax compliance.

DEFINITIONS, HISTORY, AND STRUCTURE OF THE TAX SYSTEMS
IN CHILE AND ARGENTINA

I define compliance with tax laws as strict adherence to the legal provisions of the tax code. Tax administrations and research institutions usually estimate compliance rates based on studies of the gap between the expected revenues from a given tax and the total actually collected. Therefore, tax compliance is measured using official data: *tax compliance figures reflect what the state assumes is legally owed by taxpayers.* The state and taxpayers, however, do not necessarily share the same interpretation of tax dues.

The most frequent form of tax noncompliance is *tax evasion,* which entails the deliberate nondisclosure or inaccurate disclosure of transactions for the sake of maximizing profits. It shares the basic components of other forms of white-collar crime: cheating, lying, and theft (Wheeler et al. 1988; Croall 1992; Weisburd et al. 1991). The victim in this case is the state. Another form of noncompliance is *tax avoidance,* which is perceived as a legal form of dodging the system. Tax avoidance involves taking advantage of legal ambiguities and legal procedures to find loopholes and reduce tax liabilities.[1]

Compliance, then, is the accurate and timely *reporting* of tax liabilities according to the pertinent legal statutes. Unlike conformance to many other laws, in which citizens are required to refrain from engaging in proscribed behaviors, tax compliance requires action in the form of the periodic filing of a tax return. This requirement of active behavior makes it difficult to apply to tax evasion or avoidance the definitions of intention used to evaluate compliance with other types of laws.[2] Penal codes worldwide contain monetary thresholds that must be breached in order for evasion to be considered a crime.

Other forms of noncompliance are tax arrears and inadvertent tax errors. In the United States, for instance, seventeen million federal tax

1. Corporations and individuals with large tax dues generally use avoidance; Sutherland (1949) considers them the typical prototypes of what he defines as prestigious, honorable, and powerful offenders. The difference between tax evasion and tax avoidance lies not only in the interpretation of tax codes but also in the exploitation of the legal provisions by the powerful, who blur the criteria for disclosing transactions to avoid charges of deliberation and premeditation. As McBarnet (1991) states, although tax avoidance is technically legal, it is "whiter than white collar crime." See chapter 5.

2. For instance, Kidder and McEwen (1989) differentiate between lazy evasion, which results from slightly underreported income caused by the decision not to make the effort required for accurate reporting, and conventional evasion, in which there is a calculated intention to evade.

returns (one in every six) each year are submitted with clerical or mathematical errors that affect the total level of compliance (Long and Swingen 1991). Tax errors can lead to both underreporting and overreporting by taxpayers. No estimation of the magnitude of noncompliance due to errors has been made for Argentina and Chile. Tax errors are not seen as serious tax violations; taxpayers who make errors nonetheless implicitly recognize their tax liabilities, even if, due to error, they do not pay the correct amount at the designated time.

Thus, tax noncompliance may or may not be illegal, according to the shifting definitions of legality. Even when illegal forms of noncompliance occur, not every tax violation is a penal offense. In order to be defined as a crime, tax evasion must be based on the wrongful concealment of transactions and information, deliberate deception, or premeditated intent. Such criteria make tax evasion very difficult to prove (see Braithwaite and Geis 1982; Mann 1985).

Causes of tax noncompliance differ among individuals. For some taxpayers, the failure to comply stems from a willful act of evasion; for others, it results from ignorance of tax provisions or simple mistakes, laziness, and negligence. We can be certain, however, that the lion's share of tax noncompliance in Argentina and Chile is due to tax evasion; these nations rely heavily on the VAT, and tax avoidance is a very minimal problem in systems that use the VAT (see Tait 1988).

A Brief History of Taxation in Argentina and Chile

Tax policies are based on political needs and social conditions; the nature of a tax system is not necessarily determined by any economic rationale. Very rarely do policy makers prioritize efficiency, better allocation of resources, or the optimization of markets. Scholars who have studied the emergence of the tax system in Europe have shown that the ability of governments to tax was based on their ability to command conformity from subordinates, generally under adverse conditions (Bendix 1978; Tilly 1990; Levi 1988; Barzel 2002). The tax structures that emerged reflected the resolution of social disputes, such as the power struggle between kings and aristocrats, and, to a much lesser extent, measures of economic rationality.

Historically, the tax system of Argentina has been the locus of major confrontations. The fight to control the revenues generated by the port of Buenos Aires, the main trade gate to Europe, dominated the political life of the country throughout the nineteenth century. Statehood was only established between the 1860s and the 1880s after a compromise between the elite of Buenos Aires and the rest of the provinces enabled the creation of a tax system capable of extracting a stable flow of revenues from Argentina's expanding trade. These revenues were crucial for the foundation of a national army and a national school system (Oszlak 1982).[3] Centeno (2002) persuasively argues that "limited wars," as opposed to "total wars," were characteristic of nineteenth-century Latin America. Limited wars do not require encompassing organizations to extract revenues, and they do not create strong incentives to centralize power and build institutional capacity. Limited wars can be funded by debt, and in a context of limited wars tax systems grow weaker and rely mostly on international-trade taxes. Limited wars therefore produced "limited states." Of our two case studies, Argentina more closely resembles Centeno's limited-war model, though it is not an extreme case compared to the Andean nations, Brazil, or Mexico.[4]

The first Argentine tax system consisted of several indirect taxes levied mainly on international trade. A direct income tax was first legislated in 1932 to address the fiscal crisis generated by the Depression. Throughout the 1930s, the income tax had moderate marginal rates and did not include capital gains. This tax was further reformed in 1946 after Juan Perón was elected president. In 1951, additional direct taxes on property and wealth were levied in order to fund the nation's expanding and debt-ridden welfare programs. Shortly thereafter, social security and labor taxes were introduced and then expanded to meet the increasing demand for new social programs (which were fiscally unviable). Though Perón was overthrown in 1955, the tax system did not change significantly until 1975, when the value-added tax replaced the sales tax. Finally, a major overhaul of the tax system was launched in the early 1990s, which included changes in tax rates, the revision of the structure and provisions of current taxes, and the structure of the administration.[5]

Taxation policy in modern Argentina, then, can be divided into three

3. This provides support for Charles Tilly's proposition that taxes are levied to create armies, the foundation of modern states (1975, 1992).

4. The legacy of "blood and debt," instead of one of "blood and iron," undermined the ability to create strong organizations capable of extracting revenues and mobilizing their subjects for wars. "Latin Americans *have* frequently tried to kill one another, but they have generally not attempted to organize their societies with such a goal in mind," Centeno writes (2002, 35). For Centeno, however, wars "provide the stimulus for state growth. Wars can only make states if they are preceded by at least a modicum of political organization" (106). Chile appears to have a head start compared to Argentina.

5. For an encompassing analysis of the tax-reform policies and administration in the 1990s in Argentina from the legislative perspective, see Eaton 2002.

broad periods. The first period, from the 1870s to the 1940s, was characterized by moderate state intervention and reliance on indirect taxes. The second period, between the 1940s and 1990, coincided with the expansion of state welfare programs and displayed a mixed structure of direct and indirect taxes. The third period, beginning in 1990, has been characterized by significant investments in tax administration (Eaton 2002).

The collection of tax revenues in Chile similarly developed as a result of the wars of independence and the conquest of the areas south of Santiago, originally inhabited by the Mapuche. The successful political organization of Chile was due in part to the ability of the early governments in the 1820s and 1830s to create a decent army, funded by local criollos working on crops that would ultimately find their way to California.[6] Again, foreign-trade taxes became a good source of revenue that increased dramatically when, in the second half of the century, Chile began to exploit copper and saltpeter. With its strong army directed by a centralized and well-organized state (which made it a Latin American outlier, following Centeno's argument), Chile was able to win wars against Bolivia and Peru, gaining both land and wealth. At the turn of the century, more than 40 percent of government revenues came from export duties (particularly from the mining sector).

But rapid mobilization and new flows of immigration into central and southern Chile (albeit less significant in scope than those of Argentina) put some pressure on foreign trade as the sole source of revenue. This pressure was particularly acute because the Chilean armed forces were occupying foreign land and suppressing internal strife. New taxes began to be levied. The first income-tax laws were enacted in 1924–25, with modest marginal rates ranging from 2 percent to 9 percent; these laws affected capital rents and foreign enterprises in addition to personal income (impuesto global complementario; see Arellano and Marfán 1987).

Recurring fiscal deficits along with calls for a more state participation in education, infrastructure, and social spending led to slight increases in marginal rates and the introduction of taxes on alcohol, tobacco, and other consumption goods. In 1954, Chile enacted a sales tax with a base rate of 3 percent and a top rate of 10 percent; a year later, this tax was raising revenues equal to those of the mining sector. Problems of centralized control and inflation ushered in the tax reforms of 1964, which

6. The state in Chile preceded wars. According to Centeno (2002), however, the Chilean "exception" still fit the general Latin American pattern of limited "extraction" of resources from the domestic economy, as Chile was able to enter international commerce and gain access to external finance and debt.

focused on tax simplification (mainly for the income tax) and introduced a very innovative and successful inflationary adjustment.

In 1975, a new cadre of economists and technocrats (known as the "Chicago Boys" for the prestigious American university where many of them obtained their Ph.D.s) revamped the tax system. They introduced the VAT and dismantled exemptions and promotional activities, the cornerstones of decades of interventionist policies. The new system was designed to be neutral and expand the free market. Many enterprises were privatized, although the copper industry remained under public ownership. In the 1980s, the income tax was reformed: the number of exemptions was reduced, and investment incentives were added. Finally, in 1990, the new democratic government raised VAT and income-tax rates in order to finance increases in social spending. Throughout this period, the tax administration improved its organizational capacities significantly.

Three broad periods of taxation, then, can also be identified in Chile. The first, extending from the 1830s to 1925, was characterized by an increasingly centralized state that began to successfully monitor an expanding foreign trade. From 1925 to 1973, the tax system adjusted to meet increasing demands for social expenditures, and it remained a contested arena among social and political groups. In the last period, which began in 1975, the tax system has been based on a mix of direct taxes and indirect taxes with very few rates, and it has featured a heavily centralized tax administration.

The Structure of the Tax Systems

Argentina and Chile have very comparable tax systems. Both countries enjoy large tax bases and rely heavily on two main sources of revenues, the VAT and income tax.[7] They also levy a range of other taxes, most notably the social security payroll tax and many excise taxes, as well as a small share of property taxes (see tables 2.1A and 2.1B for the share of these taxes in total country revenues). These two countries were among the leaders in the region in introducing encompassing tax reforms.[8] The following is a brief description of the most important taxes in Argentina and Chile.

7. Alesina and Spolaore (2003) contend that large nations rely on increasing numbers of taxpayers to reduce the per-capita cost of public goods. These two countries are relatively large within the Latin American context.

8. For an in-depth study of the determinants of tax reforms in the region over the last decades, see Mahon 2004.

The *VAT* is recognized worldwide as efficient and relatively easy to administer, and it became the cornerstone of tax reform in Latin America (Mahon 2004; Durand and Thorp 1998; Edwards 1995; Cassanegra de Jantscher 1990). It taxes the aggregate value at every stage of production and commercialization of goods and services. Its strength is its simple reporting procedure: taxpayers charge their clients the stipulated rate and deduct the taxes paid to their suppliers. Because the production-consumption link generates a chain of traceable documentation, the VAT is difficult to evade. In order to evade VAT effectively, taxpayers need to generate a "black" chain (a conspicuous agreement between taxpayers). If the tax administration successfully controls the final link of the chain—that is, if final consumption produces proper documentation—this automatically "trickles up" the burden of taxpaying for the production and commercialization chain. Although the strength of this tax is its simplicity, its main weakness lies in political manipulation via tax credits to special interests, which leads to distortions and adversely affects its progressiveness.[9]

Historically, in both Argentina and Chile, *income taxes* have been paid by the wealthy. In Argentina, there are four brackets, which exclude the vast majority of wage earners. Chile's income tax has generally had two to three brackets, and, again, most wage earners are exempted. Until recently, no significant withholding system was in place (a crucial tool for fighting tax evasion), and taxes were voluntarily reported once or twice a year. The reforms that took place in the 1980s in Chile and during the 1990s in Argentina broadened the tax base. The minimum taxable income was lowered, and most middle-level wage earners began to be taxed. Withholdings for employees and monthly tax payments for professionals and independents were instituted, and a final annual tax return is now required. Still, the vast majority of Argentines, and many Chileans, do not pay income taxes. In Argentina, the marginal tax rates are moder-

9. There is an ongoing debate on the progressiveness of VAT. Its supporters contend that the tax is potentially very progressive if generalized and sustained over time. If applied to all goods and services at the same rate and kept constant, it will ultimately tax all consumption regardless of taxpayer income. If these two conditions are met, then the tax is not regressive, because the difference in income will be translated entirely into a difference in spending. Savings not spent by the earner will be spent by the heirs. If income is invested, the benefits will ultimately translate into higher consumption. According to this argument, the actual lack of progressiveness in the VAT is because the two conditions are not met: (a) the rate has constantly changed, and some taxpayers' revenue in higher brackets is diverted abroad and therefore not ultimately taxed; and (b) many goods and services are exempted from the tax, thereby distorting the allocation of resources.

ate. Over the last twenty years, the higher bracket has not exceeded 35 percent. In Chile, tax rates are slightly higher, reaching 45 percent.[10]

Social security and payroll taxes were launched and expanded during the presidencies of Perón in Argentina and Ibañez in Chile to fund pension plans and benefits for workers. They accounted for 15 to 25 percent of total tax revenues, although their importance has recently diminished, particularly in Chile. These taxes were levied at a fixed rate that has changed over the years. In Argentina, the payroll tax rate ranged between 30 and 40 percent of nominal salaries. In Chile, the payroll tax's share of total revenues decreased from an average of 7.1 percent of GDP in 1960–64 to 6.4 percent between 1965 and 1971 and 3.5 percent in 1974–84 (Arellano and Marfán, 1987). This tax has always been a locus of debate and political struggle, with many analysts arguing that employers' tax burdens need to be reduced.[11] In fact, the payroll tax is a very inefficient form of income tax for low-income earners.

An array of *taxes on goods and services* has contributed significantly to revenues in both Argentina and Chile. Traditionally, governments taxed tobacco, alcohol, and luxury goods. But the fuel tax, in its different forms, is the most important of the excise taxes. This tax is easy to collect because it only requires strict control over major companies. Fuel taxes are usually levied to alleviate severe and immediate fiscal deficits, particularly in situations of economic crisis, when tax evasion usually expands. In Chile, for example, excise taxes accounted for 40 percent of total revenues in 1974 (the year after Allende was overthrown), and in Argentina they approached 50 percent of total revenues in 1988 (just before the hyperinflation of 1989). After 1990, their share of total taxes decreased in both countries.

In Argentina, the provinces levy a *property tax*, which is their main source of revenue. In Chile, its relative importance is smaller. From the revenue standpoint, the key to successful property-tax collection is the periodic adjustment of property values and the control of accurate reporting. Although this would appear to be a relatively simple task for local administrations, it has proved a difficult endeavor. In Argentina, there are important variations in the level of compliance among provinces,

10. The Impuesto Global Complementario (Global Complementary Tax) is levied on the individual earnings of executives or employees after they have paid corporate tax. It reached a maximum of 45 percent in the 1980s and 1990s.

11. Over the last decade, several tax reforms have been debated in Argentina, centering on the gradual elimination or drastic reduction of employers' tax contributions.

but the estimated evasion rate has generally exceeded 60 percent (FIEL 1991). An overall study of the level of property-tax noncompliance in Chile has yet to be undertaken, but such behavior is believed to be much less prevalent than in Argentina.

Foreign-trade revenues have historically been significant for both Chile and Argentina. For instance, in Argentina, during the second period (1940s–80s) as well as during the period immediately following the default (2002–4), a withholding tax on exports was crucial to offsetting the sharp decline in government revenues from other sources. Direct taxes on wealth, assets, and interests, as well as indirect taxes on earmarked consumption, have had mixed results in recent years. In Chile, a tax levied during the 1990s on mobile capital to restrict short-term speculative investment is considered to have been moderately effective. On the other hand, in both countries taxes on conspicuous consumption, wealth, presumed rents, and so forth have been less successful. These taxes, particularly direct taxes, require an administration capable of identifying potential taxpayers, assessing the appropriate tax, and effectively collecting it. As Bird (1992a) summarizes, there is a need for the "three E's": to enumerate, estimate, and enforce. Argentina's tax administration historically has not been very strong in any of the three areas, and Chile's has not been much better.

The Centralization of Tax Collection

Chile is a very centralized state. As such, the Internal Tax Service (Servicio de Impuestos Internos, or SII) has become a very powerful agency; its offices in Santiago boast a high degree of cohesion and obedience. SII has been moderately successful in developing programs that enable the entire country to achieve solid institutional performance and good coordination among governmental agencies. SII adjusts faster, more easily, and more effectively than its Argentine counterpart to changing environments and is therefore better poised to accomplish policy goals.

In Argentina, the only significant tax collected by the provinces is the property tax; cities and counties levy other minor municipal taxes. Nonetheless, provinces receive a share of taxes collected by the central government according to changing allocation criteria—particularly population share but also lobbying efforts based on each province's political strength. Economically backward provinces receive a disproportionately large share of revenues, a fact that tends to diminish the incentives for improving local tax collection. Argentina's system of "co-participation" is rooted in a federal tradition designed to help provinces. Unfortunately, it has created a distorted mechanism of resource allocation.[12] The central government's Federal Administration of Public Revenues (Administración Federal de Ingresos Públicos, or AFIP)—a large organization that resulted from the merger in 1997 of DGI (Dirección General Impositiva) and the Customs Authority—collects the majority of tax revenues. Social spending, however, is run by provinces and funded mainly by the federal government. The lack of incentives for provincial administrations to levy taxes has created a weak and inefficient local tax system.

The Structure of Tax Revenues

Comparing total revenues of each type of tax as a share of the GDP provides a good description of the relative importance of each tax, its share of total taxes collected, and the real revenue size of each tax. Tables 2.1A and 2.1B describe the tax history of Chile and Argentina over the last thirty years.[13] As these tables show, the VAT has become the main source of tax revenues in both countries. It is the "workhorse" of fiscal revenues. From the 1980s onward, it has accounted for at least 25 percent of tax revenues in Argentina and 40 percent in Chile. Throughout this period, social security and payroll taxes accounted for approximately another quarter of total central-government tax revenue in Argentina. Their collection has decreased in Chile since the reforms of the early 1980s. Social security, VAT, and fuel taxes have together raised at least 60 percent, and up to 75 percent, of total revenues in both countries. Until 2002 the role of foreign-trade tax diminished in Argentina but has been a steady source of income in Chile. Argentina's income-tax revenues have been historically very modest, whereas in Chile they have been higher, particularly from the 1980s onward. Until very recently, Argentina's income-tax revenues were equal to about one-third of social security tax revenues and between 20 percent and 35 percent of VAT revenues, whereas in Chile the revenue from income tax was close to 50 percent of VAT collections.

These tables allow for some tentative conclusions: Despite reforms and adjustments in Argentina, there have been no major increases or changes

12. A very rich literature has developed lately, particularly for the analysis regarding the sources of the fiscal crisis that led to the Argentine economic debacle and default in 2002. For a good review, see Jones, Sanguinetti, and Tommasi 2000. For a study of the political incentives of legislators and the sharing of tax revenues, see Eaton 2002; for the "reemergence" of local power in revenue sharing, see Eaton 2004b, chap. 6; 2004a.

13. It was difficult to get comparable data for earlier years. Therefore, in some cases, the information does not coincide.

TABLE 2.1A Federal Tax Revenues in Argentina as a Percentage of GDP

	1964	1971	1976	1981	1986	1991	1996	2001
VAT	—	—	2.72	5.14	3.31	3.45	6.2	6.4
Sales Tax	1.28	1.77	—	—	—	—	—	—
Fuel Tax	—	1.03	0.73	1.81	1.68	0.63	0.8	1.2
Other Indirect	1.75*	—	—	—	—	—	—	—
Income Tax	1.44	1.77	1.14	1.58	1.20	0.6	2.3	3.5
Assets	0.21	0.89	0.62	1.15	1.64	0.6	0.2	0.2
Social Security and Payroll	3.64	4.53	3.9	2.51	3.93	4.3	3.4	2.9
Foreign Trade	1.51	1.89	2.56	1.86	2.83	0.9	0.8	0.6
Other	0.51	2.41	1.54	3.63	4.72	3.84	0.9	1.6
Total	10.86	14.29	13.21	17.68	19.31	14.32	14.6	16.6

SOURCES: My own elaboration based on Unión Panamericana 1966; FIEL 1991, 1998; IMF 1995; INDEC 1998; AFIP 2002.

NOTE: Does not include provincial revenues, which average 4 percent of GDP, and social security transferred to retirement funds.

*Presumably this is mainly from the fuel tax, but the available data does not specify.

in the structure of revenues over the past thirty years. The different reforms undertaken did not yield significant transformations in the structure of the tax system, and an element of inertia appears to be present. In Chile, conversely, tax revenues have increased steadily from the 1980s; the tax system has been stable, relying mainly on income taxes and the VAT; and major efforts to reduce evasion appear to have been successful.

MEASURING TAX COMPLIANCE IN CHILE AND ARGENTINA

As the data above indicates, Argentina and Chile have fairly similar tax systems. The level of development of the two countries is also similar: both countries' 1990s GDP per capita ranged between four thousand dollars and nine thousand dollars. This section uses the available published and unpublished aggregate data to evaluate and compare the tax performance of each country and to provide an intuitive explanation for the differences in levels of tax evasion. I also develop different measures of compliance and describe the methodologies used to generate the different estimations.

The Magnitude of Noncompliance

In order to assess the efficacy of tax collection, it is necessary to estimate a uniform measure of compliance. Some studies attempt to understand

TABLE 2.1B Tax Revenues in Chile as a Percentage of GDP

	1969	1976	1981	1986	1991	1996	2001
VAT	—	9.9	9.5	8.4	7.8	8.0	7.9
Sales Tax	4.25	—					
Other Indirect	2.82	—	1.4	3.2	1.8	2.3	2.3
Income Tax	3.01	4.2	4.9	2.2	4.2	4.0	4.5
Assets	—		—				
Social Security and Payroll	6.2	3.3	4.0	1.5	1.5	1.3	1.5
Foreign Trade	1.97	—	1.6	2.4	2.3	1.8	1.2
Other	5.24	5.1	1.4	2.0	0.9	0.9	1.0
Total	17.12	22.5	22.8	19.7	18.5	18.3	18.4

SOURCES: My own elaboration based on SII 2007; Marcel 1986; Arellano and Marfán 1987.

state taxing capacities by analyzing the total tax burden as a percentage of GDP. Such a comparison indicates the actual revenues, but it does not account for distortions and differences in the nature of the taxes. Moreover, a systematic comparison of total tax burdens between countries is problematic, because the composition of each country's tax structure differs markedly. For instance, Chile's total tax revenues as a percentage of GDP do not include social security taxes, which were partially eliminated in 1981 and replaced by individual retirement accounts. In contrast, Argentina's tax burden includes the mixed social security funds, based on the new model introduced in 1993, which did not entirely replace the retirement and payroll taxes of the old state pension system (Arenas de Mesa and Bertranau 1997; ECLAC 1998).

In addition, the structure of tax collection also leads to differences in tax burdens. Some official publications, such as the government statistical reports published by the IMF, do not clearly discriminate between central and local government tax revenues.[14] These different structures pose difficulties for a systematic comparison between governments' tax-collection capacities. Therefore, a comparison of the tax burden must be made with extreme care. The total tax burden for Chile in 1992 was 17.5 percent of its GDP, whereas for Argentina it was 16.4 percent of GDP. But 4.8 percent of Argentina's tax revenues were social security and payroll

14. The IMF's *Government Financial Statistics Yearbook* (1996) discriminates between central-government tax revenues and regional-government tax revenues, but it is not clear whether the taxes allocated to the local authorities were indeed collected by the regional tax agencies. A large part of the "other taxes" in the statistical tables in this publication, which constitute close to 50 percent of the total regional revenues, were in fact collected by the central government and "transferred" to local governments.

TABLE 2.2 Tax Revenues in Chile and Argentina as a Percentage of GDP, 1992 and 1997

	Chile		Argentina	
	1992	1997	1992	1997
Value-Added Tax	8.50	9.16	5.89	6.20
Income Tax	4.20	4.17	1.60*	2.75
International Trade	2.01	1.91	0.95	0.90
Excise Taxes	1.90	1.87	2.77**	1.84

SOURCES: Etcheberry 1993; Larrañaga 1995; Durán and Gómez Sabaini 1995.
*For Argentina, income tax and property tax are both included.
**Argentina's gas tax is not included.

taxes, which are excluded from the total tax burden of Chile. Table 2.2 presents a comparison of the shares of relevant taxes as percentages of GDP. This first comparative analysis shows Chile's greater ability to collect VAT and income taxes and Argentina's moderate reliance on excise taxes. For both countries, the VAT is the main source of revenues. Table 2.3 shows the total tax burden for both countries. Argentina has lower and more fluctuating revenues than Chile.[15]

An in-depth examination of each country's efficacy in collecting taxes requires a finer analysis of levels of tax compliance based on the systematic comparison of the yields of a particular tax in each country. The logical candidate for such analysis is the VAT. In 1992, Chile's VAT revenues represented 47 percent of its total tax revenues and 8.5 percent of its GDP, whereas in 1997 it increased to 50.9 percent and 9.16 percent respectively (SII 2001a). In Argentina, 1992 VAT revenues represented 35.9 percent of total tax revenues and 5.9 percent of its GDP (Durán and Gómez Sabaini 1995), whereas for 1997 they equaled 35.7 percent of total revenues and 6.1 percent of GDP (AFIP 1998). Although the importance of the income tax has increased over the last ten years, it did not play a central role in total revenues in Argentina.

Three Indexes of Tax Compliance

VAT Productivity Index (PVAT)

One way of using VAT to measure the extent of compliance is to consider the *productivity of the VAT (PVAT)*. PVAT measures the yield of each per-

---

15. Some changes have been noticed in more recent years. For example in Argentina, for the period 2000–2005, the central-government tax burden has been 19.7 percent; in Chile, the 2002 rate was 19.9 percent. Both cases include social security taxes (FIEL 2006, 85).

TABLE 2.3 Central Government Tax Revenues in Argentina and Chile as a Percentage of GDP

	1992	1993	1994	1995	1996	1997
Argentina	16.4	15.6	15.5	15.1	14.4	15.1
Chile	18.9	19.4	19.0	18.4	18.4	19.1

SOURCES: For Argentina, Silvani 1995; *El Cronista*, January 6, 1997; IMF 2001a. For Chile, IMF 2001a; Jorrat 1996.

centage point of tax rate as a share of GDP.[16] Because the tax base and the tax rates directly affect its productivity level, for compliance purposes a comparison of PVAT between countries must be based on compatible tax bases and tax rates; indeed, the tax bases and rates of Chile and Argentina are compatible. The productivity rate in Chile is 49 percent and in Argentina it is only 33 percent. In other words, in Chile every percentage point of the VAT rate generates revenues worth close to 0.5 percent of Chile's GDP, whereas for Argentina every VAT percentage point yields revenues worth only 0.33 percent of the country's GDP. Although the Chilean tax base is slightly larger, which raises VAT productivity, this difference is only marginal (less than 8 percent difference between the tax bases of the two countries). Thus, the size of the tax base is compatible, although the yields differ markedly (Silvani and Brondolo 1993).

Another way to observe this difference in levels of tax compliance is to analyze lost VAT revenues by comparing revenues to the amount of taxes that would have been collected had no evasion taken place. Table 2.4 displays this comparison for five Latin American countries. Tax rates do not appear to have a major impact on this level of compliance coefficient. Throughout most of the period under study, VAT rates changed in both countries, but they remained mostly between 16 and 18 percent.[17] Thus, the differences in the level of VAT rates between these two countries do not explain the differences in tax compliance.

Compliance Coefficient (CC)

Several studies measure VAT compliance by constructing a *compliance-coefficient index* that compares the gap between expected and actual tax revenues. In fact, the IMF generally uses this index.[18] This measure

16. This methodology provides an estimation of compliance: the higher the productivity rate, the lower the noncompliance.

17. In Argentina, the VAT reached 21 percent by mid-1995 to alleviate the fiscal deficit created by the "Tequila Effect."

18. For further reference, plus a review of the methodology most commonly used by the IMF, see Tanzi and Shome 1993.

TABLE 2.4 Potential and Actual VAT Revenues as a Percentage of GDP for
Five Latin American Countries (1992)

	VAT Revenues	Potential VAT Revenues	Lost Revenues
Argentina*	6.1	9.1	3.0
Bolivia	4.3	7.7	3.4
Chile	8.5	10.4	1.9
Ecuador	3.3	5.3	2.0
Mexico	2.9	4.6	1.7

SOURCES: Jorrat 1996; based on Silvani and Brondolo 1993 and IMF 1995.
*Estimation was made using 1992 data, when Argentina had its highest compliance rate
of the last twenty-five years.

estimates potential tax revenues by using national accounts to calculate
the total tax base. Once the base is estimated, it is multiplied by the tax
rates. This produces the potential, or "expected," VAT revenues. The difference between the potential and the actual revenues generates the tax
gap.[19] The tax compliance coefficient must be accepted with certain reser-
vations, because the tax base is calculated using national accounts, which
at times are not entirely accurate (Bird 1992b) or up-to-date (Friedman
1991; Serra 1991). Therefore, any tax compliance coefficient represents
an approximation of the differences between potential and actual revenue. Figure 2.1 plots the tax compliance coefficients for Chile and Argentina over a span of fifteen years.

Tax-evasion analysis should be based on several years of tracked performance.[20] Focusing on single years, such as 1992 (a particularly good year
for Argentina due the reduction of inflation; see Tanzi and Shome 1993),
can produce false conclusions. For the years presented in figure 2.1, the
average VAT-compliance coefficient for Argentina was 54.3 percent (61.2
percent for the last years), whereas for Chile it was 78.1 percent (80.5
percent for the last ten years). These estimates, even if the last ten years
are taken into account, further reinforce my thesis that Chile has a much
lower tax-evasion rate than Argentina.[21] Several independent studies lend

19. Many models estimate compliance coefficients. They are based on an estimation of
the tax base, calculated from national accounts. Because tax laws differ between countries,
it is necessary to calculate the taxable portion of each country's GDP. This estimation must
be done annually because there are many changes in the legislation that directly affect the
tax base. Variations in the potential VAT may also stem from the inclusion or exclusion of
exports, which are generally exempted from this tax.

20. I thank a Penn State University Press reader for inviting me to clarify this point.

21. There are two studies by AFIP that have found lower tax-noncompliance rates for
Argentina. A 1997 study that found a tax-evasion rate of 27 percent has a crucial technical error: it deducts from the tax base the export-exempted VAT but leaves intact the gross

support to these findings. For instance, in Argentina one study found that noncompliance with the VAT in the 1990s occurred at a rate of at least 30 percent (FIEL 1998, 2006). In a more recent and comprehensive study by Fundación Mediterranea, VAT noncompliance in Argentina averaged 46 percent for the period 1993–2003, and was still above 40 percent in 2004 in the midst of economic recovery after the crisis.[22]

Index of Tax-Agency Efficiency or Net Voluntary Compliance (NVC)

An accurate estimation of the real capacity of the state to increase voluntary tax compliance must exclude taxes collected either when there is a genuine taxpayer incentive to pay them or when taxpayers lack a real way to avoid them. A real measure of voluntary compliance, in other words, must be based on an understanding of the antagonistic interests of the tax administration and the taxpayer, where taxpayers' real aim is to avoid taxation and the TA's goal is to effectively collect. Also, "voluntary compliance" refers to a proactive and conscious decision by the taxpayer to comply. Therefore, withholding excludes net voluntary

---

revenue. Revenues should have been deducted from the VAT export activities, and the tax compliance rate should have been estimated with net (and not gross) revenue. After correcting this error, the estimation yields a 36.1 percent rate of tax noncompliance.

A second study, currently conducted yearly by AFIP, yielded a 24.8 percent tax-evasion rate for 2004. This study, however, should be taken with extreme care for several reasons that transcend the scope of this book. The most important one is that according to this study, the tax base—that is, the portion of GDP that is VAT-taxable and therefore constitutes the base for the potential revenues to be collected—averaged only 43 percent of GDP between 2000 and 2005. This is questionable at best in a country such as Argentina, where final consumption constitutes more than two-thirds of GDP, tax exceptions are few, savings are minimal, and the investment rate is relatively low. Therefore, potential revenues from such an underestimated base are small relative to the size of the economy; consequently, actual collection looks "high" against such a small tax base.

More important for the case of the Argentina-Chile comparison, although the methodology of estimation is similar, the AFIP study includes deductions from the tax base (particularly quasi-rent for homeowners and special taxpayer category exclusion deductions) that are not applied to Chile. Thus, the tax base in Chile is 56 percent of GDP, whereas in Argentina it is 43 percent. Using the same result of the Argentine study but with a more realistic tax base of at least 50 percent of GDP, 2004 tax evasion would have been at least 37 percent. As can be seen, the evasion rate is very sensible in light of the size of the tax base, and for comparative purposes the AFIP study shows a very small tax base.

Additionally, in support of my claim, and as shown in the right column of table 2.7, most countries far exceed such a tax base. Moreover, for a sample of twenty-five European countries and fourteen Latin American countries, the productivity of VAT in Argentina is the absolute lowest, below 30 percent (FIEL 2004, 357). It is hard to reconcile good tax compliance rates (as shown in the AFIP study) with very poor VAT productivity. It appears that problems with out-of-date national-accounts estimations and questionable exemptions cast some doubt on the AFIP results.

22. See Argañaraz 2004.

Fig. 2.1 Compliance Coefficient (Percentage of Potential VAT Revenues)

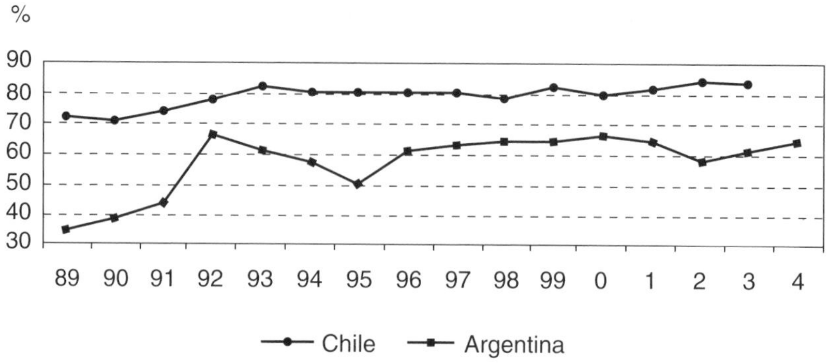

%

—•— Chile   —■— Argentina

SOURCE: My own elaboration based on official data from Chile and Argentina.

compliance, given that choices are not made voluntarily. Nor does voluntary tax compliance include VAT-export reimbursements. Exporters have incentives to report accurately (and even sometimes overreport) in order to get reimbursed for export-exempted VAT.[23] Thus, it can be assumed that the level of VAT evasion in export activities is very small.

Import-tax collection is relatively easy to administer and consequently difficult to evade. It is presumed that the vast majority of VAT collected from imports is indeed reported. In Argentina, the VAT collected by customs accounts for a large share of total VAT revenues. Particularly in periods of economic expansion, when there is a considerable growth in foreign trade, the VAT paid on imports accounts directly for a significant improvement in compliance. As shown, the average revenues collected by Argentine customs via the VAT are equal to 29 percent of total VAT revenues.

I have constructed a more reliable coefficient, based on the NVC *(net voluntary compliance) index,* which excludes export reimbursements from the tax base and from tax revenues, as well as subtracting from the tax base and tax receipts the import VAT collected in customs, which has to be paid before imports leave the port of entry.[24] This index yields a yearly

23. VAT does not include tax exports because it would increase the prices of goods, making them less competitive in world markets. Exporters claim refunds for VAT already paid at different stages. This mechanism helps tax agencies fight evasion, because exporters do not have an incentive to evade VAT (although they do have incentives to evade income tax) and they do not engage in agreed-on evasion with their providers. A "line of documentation" can be traced by the tax agency to verify the accuracy of exporters' and suppliers' bookkeeping.

24. The assumption is that imports for which taxes have not been paid cannot leave the port of entry. As a judicial investigation in Argentina revealed, however, during a five-year period (1992–96) goods worth one billion dollars were smuggled into the country.

TABLE 2.5   Share of Argentine and Chilean VAT Collected from Import Activities as a Percentage of Total VAT Collected

	1993	1995	1997	1999	2001
Argentina*	25	29	32	31	28
Chile**	37	36	38	34	36

SOURCES: For Argentina, Estado de la Recaudación, Ministerio de Economía, http:// www.mecon.gov.ar/sip/basehome/pormes.htm. For Chile, Serie Ingresos Tributarios, http://www.sii.cl.
*Includes only the VAT collected at customs premises.
**Includes all VAT related to imports collected at customs and on imports voluntarily reported at SII agencies.

coefficient that indicates the VAT voluntarily reported and paid by tax-payers.[25] Indices for Argentina and Chile, constructed from the available data, are displayed in figure 2.2.

The trend is very clear. Whereas in Argentina the deterrence capability of AFIP has been diminishing since 1993, Chile's SII has been able to increase its revenue-enhancing capacity. The "Tequila Effect" in 1995 (the "spillover" of the Mexican economic crisis) might explain part of the increase in tax noncompliance in Argentina. Two years prior to the Mexican financial crisis (in fact, from the fourth quarter of 1992 onward), however, this index already shows a decline in levels of voluntary compliance. By constructing these two coefficients using official data, I show that tax evasion in Chile is significantly lower than in Argentina.

I provide here an additional proof of the larger extent of tax evasion in Argentina: I analyze VAT collection for 1997 to deduct the VAT revenues not voluntarily reported. Unfortunately, the information needed to construct a time series is not available, but table 2.6 clearly indicates that— excluding large taxpayers, some withholding systems, and a fraction of foreign trade—only a quarter of all revenue is voluntarily reported in Argentina.

In sum, all three compliance coefficients (PVAT, CC, and NVC) indicate that tax compliance in Chile is much higher than in Argentina. Although in 1992 Argentina enjoyed lower rates of tax evasion, this success was short-lived. In contrast, Chile shows a trend of improving tax compliance.

Smuggled products are technically not registered in the national accounts and are not included in the potential VAT to be levied, and they consequently do not affect the rate of compliance (see Serra 1991).

25. In addition to foreign-trade incentives and constraints on compliance, a net voluntary measure could be improved by including the effect of withholding. Unfortunately, the available data was not conducive to a comparison between these two countries.

Fig. 2.2 Net Voluntary Compliance Coefficient (Percentage of Compliance VAT Revenues)

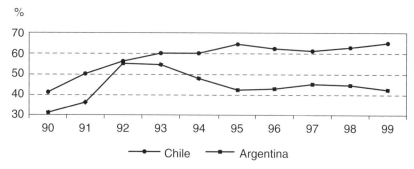

SOURCE: My own elaboration based on official data for both countries.

TABLE 2.6 Voluntary Compliance in Argentina, 1997

	Thousand of Millions of Pesos
Gross Potential Revenues (1)	36,500,000
Revenues at Source (2)	17,485,000
Net Potential Voluntary Revenues (3)	19,015,000
Real Net Revenues (4)	4,815,000
Net Voluntary Compliance (5)	25%

SOURCES: My own elaboration based on AFIP 1998 and AFIP internal documents.

(1) On a taxable 50 percent GDP base, including VAT reimbursements.

(2) Customs and withholdings VAT collected by large (2,100) and medium-sized (approximately 400,000) companies.

(3) (1) – (2).

(4) Gross actual VAT revenues – (2).

(5) (4)/(3).

Compliance Worldwide

VAT. Extending some of the indices of compliance to a wider group of countries allows us to place Argentina and Chile in an international context. As noted above, the tax-collection percentage alone does not reflect actual compliance; therefore, the productivity index based on official published data becomes the best approximation of compliance. Table 2.7 displays the collection capacity and the PVAT (with the percentage of the tax base) for several countries at the beginning of the 1990s. The table shows Chile in sixth place and Argentina in ninth place among the twenty countries for which VAT compliance and the PVAT can be calculated.

This comparison of VAT yield should be interpreted cautiously, however, as the percentage of potential tax collection does not provide an

TABLE 2.7 VAT Compliance and Productivity of VAT for Selected Countries

	% of Collection	PVAT (% base)
New Zealand (1992/1993)	94.9	0.67 (70)
Sweden (1992)	94.6	0.35 (36)
Israel (1992)	92.2	0.54 (58)
Portugal (1991)	86.0	0.71 (82)
South Africa (1992/1993)	85.4	0.52 (61)
Canada (1991)	77.0	0.32 (41)
Chile (1991)	76.7	0.49 (59)
Spain (1989)	74.0	0.52 (69)
Uruguay (1991)	70.3	0.34 (49)
Argentina (1992)	68.5	0.33 (49)
Honduras (1992)	64.6	0.42 (65)
Colombia (1991)	64.2	0.19 (30)
Hungary (1991)	63.7	0.44 (68)
Mexico (1992)	62.9	0.30 (48)
Ecuador (1991)	61.8	0.31 (50)
Philippines (1992)	59.3	0.24 (41)
Bolivia (1990)	56.1	0.28 (49)
Guatemala (1992)	47.5	0.36 (76)
Panama (1991)	46.5	0.36 (76)
Peru (1991)	31.8	0.17 (53)

SOURCES: Silvani and Brondolo 1993; IMF 1995; my own elaboration.

accurate assessment of net voluntary compliance. As I have mentioned, PVAT is useful in comparing tax compliance only when tax bases and tax rates are comparable. Countries that import a great deal, such as Israel and Portugal, have a considerable advantage in the administration of taxes, which leads to better overall compliance. In addition, the PVAT has comparative limitations because countries have different rates and tax bases. Sweden, for instance, has a high compliance coefficient but a lower PVAT because its tax base is half the size of New Zealand's.

It should also be noted that 1992 was a particularly good year for Argentina. From 1992 to 1997, the average compliance coefficient was 55 percent and the PVAT 0.30. Thus, for those years, Argentina would likely have been ranked between twelfth and fourteenth among these twenty countries. Conversely, the CC of Chile during this period averaged 77 percent and the PVAT 0.50, so it probably would have remained in sixth place. An accurate estimation of voluntary compliance would be possible by comparing the NVC for each country, but the available information is insufficient.

Income Tax. Data that would allow the systematic comparison of compliance for income-tax systems is unavailable, and estimations are intricate and contradictory. Estimations based on the size of the underground economy served as first proxies for the magnitude of noncompliance (Tanzi 1982; Gutman 1977), but they fail to provide an accurate description. Thus, figures for noncompliance are generally "guesstimates." In the United States, compliance with the income tax in the 1980s has been estimated around 82 percent (Roth, Scholz, and Witte 1989). In the 1990s, this rate had apparently not changed significantly, but there has been a trend of decreasing compliance since the late 1990s, and a 1998 study estimates the tax gap (the difference between legally expected and actual revenues) at slightly over 15 percent (Plumley 2002). In the United Kingdom, the black market economy is estimated to be equal to 7.5 percent of GDP, and an Inland Revenue Commissioners' report estimated noncompliance at close to 28 percent (Cook 1989).

In Chile, a study by SII estimated income-tax evasion for 1997 at 39 percent. The largest share of noncompliance was found in the first category (corporations and large firms), where 41.7 percent of expected revenues failed to be collected. Presumably, a large share of such noncompliance is tax avoidance. For individuals, the second category, noncompliance was estimated at 35.8 percent (Barra and Jorrat 1999). There is no official estimation of income-tax noncompliance for Argentina. Given the structure of the tax rates and the tax base, economists agree that optimal revenues for this tax should be 6.5 percent of GDP. Because the income tax generated revenues close to 2.85 percent of GDP between 1995 and 2002, it seems that no less than 60 percent of expected income-tax revenues remained uncollected throughout this period. This estimation is plausible: if the VAT, the most closely monitored tax and the most difficult to evade, averages 42 percent noncompliance, then income-tax noncompliance could significantly exceed that rate. Two independent studies conducted in 1998 partially corroborate this high estimation of the evasion rate. One study indicates that income-tax noncompliance in Argentina for 1996 exceeded 50 percent (FIEL 1998). Another estimates the total unpaid income taxes in Argentina at more than nine billion dollars (3 percent of GDP) and a 52 percent tax gap (Bocco et al. 1999). In other words, it is safe to assume that income-tax evasion in Argentina is at least 30 percent higher than in Chile, more than two times that of Great Britain, and at least triple that of the United States.

Other Taxes. Estimations of compliance with other taxes are even more difficult. Payroll and social security taxes have better compliance rates historically, particularly among employees, who have a clear incentive to demand that employers pay the workers' dues. Trade unions,

which indirectly have access to a share of such revenues, closely monitor the level of compliance. Nonetheless, there are two main sources of
noncompliance with payroll and social security taxes. First, the category
of self-employed and liberal professionals is large, and those employed in
these categories are inclined to pay substantially lower contributions by
disclosing only a fraction of their true income. They generally self-report
in lower-income brackets. Second, many employees and employers agree
to report only a share of the employee's wage, thus avoiding additional
taxes while guaranteeing legal social security coverage with a minimum
contribution. In addition, the unemployment rate is crucial to the level
of noncompliance: the higher the rate, the lower the bargaining power
of employees and the larger the black labor market. That was the case in
Chile after the 1982 crisis and in Argentina over the last ten years.

Assessing the History of Tax Compliance in Argentina and Chile

It is virtually impossible to reconstruct Argentina's history of tax compliance. Estimates are based on incomplete and probably inaccurate data,
particularly for the 1940s–60s. Fragmented but more reliable information available for the period since the 1970s, however, allows for a better
assessment of the level of compliance. The estimates presented in table
2.8 are based on generalizations and are not intended to provide an accurate measure, but rather a general trend. Because the data of national
accounts and tax collection is available, in some instances I estimate the
size of the tax base and potential tax collection as a percentage of the
GDP; I then compare these results with actual tax collection.

Several generalizations can be made on the basis of this table. First,
compliance with the VAT is higher than with the income tax. Second, because VAT is very sensitive to economic activity, both the compliance coefficient and the PVAT clearly denote the impact of economic cycles. The
late 1970s, 1986, and 1992 were periods of economic growth, whereas
1981, 1989, and 1995 were years of economic slowdown and recession.
VAT revenues declined sharply in these latter years not only because economic activity shrank but also because tax evasion became a source of
taxpayers' personal financing. Third, compliance increased particularly
in years of economic expansion, which are generally tied to the growth
of imports. The sharp decline in compliance in 1981 is due precisely to
changes in monetary policy that significantly curtailed the flow of imports. The improvement in compliance between 1981 and 1986 resulted

TABLE 2.8 Historical Compliance Performance in Argentina

	1978–80	1981	1986	1989	1992	1995
CC VAT	60%	51%	62%	48%	65%	51%
PVAT	0.31	0.24	0.29	0.23	0.32	0.27
Inc. + Ass.*	33%	35%	33%	20%	25%	31%
	(1.67)	(1.7)	(1.7)	(1.2)	(1.45)	(2.3)

SOURCES: FIEL 1991; Durán and Gómez Sabaini 1995; my own estimations.
* Includes income tax and direct taxes on assets and capital. Total revenues are presented as a percentage of GDP in parentheses. For 1978–86, the potential tax is estimated as 5 percent of GDP; for 1989 and 1992, 6 percent; and for 1995, 7 percent. Estimations varied according to sources.

from economic growth unrelated to an increase in imports. Similarly, the 1992 VAT-revenue increases are explained largely by a return to growth in imports. Fourth, noncompliance remains high in income and asset taxes. Income tax represents more than 80 percent of the revenues in this category, with close to 50 percent of it collected through withholding. As we will see, the poor results for income taxes can be explained by the weakness of AFIP detection capabilities, by the well-developed avoidance strategies of large firms and corporations, and by an outdated withholding system. The slight progress achieved in income-tax compliance in the 1990s stems from an improvement in withholding, as well as from the revenues generated by the privatization of state-owned firms.

Data to estimate compliance coefficients for extended periods is not available for Chile either. The 1964 reforms helped to reduce evasion of the income tax. For instance, in 1962 only 2 percent of more than sixty thousand executives paid the global complementary tax (French Davis 1973). For the 1964–70 period, the noncompliance rate is estimated at 45 percent. Most noncompliance during this period, however, was attributed to the tax exemptions and promotional activities for the income and sales tax. Given that the potential income tax never exceeded 7–8 percent of GDP in the 1970s and 1980s (Arellano and Marfán 1987), tax noncompliance in these decades remained between 40 and 55 percent—much lower than in Argentina over the same period. It should be recalled, however, that these estimates are drawn from incomplete information. The statistics on VAT revenues allow for better comparisons. The VAT reform implemented in 1975 helped to reduce tax evasion. Marcel (1986) estimates that VAT noncompliance averaged 26 percent for the period 1976–82. Table 2.9 shows the noncompliance rate for the decade as reported by Larrañaga (1995). Though the information is incomplete,

TABLE 2.9 Tax-Evasion Rate for VAT in Chile

	1980	1981	1982	1983	1984	1985	1986	1987	1988	1989
Rate	19.4	20.1	31.9	23.6	22.2	21.8	20.1	22.5	23.4	23.5

SOURCES: My own estimation based on Marcel 1986 and Jorrat 1996.
NOTE: This rate is a percentage of potential revenues using national-account estimators from the 1970s. In order to compare this to the results of figure 2.1, these numbers need to be adjusted using updated national-account estimations. In this case, the rates for the 1980s will be slightly higher using the 1990s figures, and compatible with the Marcel study (1986); those adjustments produce an evasion rate of 24–29 percent, excluding 1982.

tax evasion appears to have been much lower in Chile than in Argentina during the 1970s and 1980s, as well as in the years that followed.

SUMMARY

This chapter has focused on defining the problem of noncompliance and providing a comprehensive measure of tax compliance in Chile and Argentina. As I stressed, tax compliance is a constructed concept, and its meaning can be shifted according to different legal and social criteria. I define it in practical terms, basing it on state estimates of what taxpayers should pay according to the state's interpretation of the law. Tax evasion is understood as a deliberate and premeditated act of noncompliance.

Measuring noncompliance is a difficult endeavor, and an analysis of worldwide estimations demonstrates that different measures are far from robust. The lack of reliable data constrains the interpretations of income-tax compliance. VAT data, which tends to be more reliable, allows for better comparative assessment of compliance. In this chapter, I presented a new index, the NVC, that in my view represents the best available estimation of voluntary compliance. Unfortunately, there is not enough data to estimate NVC for extended historical periods or for comparison among many countries. Nonetheless, in contrast to Chile, and based on NVC performance over good years of economic growth (1990–96), it can be concluded that Argentina experienced endemic noncompliance.

Other estimations shed light on the historical roots of tax evasion. Despite the development of a rational tax system during the 1990s and the significant progress within the tax-administration offices, tax compliance in Argentina has remained weak. The improvement in economic conditions and the launch of major tax reforms yielded results that do not radically depart from the historical pattern.

A comprehensive analysis is needed to develop an explanation for the disparities in compliance between Argentina and Chile. I begin this analysis in the next chapter—the first of three chapters dealing with aspects of enforcement—which investigates perceptions of government enforcement of tax laws in each country.

3

TAXPAYERS' PERCEPTIONS OF
GOVERNMENT ENFORCEMENT

Todos somos buenos, pero si nos vigilan somos mejores.
[We are all good people, but if we are being watched, we are
even better.]

— JUAN DOMINGO PERÓN

Chapter 1 argues that tax compliance can reach the assurance-game equilibrium if two conditions are met: First, taxpayers have to know that
others will honor their commitments to comply. Second, they must receive something of value in exchange for their contributions. The first
condition is strictly a coordination game between taxpayers, whereas the
second relates to the exchange-equity proposition. Taxpayers frequently
adopt a noncooperative strategy when these two conditions are not met.
This chapter undertakes the study of the first condition. In order to guarantee coordination in an N-person assurance game, players must know
that there is a capable enforcer that will oblige others to cooperate. In
short, taxpayers will comply initially to the extent that they believe the
enforcer is capable of deterring potential free riders.

Throughout this book I claim that the success of enforcement is largely
contingent on the given equilibrium. This chapter undertakes an empirical test of this proposition. I examine the role of the enforcer in eliciting
wider compliance, and I conclude that the effective threat of sanctions
for noncompliance exceeds the technical capacities and expertise of the
enforcement agencies. I show that Chile and Argentina have quite similar tax administrations, yet taxpayers in the former perceive their enforcement agency as very capable of detecting tax evasion. Moreover, I
suggest that the liabilities of the Argentine tax administration stem from
a "trapped" enforcement strategy. Because there are so many cheaters (as
opposed to Chile), the tax administration must opt for fewer in-depth
audits in exchange for wider coverage. This leads to fewer detections of
noncompliance. A badly performed audit, however, actually decreases
future compliance, fueling the exchange of information among cheaters
that the dog is all bark but no bite. I show that weak enforcement is endogenous to the noncompliance equilibria.

Other enforcement strategies might reverse this path-dependent trap,
and they are examined in following chapters. Here I start by challenging

the more conventional assumption that rule abidance requires organizational expertise and solid technical capabilities. By showing that Argentina has a quite competent tax administration, I pose a critical question: what is the role of tax enforcement in tax compliance? As this and other chapters will show, the effect is rather indirect: taxpayers are deterred from deviating from norms to the extent they perceive that others refrain as well. Tax-administration agencies that gear their enforcement measures toward signaling that only few people cheat, and that the likelihood of getting caught cheating is high, stand a better chance of achieving solid performance.

In this chapter, I examine both the actual effectiveness of the tax administration in Chile and Argentina and how taxpayers perceive the threat of sanctions in these two nations. I maintain that Chile has only a slightly more developed enforcement agency than Argentina, and that even this has not always been the case; that the difference in tax-administration capacities in Chile and Argentina is not large enough to explain the difference in compliance between the two countries; that Chileans believe in the efficiency of their tax administration more than Argentines do; and that deterrence therefore is more effective in Chile because risk aversion among its taxpayers is greater. In short, the tax administrations are comparable but deterrence in Chile is higher. Compliance is wider because authorities in Chile have succeeded in showing compliers that cheaters might get caught and punished. This has been possible because the extent of cheating is relatively small; therefore, it pays for taxpayers to be legalists.

I begin by describing the institutional capacities of Chile and Argentina's TAS, putting special emphasis on audits. I review several indicators of performance in order to show that SII and AFIP have comparable deterrence capabilities. The second section analyzes survey data to gauge the disparities between taxpayers' perceptions of their TAS in both countries. In a brief conclusion, I weave the chapter's analysis of the state's enforcement capacities and of taxpayers' perceptions into a coherent argument about the general-deterrence effects of enforcement.

INSTITUTIONAL CAPACITIES

Tax Administration in Chile and Argentina

The current Argentine tax administration organization resulted from a merger of DGI (18,000 employees from the Argentine tax administration) with DGA (4,500 employees from the customs agency). The president of the country nominates the director without much scrutiny from other institutions. AFIP has a hierarchical structure headed by nine to ten directors and is divided into twenty-two to twenty-seven regions or tax districts, including a special large-taxpayer unit. Each region has several agencies. Control and monitoring (including audits) are administered from the region's headquarters, and registration, collections, and customer service are run by local agencies.[1] Other divisions in the head office, such as IT, revenue collection, comptroller, audit department, and human resources, provide technical and logistical support. Taxpayers file VAT returns monthly and income-tax returns yearly, although they pay monthly installments toward the final return based on their previous year's tax reports. Filing can be done electronically or at an AFIP agency. Taxpayers must regularly solicit authorization for issuing invoices and other formal requirements; therefore, they have regular contact with AFIP.

The Chilean tax administration is much more centralized. Taxes are collected by the treasury department, which is structurally separated from the TA. The treasury provides SII with a detailed monthly account for each taxpayer. Customs are under another directorate, but taxpayers' information flows between the agencies. The president of the country appoints the general director. SII has nine divisions, and each division head reports directly to the general director of SII. Annual budgets and major yearly program decisions, including revenue targets and evasion rates, are debated in Congress. There are sixteen regions or tax districts for SII: twelve districts correspond to the country's regions, and the remaining four are for Santiago and the metropolitan area. Routine operations are concentrated in Chile's regions, as they are in Argentina, but programs of control and monitoring are centrally designed.[2] Taxpayers in Chile have steady contacts with tax agencies, particularly for invoicing authorization and registration procedures.

The Argentine tax administration is larger and functionally more diversified than the Chilean administration. But Chile's centralization, as well as its functional uniformity, makes it unique. Other successful tax administrations, such as the U.S. IRS, the French DGI, the British Inland Revenue, and the Spanish tax authority, follow the Argentine, rather than

---

1. Heads of agencies (four to eight per tax district) report to a regional director, who in turn reports to one of the two general directors of operations (one for metropolitan Buenos Aires, the other for the rest of the country). Regions are strategic for daily operations, overseeing filing, registration, assessments, and audits.

2. For example, audit programs or income tax-return supervision programs (Operación Renta) are run from central operation centers (see table 3.3). Regional directors execute central commands based on state-run programs.

the Chilean, makeup. Current trends in effective administrations call for decentralization and institutional coordination conducted by a single organization (Poterba and Hagen 1999; Bird and Oldman 1990). Despite that, Chile's tax administration has an adequate performance and a good institutional coordination.

Finally, over the years both administrations have been relatively "shielded" from political appointments at the middle and lower levels. That has not always been the case, particularly in Argentina, where in the 1970s and 1980s some appointments were politically driven. Since 1990, however, 95 percent of the top managerial posts have been professionally oriented and internally promoted. In Chile, during the military dictatorship, some positions were staffed by political appointments, but for the most part the organization remained highly professional. One important difference between the two nations is the number of TA chairpersons: whereas in Chile there have been four SII directors since 1985, in Argentina over the same period there were eleven.[3] It appears that although the Argentine political partisanship had some effect on the TA professional cadre, this influence had almost disappeared by the late 1980s.

Audits, Deterrence, and Tax Compliance

Initial research on tax evasion assumed that people comply with tax laws when to do so is affordable and when sanctions and detection are perceived as severe. According to this paradigm, in order to reduce tax evasion states need to lower taxes and foster good tax administrations (Brennan and Buchanan 1980; Harberger 1987; Stigler 1970; Allingham and Sandmo 1972). Audits are conceived of in this understanding as the most efficient instrument to fight tax evasion. Their role is equivalent to that of surveillance in general crime prevention. Good audits depend on solid administrations. In addition to the auditor's good technical skills and work ethic, an optimal audit requires dependable support systems (third-party reports, computerized and reliable information, well-trained auditors, etc.). The effectiveness of a tax administration is measured by its capacity to develop these systems. For this reason, my analysis of the effectiveness of the Argentine and Chilean TAs centers on audits.

Still, the emphasis on audits as an indicator of TA effectiveness has limitations. Several studies have failed to identify a clear and consistent trend

3. Still, three general directors served with a highly trained professional staff and were insulated from political appointments for extended periods: Ricardo Cossio (1990–95), Carlos Silvani (1996–2000), and Alberto Abad (2003–8).

between the audit rate and the level of voluntary compliance with taxation law (Witte and Woodbury 1985; Dubin and Wilde 1988; Tauchen and Witte 1986; Beron, Tauchen, and Witte 1992). They have found modest associations, particularly under certain model specifications. According to deterrence theory, the effect of audits is first and foremost to cause taxpayers to internalize the possibility of an audit. Almost every survey has found that taxpayers overestimate the probability of being audited (Kinsey 1992; Mason and Calvin 1984). For Argentina and Chile, all the surveys corroborate this result. Overestimation, however, is not uniform. For example, taxpayers in the service sector have larger opportunities to hide income and cheat compared to those in the manufacturing sector, and taxpayers with high taxable income have a higher probability of being audited.[4] Because taxpayers with higher income visibility are more likely to be selected for an audit, they adjust their estimations accordingly. In order to validate the correlation between a higher probability of being audited and compliance, one must control for income, opportunities, and other variables that affect the odds of being selected.

Beron, Tauchen, and Witte (1992), Tauchen and Witte (1986), and others have further developed the deterrence-theory proposition. They suggest that perceptions of the likelihood of being audited are not shaped by the absolute odds of being selected (the ratio between the number of audits and the number of returns, even controlling for variables such as income) but rather by how the individual characteristics of taxpayers *are known* to the tax administration. This explains why research on the effects of tax audits on tax compliance has shown only a modest correlation with deterrence. To estimate the effect of deterrence, it becomes crucial to study how taxpayers estimate their own perceived audit probabilities based on the information that they assume the tax agency has, and how such detection of noncompliance translates into effective sanctions.[5] Such estimations are measured by surveys or by experimental designs. I will return to this question, and advance my own theory of what influences audit effectiveness, in this chapter's conclusion. For the moment, it is sufficient to emphasize that although the effectiveness of audits does not directly determine the extent of compliance, audits nonetheless serve as a good proxy for overall TA effectiveness.

---

4. In the United States in 1989, a tax return for an income over one hundred thousand dollars had an audit probability of 5 percent, compared to 0.03 percent for an income of thirty thousand dollars or less. There is no comparable information for Argentina and Chile.

5. Corruption must also be taken into account, because bribes reduce the "costs" of punishment for noncompliance.

Audit Policy and Tax Administration in Argentina and Chile

Argentina and Chile do not provide public information on audits. Each year, AFIP audits less than 2 percent of returns, whereas SII audits between 1 percent and 1.5 percent. In-depth audits are fewer. In 1997, AFIP conducted 19,420 external (in-depth) audits, which represent 0.5 percent of total tax returns. In Chile, there are approximately 3,300 audits per year of income-tax returns, which represent 0.8 percent of the active-taxpayer register (Trujillo 1998).[6]

During the 1990s, Argentina increased the number of audits from an average of 360 a month in 1989 to 1,800 a month by 1992 (Durán and Gómez Sabaini 1995),[7] then decreased this figure slightly to a monthly average of 1,600 in 1997 (SARC/SELECCIO 1998). Very likely, these last audits were more in-depth and extensive than the ones conducted in 1992. In other words, throughout this period there was an improvement in quality and audit coverage. The personnel allocated to auditing tasks also increased significantly, from 1,400 employees who worked in audit-related duties in 1989 to 6,500, among them 1,290 auditors, in 1992 (Durán and Gómez Sabaini 1995); by 1997 there were more than 8,000 employees, including 1,751 tax auditors (SARC/SELECCIO; my own estimates).

Conversely, audit rates in Chile have remained stable, and only minor changes in resource allocation were noticeable throughout the 1990s. Whereas in 1990 there were 734 tax inspectors for 982,000 income-tax returns and 475,000 yearly VAT returns (1,339 taxpayers per auditor in income tax and 647 per auditor for VAT), in 1999 there were 1,021 auditors for a total of 1.8 million income-tax returns and 671,000 yearly VAT returns. Although the ratio for the income tax has increased slightly, it remained constant for the VAT (SII 1999).

Personnel allocation to audits in Latin American tax administrations averages 13 percent (IMF 1995). In Chile, nearly 3,000 officers (approximately 40 percent of SII's 6,900 employees) are assigned to tax inspections.[8]

---

6. Audits can be triggered by suspicion or by unmatched third-party information. A typical audit includes at least two taxes: VAT and income tax. In Argentina, it usually includes social security and payroll taxes as well. By finding noncompliance in one tax, a well-rounded audit usually generates an adjustment of the other taxes as well.

7. There is no specification of the nature of such audits. During the early 1990s, an extensive effort was centered on the process of tax registration and invoicing. Therefore, many audits were faster and targeted better compliance in these fields.

8. As mentioned, the treasury department runs tax collection. Thus, most SII duties involve monitoring and control.

TABLE 3.1A Indicators of Audits and Tax-Return Processing for Three Latin American Tax Administrations

	Annual Audits*	Cases per Tax Auditor	# of Inhabitants per Tax Official	# of Officials for Each GDP Percentage Point of Revenues Collected	# of Returns per Tax Officials**
Argentina	19,000	11.2	1.890	1.000	277
Chile	9,152***	50	4.051	146	899
Mexico	10,000	—	3.064	1.962	—

SOURCES: My own elaboration based on, for Argentina, Control de Gestion 1998; for Chile, SII 2001a; and for Mexico, Das-Gupta and Mookherjee 1997.
*Includes only in-depth audits.
**Includes only the number of active taxpayers who file VAT or income tax.
***Includes audits of firms, controls of export franchises, and other special permits.

Considering that Chile has a similar tax structure to Argentina but roughly half the number of taxpayers, the difference between these two countries indicates that the ratio of personnel to taxpayers is smaller in Chile. Tables 3.1A and 3.1B present comparative indicators.

Audit policies, of course, do not depend on the number of officials but on their effectiveness, which includes the optimal allocation of resources and the analysis of available data. Audit policies are successful to the extent that they meet several operational standards. In order to evaluate audit policy performance, I present a brief comparative, qualitative assessment for Chile and Argentina based on fieldwork, interviews, and participatory observation in both tax-administration agencies.

Goals. Audits in Argentina and Chile are conceived of as a way of improving revenue collection. Audits are used only to a lesser extent as a strategic weapon to enhance compliance.[9] This slowly began to change throughout the 1990s, moving toward compliance.

Selection. Selection criteria are far from optimal. In Chile, a predetermined centralized plan selects cases for audits. Also, the Operación Renta (a massive annual program for checking income taxes with third-party information) triggers cases for in-depth audits. In the late 1990s Argentina developed a computerized information system for the tax districts that matches tax returns with third-party information. In both countries, there is a lack of clear and well-thought-out selection guidelines, and

---

9. Audits are measured in both countries by the additional revenues that they raise, creating incentives for auditors to generate more revenues rather than enhance deterrence.

TABLE 3.1B Comparison of Indicators of Cost and Number of Officials for Four Tax Administrations

	TA Cost/GDP	Inhabitants per Tax Official
Argentina	0.37	1.890
Chile	0.12	4.051
United States	0.10	2,657
Spain	0.16	650

SOURCES: My own elaboration based on Control de Gestion 1998 and SII 2001a.

neither country has a methodology similar to the U.S. DIF.[10] SII and AFIP still select cases for audits based on a taxpayer's visibility or the expectation of additional revenues.[11]

Control. Internal controls are weak. Supervisors and managers are more concerned with formalities and hierarchical requirements than with improving efficiency and effectiveness. In Argentina, some supervisors are thought to be allies of auditors in corrupt "arrangements" with taxpayers. Surprisingly, both the internal-audit divisions and the comptrollers have weak supervision programs in both countries.

Evaluation. Evaluation criteria have been ineffectual in Argentina but are somewhat better run in Chile. As mentioned, the most widely used criterion for evaluation is the yield of the audit, measured by the additional taxes assessed. Until the late 1990s, nobody in AFIP readily evaluated the scope and effectiveness of audits. Chile has a slightly more elaborate reporting system, but the emphasis is still on the possibility of gaining additional assessed revenues and not on the type of noncompliance found.

Analysis. There is no statistical analysis of data collected at audits, and there is not a systematic report of the aggregate findings of the audit program. Surveys conducted with managers of AFIP indicate that regional officers are unaware of any measuring criteria other than the amount raised by audits. In Chile, the central offices of SII in Santiago have a modest grasp of audit outcomes.

Database. Although it has been increasing, the use of databases of third-party sources has been very limited in Argentina during the 1990s. Auditors and supervisors have resisted new modalities of work, like those

10. Differential Index Factor. This is the formula that the IRS uses to select cases for audits, estimated on the basis of the TCMP (tax compliance measurement program). It has been the IRS's most closely guarded secret. The formula's goal was to select only tax returns likely to exhibit noncompliance.

11. Although third-party sources of information are improving, many cases are still selected on the basis of whistle-blowers or an auditor's intuition.

based on cross-checks of electronically filed information or analysis of third-party sources (although this has changed recently). In Chile, the transition has been smoother, perhaps due to the effect of centralized programs.

In sum, the tax organizations of Chile and Argentina house good human resources and are in transition toward a well-organized tax administration. Chile has a more developed audit department, introduced information technology earlier, and has managed to incorporate third-party information into selection and cross-check procedures. But Chile is perhaps only three to four years ahead of Argentina in terms of management and IT. Neither has a very sophisticated or highly effective audit department. It is unlikely that small differences between the two departments can account for disparities in compliance.

Aggregate Results from Audits and Control

The Argentine Congress and the president were very active in revamping fiscal policies and strengthening tax administration, particularly during the first half of the 1990s (Eaton 2002).[12] Despite these broad changes, audit and tax enforcement efforts were not impressive. Table 3.2 presents a brief summary for 1997, which is also the most disaggregated information that many top executives in AFIP had access to in 1998. This data is also disaggregated by tax districts, but there is no precise information regarding the nature of audits, the type of taxes they involve, or the ratio between additional assessments and the size of audited firms.

From the available information, several conclusions can be drawn. First, the large amount of nonconformity (43 percent of non-admitted noncompliance) suggests that taxpayers rely heavily on delay tactics.[13] Second, only 6 percent of audits did not yield additional assessments of tax liabilities; in other words, 94 percent of the audited taxpayers were *found noncompliant*—a remarkable result, particularly for a country that lacks a developed system for audit selection. This indicates that the vast majority of Argentina's taxpayers are noncompliant. In comparison, in the United States only 28 percent of taxpayer returns are found to

12. Menem's second term (after 1995) has been less successful in advancing tax reforms because, according to Eaton (2002), the legislators' incentives to delegate to the executive diminished considerably due to the alignment of party delegates in Congress. The struggle of succession in the Peronist Party began at the start of his second presidency.

13. Even though a large sum (three hundred million dollars) is part of a contentious case in the province of San Luis, the data still signals that taxpayers have a large degree of success in tax courts.

TABLE 3.2 Aggregate Data of Tax Audit Results in Argentina, 1997

Annual Number of Audits: 19,420	Total Number of Hours: 1,515,318
Number of Inspectors: 1,751	Number of Cases SIF: 1,147 (5.9%)*
Average Length of the Audit: 209 Days	Large Taxpayers SIF: 29% Average Cases by Auditor per Year: 11,1
Total Tax Assessments: $3,664,508,000	Total Tax Liabilities: $6,521,105,000
Assessments Conformed: 57%	Assessments Nonconformed: 43%**

SOURCES: AFIP 1998; Control de Gestion 1998.

NOTE: For 2006, the numbers had not changed significantly. There have been 21,353 in-depth audits, accounting for 85 percent of total new assessments due to enforcement (*La Nación*, January 3, 2007). These new assessments constituted 3 percent of tax collection for the year, which represents a very high proportion of noncompliance found in relatively few cases. This suggest that noncompliance in 2006 was still very high.

*SIF = Sin Interés Fiscal (Without Fiscal Gain); in other words, without assessments of additional revenues.

**Conformity or nonconformity relates to taxpayer acceptance of the auditor's assessments. Nonconformity will lead the case to tax court. In the United States, less than 18 percent of cases reach tax court (*USA Today*, April 17, 1998).

include some type of noncompliance (Kinsey 1992). Third, 29 percent of the two thousand larger taxpayers had no additional assessments made (SIF), compared to 5.9 percent of the general population. This suggests that even though large taxpayers are more closely monitored, about 70 percent were still found in noncompliance; the ratio of conformity and nonconformity is the opposite of that for the general population (35 percent against 65 percent), suggesting that most noncompliance stems from tax avoidance, in line with classic models of white-collar crime. Finally, the ratio between paid taxes filed in the original returns and the additional liabilities assessed by auditors is very high. Assessments account for more than 50 percent (3.6 billion out of 6.5 billion) of the true tax liabilities. Even if parts of these assessments are disputed, the admitted and undisputed additional liabilities represent 32 percent of total tax liabilities assessed by auditors. This large amount does not cast any doubt as to the seriousness of tax noncompliance in Argentina.

Because the data for Chile does not replicate that for Argentina, no exact comparison can be made. The information of table 3.3 summarizes the fiscalization efforts for 1996, including all contacts that the audit department had with taxpayers. The two larger programs, monitoring (*fiscalización*) and Operación Renta, are not in-depth audits. The first one includes inspections on businesses premises, mainly to check invoicing procedures. The amounts raised are mostly fines and penalties. The

TABLE 3.3 Aggregate Enforcement Results for Chile, 1996

Program	# of Cases	Yield
Fiscalization Presence	34,776	13,164
Massive Programs		
Operación Renta 1996	109,697	13,803
National Programs		
Personal Expenses Imputed to Corporations	599	1,966
Anticipated VAT	36	1,529
Use of Personal Cars and Jeeps	522	1,844
Builders and Contractors	303	1,834
Rents of Tax Funds	612	2,104
Export Reimbursement Control	1,553	8,734
Regional Programs		
Export Suppliers	81	2,599
Investments	265	6,399
Lumber and Forest Products	66	477
Agriculture	62	569
Change in Withholding Sources	1,778	15,497
Transport	82	297
Investment Funds	263	3,320
Invoicing	38	260
Contractors	162	1,518
Reimbursement	197	1,735
Investment Funds	11	2,273
Total	151,103	79,922

SOURCE: Trujillo 1998.
NOTE: Yield figures in millions of pesos for January 1997 (US$1 = 4.20 pesos).

second is a computerized matrix of fast cross-checks that matches individual income-tax returns with third-party information on a yearly basis. These checks generate a list of tax returns with inconsistencies. Taxpayers are notified about the discrepancies and are asked to either provide proof that their original return is correct or adjust their tax return and pay the difference; this process raised 13.803 million pesos.

As mentioned, audit programs in Chile are centrally launched. For example, in 1996 SII decided to target returns that had questionable items, such as personal expenses attributed to business; they initiated another general program that targeted builders and contractors.[14] Many regional

14. Usually, once the program is decided, cases for audits are selected on the basis of taxpayers' return information in a given category, with those returns selected whose ratios substantially deviate from the group median. Also, after an audit is initiated on a particular line item, an auditor reviews other items as well. Thus, the yield of an audit does not necessarily reflect a tax evasion on the item that triggered the audit; it might result from other items in the tax return.

programs are centrally defined as well, but they target a particular region. On average, the financial results do not show high levels of tax evasion in the different programs.

The analysis above suggests that the tax administrations of Chile and Argentina are moderately effective organizations, particularly for the scale of operations that they run. They are among the most developed public organizations in their respective countries. Still, the scale of their operations, the complexities and number of taxes that they administer, their functional diversity, and the complexities of the tax field inhibit them from reaching a high level of effectiveness. Chile's sii is smaller and functionally more efficient, but differences between it and afip in Argentina are not dramatic. afip in the late 1990s was as developed as sii in the mid-1990s, but the noncompliance rate in Argentina for the late 1990s was double that of Chile in the early part of the decade. Both countries have mounted considerable efforts to increase fiscal presence, and enforcement has been a priority. Other variables must be examined to explain variations in compliance between the two countries.

TAXPAYER PERCEPTIONS OF TA EFFECTIVENESS IN ARGENTINA AND CHILE

Deterrence is effective to the extent that taxpayers believe that there is a strong probability that tax evasion will be detected. In this section, I present an analysis of perceptions of TA effectiveness in Chile and Argentina. I begin with the information-gathering process, which is crucial to measuring the individual construction of beliefs about the tax administration's effectiveness.

Information

Several studies have found that taxpayers who know cheaters are more likely to engage in tax evasion themselves (Grasmick and Scott 1982; Westat 1980; Alm, Sanchez, and de Juan 1995); hence, firsthand information is crucial for tax compliance decision making. Because information about enforcement is imperfect, taxpayers adopt strategies that best serve their interests. Two basic strategies are imitation and experimentation. Imitators are constantly adjusting their decisions to mimic the average action in the population, and experimenters adjust more quickly or slowly depending on their distance from and dissatisfaction with the general compliance or noncompliance equilibrium. For both imitators and experimenters, available information is crucial to making a rational decision.[15] Because the probability of being selected for an audit is small but the cost of sanctions might be high, taxpayers need information to help them decide to cheat or comply. I assume that individual experiences of contacts and enforcements on the one hand and the effects of peer behavior on the other are the two most valuable tools to help taxpayers design their best strategies. In this section, I present data on what information taxpayers perceive that the TA has about them; I also evaluate how shared information affects decisions.

In the surveys administered for this study, several questions measured taxpayer assumptions regarding the TA's access to personal information. A general question asked, "Please determine whether DGI or SII has (*dispone*) the following information for an average taxpayer." Table 3.4 shows the results. The data suggests that Argentine taxpayers perceive that AFIP does not have much information about their basic business transactions.[16]

Conversely, Chileans believe that SII has more information. The percentage of respondents who stated that the TA in Chile has no information is significantly smaller than the percentage who made the same statement in Argentina. Only 45 percent of Argentine taxpayers believe that the TA has full information about foreign-trade transactions, despite the fact that all such transactions should be registered with customs. In Chile, banking and other formal transactions are perceived as known to the authorities.

Taxpayers are more likely to comply with tax law if they believe that a TA is capable of matching tax-return data with third-party information. Sixty-one percent of those surveyed in Argentina answered that it is either unlikely or very unlikely that such information is matched, whereas in Chile 49 percent of respondents said that there is a strong likelihood that their declarations of income are cross-checked against other sources.

Additional survey questions measure and rank the types of transactions about which information might be available to AFIP and SII. One strategy that I adopted was to ask taxpayers to imagine themselves as

15. I define "imitation" as a fully rational behavior to contrast with herd behavior, wherein agents ignore their own information and base their decisions on the public information revealed by the actions of their predecessors (Banerjee 1992).

16. The validity of the questions is high, because the question on deposits in foreign banks scored significantly differently. It is well known that the TA does not have information about deposits in foreign countries.

TABLE 3.4 Taxpayers' Perceptions About Information Known to AFIP and SII

| | Perceived Known Information | | | | | |
| | Full | | Partial | | None | |
Types of Transactions	Arg.	Chile	Arg.	Chile	Arg.	Chile
Income, Rents, Salaries	35	58	49	39	16	3
Real Estate Transactions	53	63	35	34	12	3
Registries of Foreign Trade	45	—	39	—	16	—
Stocks Transactions	47	—	36	—	17	—
Certificates of Deposit	57	—	28	—	15	—
Vehicles Transactions	51	61	37	37	12	2
Checking-Accounts Transactions	56	49	31	48	13	3
Deposits in Foreign Banks	6	22	22	48	72	30

SOURCES: Surveys 1 and 6 (see appendix A for details on surveys).
NOTE: Valid n for Argentina = 522, for Chile = 518.

the director of the TA and charged with the specific assignment of fighting tax evasion. Respondents were asked, "Which type of tax evasion do you believe AFIP or SII should scrutinize more?" Table 3.5 reports the results. Overall, Chileans were more likely to believe that all categories of taxation required greater enforcement than were Argentines, indicating that Chileans, on average, believe that good compliance requires better policing. Because Chileans comply more than Argentines, there is a positive correlation between higher compliance and demands for strong enforcement. Interestingly, fake invoicing in both countries has the high mean, denoting that taxpayers believe that it is a major source of tax evasion. Other underreported income also scores higher averages. Conversely, the lower (but still high) mean of overstated deductions supports what is already known in the tax-audit literature: audits are moderately efficient in detecting overstated deductions but relatively ineffective in detecting underreported income.

To evaluate the effectiveness of the two countries' cross-check programs, respondents were asked to evaluate Operación Renta in Chile and the Peine Informático in Argentina.[17] In Chile, 93 percent said that the current level of monitoring was either adequate or very good. In Argentina, just 16 percent considered the efficiency of their program very high or high, and 28 percent considered it adequate.

To measure individual perceptions, audited and non-audited taxpayers were asked to determine the level of information that the TA has for an

---

17. In 1996, a new program called Peine Informático (Information Comb) was launched, with the goal of raising taxpayers' awareness of a new cross-checking policy. The TA would match third-party data with individual tax returns, thereby "combing" the information.

TABLE 3.5 Perceived Increase of Enforcement Needed to Fight Tax Evasion

Transactions	Argentina Mean (sd)	Chile Mean (sd)
Sales and Purchases Without Invoices	5.81 (3.41)	6.72 (3.57)
Search for "Fake Invoices"	6.89 (3.20)	8.39 (2.98)
Professionals Who Do Not Invoice	6.60 (3.16)	7.52 (3.19)
Personal Expenses as the Firm's	4.78 (3.12)	7.21 (3.35)
Own Investments as the Firm's	5.31 (3.29)	7.20 (3.43)

SOURCES: Surveys 1 and 6.

NOTE: Scale: 1 to 10, where 1 means maintaining the same level of surveillance and enforcement and 10 means maximum increase. Valid n for Argentina = 539, for Chile = 507.

TABLE 3.6 Audited and Non-audited Taxpayers' Perceptions About Information Known to the AFIP and SII

Sources of Information	Argentina Mean		Chile Mean	
	Audited	Non-audited	Audited	Non-audited
Income from Goods and Services	3.19	3.45	4.1	4.08
Income from Property Rent	2.42	2.47	3.36	3.18
Real Estate Transactions	3.53	3.57	4.21	4.17
Purchases or Sales of Motor Vehicles	3.44	3.51	4.17	4.08
Banking Transactions	3.82	3.87	3.79	3.73
Deposits in Foreign Countries	2.60	2.60	3.01	2.79

SOURCES: Surveys 4 and 6.

NOTE: The scale is based on 1 = nothing, 2 = a little, 3 = somewhat, 4 = quite a bit, and 5 = a lot. In other words, a score between 3 and 4 should be interpreted as an average in which the taxpayers assume that the TA has between somewhat and quite a bit of information. Valid n for Argentina = 512, for Chile = 448.

average taxpayer with similar characteristics to the respondent. The mean for every source of information is shown in table 3.6. Some conclusions can be drawn from this table. First, in Argentina no score reaches 4, which means that taxpayers estimate that AFIP has little information about them. Second, real estate and banking transactions are perceived to be the best "known." Only in this category and the category for deposits in foreign countries are Argentines' perceptions equivalent to those of Chileans. Third, the low mean score of the most common incomes denotes that respondents consider the TA to be poorly informed. Conversely, Chilean taxpayers believe that other sources of income are better known to SII, which partly accounts for the higher risk aversion of taxpayers in that country. Finally, differences between audited and non-audited taxpayers

TABLE 3.7   Mean Scores of Taxpayers' Perceived Audit Experience in the
United States (Minnesota), Chile, and Argentina

Respondents' Opinion About the Auditor/Inspector	Argentina	Chile	U.S.
General Relationship with the Auditor	7.20	7.50	8.40
Politeness and Manners	7.40	7.42	8.42
Information Had About Your Firm	6.36	7.28	8.96
Technical Skills of the Auditor	7.06	7.16	8.36
Efficiency in Dealing with Audits	5.52	6.80	8.00
Willingness to Speed up the Stages of Audit	5.70	—	8.20
Level of Objectivity	6.34	6.56	7.42
Level of Honesty	6.96	7.48	9.74
Concern for the Amount of Adjustment on Liability	6.62	6.10	5.80

SOURCES: For Argentina, survey 4; for Chile, survey 6; for the United States, the
Minnesota Survey of Taxpayers 1996.

NOTE: The scores for Argentina and Chile were reconverted from a 5-point scale to a
10-point scale, which is the U.S. standard. The lowest score possible for Argentina and
Chile is 2, and therefore comparisons with the United States should be made with care
(2 means very bad/none/very low, and 10 means very good/a lot/very high).

in both countries are not statistically significant; the small differences,
however, are in the opposite direction—that is, on average, Argentinean
non-audited taxpayers believe that the TA knows more than do those who
have been audited, whereas the opposite is true in Chile.

In table 3.7, I compare the perceptions of audited taxpayers from
Chile, Argentina, and the United States. This table is constructed using
three surveys that asked similar questions. Audited taxpayers were asked
their opinions regarding different aspects of the audits and the auditor's
job. Mean scores are different in the three countries. Regarding the information that the auditor had at the time of the audit, there is a 25 percent mean difference between Argentina and the United States and a 10
percent difference between Chile and Argentina. Whereas in the United
States and Chile the information and honesty scores were among the highest given to the auditors for any of the questions, in Argentina they were
among the lowest. Most respondents in Chile and Argentina shared other
perceptions regarding the auditors; in particular, they shared a similar
opinion of the auditors' technical skills.

Differences in taxpayers' perceptions of their TA's ability to gather information seem to be moderate but significant. This partly explains differences in levels of risk aversion between Argentines and Chileans: Chileans
believe that they are more likely to be caught and punished if they evade
their taxes than do Argentines, so they are less likely to do so. The results also suggest that taxpayers are not "reckless" in their tax behavior.

Taxpayers estimate that AFIP has a moderate ability to gather information and SII a slightly better one; thus, they adjust their behavior accordingly. Finally, the results indicate that rational taxpayers in both countries would be more cautious in overstating deductions than in underreporting income.

Detection Capabilities

The most basic assumption of deterrence theory is that tax evasion is negatively correlated with taxpayers' perception of the certainty of detection. A tax administration's enforcement strategy, then, has two goals: general and specific deterrence. General deterrence refers to the wide range of measures that a TA undertakes to increase taxpayers' perception of the certainty of detection. Public-information campaigns, fines, laws, massive checks, and return filings fall under this category. Specific deterrence (or particular deterrence) refers to measures directed at particular individuals, either to make them believe that noncompliance is likely to be detected or to rehabilitate a single taxpayer. From the tax agency's perspective, an audit is a specific-deterrence measure because it is only directed at 1–2 percent of cases each year. But it also has a general-deterrence goal because it signals the TA's willingness to review returns and take compliance seriously. In this sense, an in-depth audit strategy is usually associated with specific deterrence, and a wide-breadth audit strategy with general deterrence.

Several studies in the United States have shown that the likely detection of noncompliance has a substantial effect on compliance. The surveys conducted in Argentina and Chile provide valuable data to test the effectiveness of TA deterrence. Survey 1 in Argentina and survey 6 in Chile used a mixed technique introduced by Klepper and Nagin (1989a) in the field of taxes.[18] To neutralize personal biases, respondents were asked to estimate the probabilities of noncompliance detection, risk aversion, and sanction in several predefined situations. For Argentina, I introduced a change to the Klepper and Nagin design to further explore the effect of certain sector activities,[19] and for both countries I adjusted the survey questions for

18. They integrated an experimental approach in surveys by asking taxpayers to assume being a plumber in a particular set of situations to assess the effects of criminal punishment on tax decisions (Klepper and Nagin 1989a, 1989b).

19. The sample includes a sector of the industry. Each taxpayer was asked a question related to his or her own industry (for agriculture, he or she was asked to pretend to be small-scale wheat growers; for construction, electricians; for service, computer analysts; and so on).

TABLE 3.8 Perceived Probability of Tax-Fraud Detection by Size of Firm in Argentina and Chile

Understate Income by	Firm Size			
	Large	Medium	Small	Total
Argentina $5,000	22.57	19.01	24.8	22.45
Chile $5,000,000	66.9	71.9	73.3	70.9
Argentina $9,000	24.48	23.47	32.15	27.62
Chile $9,000,000	70.3	75.4	76.2	74.1
Fake Invoice Argentina $50,000	40.34	44.03	41.15	41.85
Fake Invoice Chile $10,000,000	67.4	71.2	74.9	71.5
Argentina $100,000	47.76	52.89	56.68	53.33

SOURCES: Surveys 1 and 6.

NOTE: The amounts for both countries were rounded. At the time of survey administration in Argentina, US$1 equaled 1 peso, whereas in Chile the exchange rate was US$1 = 700 pesos. Thus, for the first three categories the amounts for Chile equaled US$7,100, US$12,800, and US$14,200. Valid n for Argentina = 512, for Chile = 498.

the VAT, which requires a different treatment than the income-tax questionnaire used in the United States. A typical question asked taxpayers to imagine a hypothetical situation in which they had deliberately decided to underreport their income by ten thousand dollars. Respondents were asked, "What are the probabilities (on a scale from 0 percent to 100 percent) that AFIP or SII will detect this underreporting?" (For this case, in Argentina the mean was 32.4 percent, and for Chile it was 71.1 percent!) Questions varied the underreported amount and the types of taxes. Other questions inquired about the probability that the TA would detect the fraud in a tax return that included computations of "fake or bogus invoices."[20] Tables 3.8 and 3.9 show the average perceived probability of detection for the sample. Even though the questions changed slightly across sectors and according to situational evasion decisions, the findings are nonetheless robust. Differences in Chile and Argentina are noticeable. Although the results could be sensitive to the specifics of each country's tax administration and to the form of the questions (I made small

20. Fake or bogus invoices are very common in Argentina and in Chile. They look like regular invoices but are from nonexistent business. These invoices are used to overstate deductions and, more important, to reduce purchases from the balance sheet. Also, because some business purchases are done in the "black" (i.e., without invoices) and might be later retailed with real invoices, these sales generate large taxable incomes. Therefore, to reduce taxable income, some taxpayers rely on fake purchases. These are obviously fraudulent transactions and are subject to severe punishment if detected. For an in-depth explanation of fake or bogus invoices, see chapter 5.

TABLE 3.9 Perceived Probability of Tax-Fraud Detection Capabilities by
Sector or Industry for Argentina

Understated Income	Construction	Wholesale/ Retail	Services	Agriculture	Total
$5,000	12.33	32.04	23.07	—	22.45
$9,000	13.57	36.87	26.97	31.48	27.62
Fake Invoice					
$50,000	33.25	44.34	38.68	47.83	41.85
$100,000	47.65	64.76	31.82	62.04	53.33

SOURCE: Survey 1.
NOTE: Valid n = 533.

adjustments in vocabulary, and dollar amounts were 30–35 percent larger
in Chile), the results still prove conclusively that the Chileans believed that
the underreporting of significant amounts of income could very likely be
detected by their TA. In Argentina, taxpayers believed that they could fail
to report equivalent amounts without serious risk of detection. There are
smaller variations for the size of taxpayer units (the larger the firm, the
smaller the perceived probability of detection), but differences around the
mean are not significant.

Larger differences in scores regarding the perceived likelihood of detection were found among Argentine sectors (see table 3.9) and Chile's
regions (table 3.10). In the former, the construction sector had the low
score. To validate these questions, I conducted a reliability test by comparing the mean of industries with the results of a more neutral question
regarding the capability of AFIP to detect an underreported ten thousand pesos (see above). Still, services and construction scored significantly
lower than agriculture and retail sectors, although the differences were
not as large.[21]

I constructed a new variable for Argentina (adding the individual responses to the first three questions of table 3.9: nine thousand pesos, ten
thousand pesos, and fifty thousand pesos) to measure the effect of sector activity on the perceived capacity of detection (overall mean = 34
percent). I tested a one-way ANOVA; a statistically significant ($p < 0.01$)
beta square of 0.17 denotes that perception of the likelihood of tax-fraud
detection is somewhat associated to the industry. I also tested an ANOVA
to measure the effect of firm size and the role of the respondent. In both
cases, the results, although less robust, were statistically significant. Thus,

21. The mean scores were as follows: for construction, 28 percent; for commerce, 35
percent; for services, 26 percent; for agriculture, 36 percent; and overall, 32 percent.

TABLE 3.10 Perceived Probabilities of Tax-Fraud Detection by Region in Chile

	Interior (Antofagasta/ Concepción)	Metropolitan (Santiago)
$5,000,000	74.8	69.2
$9,000,000	77.5	72.4
Fake $10,000,000	75.2	69.5

SOURCE: Survey 6.
NOTE: Valid n = 508.

differences among subgroups are explained by opportunities, visibility, and the sector's structural conditions.[22] In Chile, taxpayers from the metropolitan area estimate the detection capabilities of SII somewhat lower than do nonmetropolitan taxpayers. Finally, in neither Chile nor Argentina did education affect perceptions of the likelihood of tax-fraud detection. Only taxpayers who had completed elementary school or less (a small subsample) were more likely than better-educated taxpayers to elevate the probability of tax-fraud detection. In contrast to results in the United States (Beron, Tauchen, and Witte 1992), then, education has no significant impact on perceptions of the likelihood of fraud detection.

Given that opportunity strongly influences the nature of tax misreporting, the control that tax agencies exert affects individuals' decisions to evade taxes. As mentioned above (see table 3.5), the perceived effectiveness of the TA in detecting overstated deductions or underreported income is tied to its capabilities. Therefore, I constructed an indicator to determine taxpayers' perception of the likelihood of detection of underreported revenues as compared to overstated deductions based on two questions; taxpayers were asked to estimate the likelihood of detection of an overstated deduction versus underreported income, with the levels of fraud at one thousand pesos or ten thousand pesos for Argentina and one million pesos or ten million pesos for Chile. Table 3.11 reports the results.

Smaller amounts of underreporting and small overstatements in deductions are obviously difficult to detect. The higher the level of noncompliance, the more likely taxpayers were to believe that their TA was capable of detecting overstated deductions over underreported income. This supports the hypothesis that the visibility of transactions affects compliance

22. For example, in the construction sector, a house might be sold for one hundred thousand dollars but the deed might be escrowed for fifty thousand dollars. The seller and buyer would agree to underreport to avoid taxes. The notary public (escrow agent) would participate by refusing to ask questions. This perverse underreporting could be dismantled by a good administration that validated property value. Yet property taxes are administered by the provinces, which are very inefficient.

TABLE 3.11 Perceived Probabilities of Tax-Fraud Detection by
Type of Noncompliance

	Underreport Income Small Amount	Overstate Deduction Small Amount	Underreport Income Large Amount	Overstate Deduction Small Amount
Chile	1.89	2.19	1.52	1.71
Argentina	3.21	3.22	2.63	2.53
Tax Officials				
(Argentina)	3.35	3.30	2.50	2.51

SOURCES: Surveys 1, 2, and 6.
NOTE: Scale: 1 = very likely, 4 = very unlikely. Valid n = 502 for Argentina, n = 512 for Chile.

(Kagan 1989). In addition, in Argentina the same questionnaire was administered to tax-agency officials (survey 2) and yielded similar results. As the last row of table 3.11 shows, tax officials' low estimation of their own agencies' abilities matches that of taxpayers.

The tests of detection capabilities indicate that cheaters in Argentina and Chile are rational in the sense that their perceptions regarding enforcement do not differ from those who actually enforce the laws. Perceptions of the TA's detection capabilities in Chile credit the agency with a high level of effectiveness compared to Argentina. In addition, there were no significant differences in perceived detection capabilities between audited and non-audited subsamples in both countries, which supports the hypothesis that taxpayers learn more about their TA's capabilities from the environment than from personal experiences. The large differences in tax compliance between Chile and Argentina strongly correlate with the large disparities in perceptions of the TA's detection capacities. This does not mean that detection capacities are stronger in the former country than in the latter, but simply that Chileans believe that their TA's detection capacity is stronger than Argentines do.

Risk and Tax Compliance

According to standard economic theory, the willingness to take risks is inversely associated with income (Cowell 1990). More important, risk is inversely associated with perceptions of the likelihood that tax noncompliance will be detected. Risk aversion in Argentina is low, whereas it is higher in Chile. Surveys 1, 4, and 6 tested several measures of risk using standard questions in the survey literature. In surveys 1 and 6, two hypothetical questions about underreported income (five thousand pesos and nine thousand pesos for Argentina, five million pesos and nine million

TABLE 3.12 Risk Estimation for Given Transactions in Argentina and Chile

	Argentina	Chile
$5,000 (Arg.), $5,000,000 (Chile)	67.4	45.9
$9,000 (Arg.), $9,000,000 (Chile)	58.2	45.5
Fake Invoice	45.2	38.5
VAT 50% (only Argentina)	21.4	—

SOURCES: Surveys 1 and 6.

pesos for Chile; see table 3.8) were followed by the question, "What is the probability (from 0 to 100 percent) that such an individual will take the risk of underreporting [such] income?"[23] Table 3.12 shows the means for Argentina and Chile, where the score represents the percentage average probability that taxpayers will take the risk of underreporting these amounts. For example, the value 67.4 means that for this sample, on average, the probability that the respondent would take the risk of underreporting five thousand dollars was 67.4 percent. This data suggests that Argentines were more likely than Chileans to take the risk of underreporting income, and therefore that Chilean taxpayers are more risk averse. Also, there is a very high mean for the use of fake invoices in both countries—an act considered fraudulent and punishable under penal statutes (see chap. 4). Finally, as the amount of money involved increases, risk taking decreases, presumably because visibility and the likelihood of detection increase.[24]

Table 3.13 presents an informative comparison of risk aversion between audited and non-audited taxpayers in Chile and Argentina. Audited taxpayers on average are more prone to take risks in Argentina than are non-audited taxpayers, whereas in Chile, audits have no effect on risk aversion. These results are not conclusive, but the fact that no differences in risk taking are found in Chile suggests that audits do not always lead to risk aversion, and consequently that they fail to reduce tax noncompliance. Finally, in both countries no differences were found between audited taxpayers who were assessed additional taxes and those who were fully compliant. This suggests that audits, despite their use of fines

23. The fake-invoice question was followed by the question, "What is the probability that you or a given manager would undertake the risk of reducing VAT liabilities by filing taxes with fake invoices for that amount?"

24. Two additional results are worth mentioning: (1) Individual position within the firm matters. Managers and executives are on average more prone to take risks, whereas accountants are more risk averse (see Mazur and Nagin 1987). (2) Firm size positively correlates with risk perceptions. This result also supports the hypothesis that risk is a function of disposable income.

TABLE 3.13   Risk Estimation by Previous Tax Experience

	Previous Tax Experience		
	Audited	Non-audited	Total
Argentina $5,000	69.7	61.8	67.4
Chile $5,000,000	44.7	43.1	44.9
Argentina $9,000	60.5	54.4	58.3
Chile $9,000,000	44.6	46.5	45.4
Fake Invoice Argentina $50,000	47.8	40.5	45.3
Fake Invoice Chile $10,000,000	38.1	39.1	38.5
Argentina $100,000	22.8	18.3	21.5

SOURCES: Surveys 4 and 6.
NOTE: Totals of means do not always coincide among the last four tables due to slight variations in n. Valid n for Argentina = 533, for Chile = 522.

and their production of additional tax revenue, failed to "teach a lesson" to taxpayers. Due to the small number of cases, however, the results on this point are at the limit of statistical significance.

Willingness to take risks and the perceived likelihood of detection are correlated. For Argentina, in survey 1 the correlation coefficient between the detection measure[25] and subjective risk[26] was −0.23. In survey 4 the correlation between risk and detection was −0.33, and in both cases the coefficients are statistically significant at p < .01. In Chile, correlations between three different measures (five million pesos, nine million pesos, and fake invoices) average −0.17. The inverse association suggests that the higher the perceived likelihood of detection, the less willing people are to take the risk of noncompliance.

Risk aversion increased in another simulated case studied in surveys 4 and 6. Using an experimental approach, respondents were asked to react to a hypothetical situation: An "average" taxpayer in Argentina was said to have true income-tax liabilities of twenty-five thousand pesos but to have paid only fifteen thousand pesos for the given year (underreporting by ten thousand pesos). For Chile, this amount was multiplied by one thousand; for comparison purposes, however, I will report figures for Chile divided by one thousand (i.e., equivalent to Argentina). The probability of an audit was said to be about one in fifty. Respondents were informed that for next year, the TA would double the number of audits. They were asked to decide the amount of taxes that the given taxpayer

25. The detection measure is a variable constructed by the addition of questions about the perceived detection of nine thousand dollars and fifty thousand dollars.
26. Subjective risk is a variable constructed by the addition of questions about fake invoices and risk taking on a transaction of nine thousand dollars.

TABLE 3.14A Mean of Hypothetical Tax to Be Reported According to the
Perceived Likelihood of Matching by the TA

	Hypothetical Tax	
Likelihood of Matching Information	Argentina	Chile
Very Likely	$23,095	$23,790
Likely	$21,442	$24,201
Unlikely	$21,167	$22,657
Very Unlikely	$20,547	$22,000

SOURCE: Survey 4.

NOTE: For Chile, amounts should be multiplied by 1,000. Valid n = 531.

should report the following year if the taxpayer's finances were exactly the same. The sample average for Argentina was $21,350, whereas for Chile it was $23,830. Taxpayers increased the amount of reported tax liability from the hypothetical previous year, but they remained largely in noncompliance in Argentina and substantially less so in Chile.

The different average response is associated with both the increased amount of information that the TA was perceived to have and the probability that it would match tax-return information with third-party sources. As tables 3.14A and 3.14B show, the more taxpayers believed that the TA had relevant information that it might use to screen tax returns, the more likely they were to recommend that the hypothetical individual report twenty-five thousand pesos (or something very close to it). (In fact, the vast majority of this group recommended that the individual report twenty-five thousand, but a few undertook some risk.)

Still, the question remains: what variables account for the difference in responses? To provide an answer, I constructed an index of aggressiveness-conservatism in tax compliance, based on the data from survey 4 (see Table 3.15).[27] Respondents were informed that a change in the tax-withholding system for the following year would alter the amount of taxes that had to be paid in advance. For a hypothetical taxpayer, thirty thousand pesos had already been withheld, and he or she had to request a reimbursement. Two messages were specified in the question: the taxpayer's true tax liability remained constant at twenty-five thousand pesos, and taxpayers were assured that authorities would reimburse them no later than thirty days after the returns were filed. This hypothetical question allows testing for the effect of withholding, which diminishes tax evasion because it

27. I present the results for Argentina, which had a larger variance in responses, although the trend for Chile is similar.

TABLE 3.14B Mean of Hypothetical Tax to Be Reported According to the
Perceived Information Available to the TA

Information Available to TA	Hypothetical Tax	
	Argentina	Chile
High	$24,166	$23,769
Quite a Bit	$21,710	$23,282
Some	$21,050	$23,289
None	$20,922	$23,182

SOURCE: Survey 4.
NOTE: For Chile, amounts should be multiplied by 1,000. Valid n = 531.

compels taxpayers to frame tax decisions differently. In this case, claiming
reimbursement of a true tax liability is perceived as a partial gain.[28]

The sample was then divided in two groups: respondents who decided
to be "aggressive" and claim a reimbursement that encompassed an evasion of at least $5,000 (i.e., those who hypothetically requested a reim-
bursement of $10,000 or more) and a more cautious or "conservative"
group, who decided to claim less than $10,000 (i.e., no evasion or an eva-
sion no greater than $4,999). Table 3.15 displays the results. Although
the differences in the mean for conservatives between previously audited
and non-audited taxpayers is 2 percent both for detection and risk (42
percent and 44 percent; 53 percent and 51 percent), the spread increases
significantly for the more aggressive, up to 7 percent in the risk variable
(57 percent and 50 percent) and up to 9 percent in the detection variable
(35 percent and 44 percent). Moreover, the entire effect of the spread
increase is attributable to the audited group, because the non-audited
taxpayers do not differ in their mean for either the detection or the risk
variable.

The gap between the audited and the non-audited scores increases with
the respondents' degree of aggressiveness. This indicates that taxpayers'
aggressiveness is at least partly associated with an individual's tax history. This test shows that a badly performed audit affects the willingness of taxpayers to take risks and contributes greatly to the perception
that evasion will likely go undetected. A solid audit, however, might contribute to a reduction in tax evasion, particularly among "conservative"
taxpayers.

28. Paying taxes at the tax deadline is perceived as a total loss. Cognitively, a partial
gain leads to more cautious behavior, and therefore the willingness to evade taxes decreases
(Webley et al. 1991).

TABLE 3.15 Estimation of Perceived Likelihood of Tax-Fraud Detection and Risk by Audit Experience

	Personality			
	Detection (Aggressive)	Detection (Conservative)	Risk (Aggressive)	Risk (Conservative)
Audited	35	42	57	53
Non-audited	44	44	50	51
Mean	37	43	55	51

SOURCE: Survey 4.
NOTE: Valid n = 530.

SUMMARY

In this chapter, I have presented evidence about taxpayers' perceptions of the effectiveness of their TAS. The survey data has shown a large discrepancy in taxpayers' perceptions regarding the ability of their respective tax administrations to detect and punish tax evaders. Consequently, Chilean taxpayers are more risk averse and tend to be more cautious, whereas Argentines are more aggressive. These attributes nurture stable equilibria wherein strategic decisions are governed by the perceived threat of sanctions. At the root of the discrepancy is a difference in information: despite compatible enforcement capacities, taxpayers' level of information in Chile and Argentina differs. In conditions of bounded rationality and limited information, taxpayers adopt strategies such as imitation and herd behavior that help them cope with uncertainty. When everybody cheats, taxpayers learn quickly that the tax administration lacks the ability to detect and punish; when legalists comply, taxpayers believe that tax administrations are effective. That does not imply that the true capacities of the TAS are different but rather that social learning, "experimentation," and personal experience account for the difference. In a noncompliance equilibrium (such as Argentina), cheaters rarely shift to compliance; thus, cheaters rarely "experiment" with legalist behavior. On the other hand, under a compliance equilibrium, some compliers might occasionally "test" tax evasion. The equilibrium can only be undermined, however, when the number of experimenters reaches a critical mass. To the extent that a TA fails to detect and punish new tax evaders, the equilibrium becomes unstable. The TAS are instrumental in strengthening the perception that cheaters will be caught and punished. Their task (as in Chile) is to preserve the equilibrium and deter experimentation.

In this chapter, I have also suggested that personal experience with audits has only limited (but specific) individual effects. Taxpayers in both Argentina and Chile realize that the poor detection capabilities of TAs inhibit their capacity to run effective audits. The slight difference between Argentina and Chile stems from Argentina's need to rely on wide-coverage audit policies (due to the large scale of noncompliance). Conversely, given the better compliance record in Chile, audits that are more in-depth are perceived by taxpayers as threatening. As in the United States, however, taxpayers' fear of audits is largely unwarranted (Plumley 1992). In the United States and Chile, people are more afraid of the experience of an audit than of its financial consequences. In Argentina, people fear audits less; therefore, the power of the stick diminishes.

AFIP's directorate officers hear recurrent complaints about the poor job done by auditors. In a private conversation, Ricardo Cossio, the head of DGI between 1990 and 1995, described his frustrations: "I had many successes heading the tax agency; however, I failed miserably at auditing" (*Fiscalización*). He is not alone. All of AFIP's chairpersons failed in this regard. Why? Enforcement agencies that operate in compliance environments are more effective. Moderate efficiency in law-abiding societies generates better results than good administration in a world of cheaters. This feeds a virtuous circle. President Perón was right about the effect of enforcement, but he was wrong about the country where this might work. General deterrence is effective when there are fewer people to watch. The chapter that follows takes a closer look at how particular enforcement policies influence taxpayers' perceptions of TA effectiveness in Argentina and Chile, with particular attention paid to the conditions in which general deterrence can be effective.

4

GENERAL DETERRENCE:
IMPUNITY AND SANCTIONS IN TAXATION

> ...La ley se hace para todos
> Mas sólo al pobre le rige
>
> La ley es tela de araña,
> En mi inorancia lo esplico:
> No la tema el hombre rico,
> Nunca la tema el que mande
> Pues la ruempe el bicho grande
> Y solo enrieda a los chicos
>
> Es la ley como la lluvia:
> Nunca puede ser pareja;
> El que la aguanta se queja,
> Pero el asunto es sencillo,
> La ley es como el cuchillo:
> No ofiende a quien lo maneja
>
> [... The law is created for all,
> But it only rules over the poor.
>
> The law is like a spiderweb,
> I will explain in my humble words:
> The rich man does not fear it,
> Those who rule do not tarry
> Because big bugs can tear it,
> And it only entangles the little ones.
>
> The law is like the rain,
> It is never fair to all.
> He who puts up with it complains,
> But the matter is quite simple:
> The law is like a knife
> It doesn't hurt whoever holds it.]
>
> — JOSÉ HERNÁNDEZ, *Martín Fierro* (1878); translation mine

Seventy-five percent of taxpayers in Chile believe that cheaters get caught and are severely punished. In Argentina, less than 40 percent believe this same statement, and close to two-thirds of Argentines believe that cheaters get away with their misdeeds. What are the implications of such beliefs regarding tax behavior? What can tax administrations do to reverse course in countries like Argentina and maintain stable levels of compliance in places like Chile? This chapter analyzes the role of sanctions in bolstering general compliance. If, as deterrence theory asserts, compliance depends on the ability of the enforcer to detect and punish tax evaders, we should expect that a better regime of punishment for tax evasion elicits better compliance from taxpayers. Because it is highly unlikely that an enforcer can effectively monitor most taxpayers, the credible threat of severe punishment should compensate for deficiencies in detection and control, sending the right signals to tax cheaters (that tax evasion can be costly) and to compliers (that the enforcer is fulfilling its part of the bargain). But I claim that deterrence theory falls short in explaining tax compliance because the ability to impose severe sanctions is contingent on the given equilibrium. This chapter examines the effect of sanctions on the construction and maintenance of both compliance and noncompliance environments.

Sanctions are instrumental for norm abidance. Because this book develops the argument that culture matters in compliance, there is a need to examine the role that punishment plays for individual and group deviance from preestablished norms. In the following pages, I undertake a systematic study of the institutionalization of the enforcer's threat. I study the conditions under which some threats are effective and others are not. Again, the given equilibrium matters. Effective sanctions are more common in a "bad apples" scenario. In "rotten barrel" situations, sanctions inherently lose effectiveness, inhibiting active defectors from becoming passive cooperators. Here I develop a central piece of the general theory of tax compliance: The way that the policy of sanctions is constructed and implemented nurtures the institutionalization of the given equilibrium.

This chapter demonstrates that the essential difference between Chile and Argentina in general deterrence is the rate of impunity: that relatively few people are able to cheat with impunity largely explains the success of deterrence in Chile. Because impunity seriously undermines the conditions for cooperation, compliance equilibria can only be reached if sanctions are effectively imposed. This chapter will also show that sanctions contribute to better overall compliance to the extent that they are fairly administered. Effective enforcement requires an institutional makeup that ensures fairness through constraints on state power, an efficient legal system, congressional oversight over the tax agency, a clear appeal procedures, and so forth (Barzel 2002). This contributes to a culture of compliance, because taxpayers believe that the system punishes free riders and treats fairly those who are in compliance. The institutions that protect taxpayers check the stringent tax enforcement in Chile. Chileans perceive that laws are effective and fairly handled, which is not the case with Argentines. Finally, this chapter proposes a new conceptualization of the role of sanctions by claiming that their effectiveness is tied to the given compliance equilibrium. Regardless of the type of sanctions (civil, penal, or administrative), they must be perceived as severe and, more important, very likely to be imposed.[1] As I will show, in noncompliance equilibria, policies based on severe punishment usually fail because most taxpayers are never caught; thus, paradoxically, this policy ends up promoting greater impunity and further undermines the basis of trust and reciprocity in cooperative actions. There is a need to address the problem of severe deviance where conditions for cooperation are already broken, because impunity is endogenous to noncompliance environments. I contend that the study of sanctions under different equilibria allows for a better understanding of the conditions that explain whether the level of impunity can be reduced.

The chapter begins with a brief discussion of sanctions and punishment in tax evasion. I then turn to the empirical analysis of the sanctions policy in Argentina and Chile, the criminalization of certain types of tax evasion in Argentina, and the administration of the prosecution of tax charges in Chile. The last section presents a statistical analysis of taxpayers' perceptions of the likelihood of severe punishment for tax fraud in each country. Although threats of criminal punishment for tax evasion have clearly failed in Argentina, they have been moderately successful in Chile, demonstrating that general deterrence can be somewhat effective only in a compliance environment.

SANCTIONS AND PUNISHMENT IN TAX EVASION

Tax evasion has historically been conceived as a civil rather than criminal violation. As such, the types of penalties have been overwhelmingly monetary. In the last decades, as a result of fiscal deficits and growing tax evasion, many countries have begun to treat tax evasion as a type of fraud, in itself an illegal act socially constructed as a crime. The ultimate goal has been to deter tax evaders with the severest of penalties: incarceration.[2]

1. Certainty of imposition appears to be more important than severity of punishment (above a minimal threshold of penalties). This is probably because an increase in penalties might signal to potential cooperators that authorities are having a hard time detecting offenders. Further research is needed to ascertain whether this proposition is true (see Triest and Shefrien 1992; Frey and Feld 2002).

2. Crimes are distinguished from other law violations by the origin of the act (*mala in se*) and by the intent of the offender (*mens rea*; see Newman 1958). Sociologists have challenged the notion of crime as simply the result of the text of the law (Braithwaite 1989; McBarnet 1991, 1992; Croall 1992); crime is a social construction that is reproduced and constantly challenged. For a full discussion of white-collar crime and the criminalization of tax offenses, see Bergman (1998).

Even though tax codes and legal statutes worldwide have specific provisions that allow tax authorities to penalize tax evasion, only a small fraction of these cases are indeed pursued criminally. The majority of detected tax evasion is punished at the administrative level. In the United States, the Criminal Investigation Division (CID) investigated and prosecuted an average of five thousand cases yearly in the 1970s and 1980s. These cases accounted for less than 3 percent of the presumed two hundred thousand annual criminal tax offenses (Long 1981; IRS 1992). In the 1990s, prosecutions ranged between two thousand and three thousand cases yearly, roughly half of them for money laundering and the other half for tax evasion, and these figures have increased slightly over the last few years.[3] In Britain, courts adjudicated a yearly average of 373 criminal tax cases between 1981 and 1987 (Cook 1989). In Chile, only eighty-five criminal charges out of five thousand potential tax evasion cases were brought against tax violators in 1995 (SII 1996).

There is only scattered evidence that criminal prosecution and incarceration are effective for general deterrence (Plumley 1992, 2002). One study for the United States (Dubin 2004) shows that it is not the rates of sentences per number of tax returns but the absolute number of criminal prosecutions by the CID that has the largest influence on general compliance. Criminal prosecution is somewhat more cost-effective than audits in increasing tax collection, but both contribute significantly to the spillover effect of enforcement on general tax compliance. Furthermore, the publicity of such convictions has a moderate effect because it helps to disseminate information about the risks that tax cheaters incur.[4] Scholars have proposed alternative approaches to criminal prosecution: Ostrom (1990) suggests that graduated sanctions should be imposed according to the seriousness and context of the infraction, starting from light and informative reprimands for occasional norm violators and progressing to harsh penalties for repeat offenders. Kahan (2000) argues that "gentle nudges" should be preferred to "hard shoves" because they are more likely to be imposed by law enforcers, whereas Frey and Feld (2002) emphasize that harsh punishment might even be counterproductive because it signals that others do not fully cooperate in taxation. But these works of scholarship

---

3. In 2000, 3,372; in 2001, 3,284; and in 2002, 3,906. The number of convictions for these years was 2,249, 2,251, and 1,926, respectively. It should be remembered that convictions relate to cases filed many years before (reported by Lederman 2003, n25). The average conviction rate is above 88 percent.

4. This study was conducted in the United States, a compliant country. It is unclear what results would be obtained in a country where most people cheat.

are case studies regarding single or few deviants in compliance environ-ments. Noncompliance equilibria call for different strategies.

For a criminal threat to be effective, taxpayers must believe that levels of detection and prosecution are high—that is, that impunity is being effectively curtailed. Tax administrations can enhance their image as effective detectors of cheaters by instituting an efficient auditing-control process. Successful criminal prosecutions also require an effec-tive criminal-justice administration. Tax administrations, however, avoid criminal sanctions because they are too costly, require other govern-ment agencies' intervention, and are extremely time-consuming. Thus, problems of coordination, resources, and scale inhibit wider reliance on criminal deterrence. Selective enforcement of the threat of criminal pros-ecution has shown moderate success, but this strategy is effective only within a compliance environment.

Severe punishment can take many forms. In this chapter, I concentrate on closure of businesses, penal prosecution, and fines. I evaluate the ef-fect of these instruments in both Chile and Argentina, paying particular attention to the way that the threat of severe sanction is perceived. I examine Argentina's difficulties in implementing an effective penal policy related to taxation within the context of a weak state, and I compare the Argentine case to the achievements of Chile. The success of a penal policy (severe punishment) for tax fraud in the United States, Chile, and many western European nations is tied to the careful selection of cases to be prosecuted, the exemplary significance of the punishment, the prob-ability that a case will successfully reach conviction, and the potential revenues that a case might generate. The goal of a penal policy for tax fraud is to demonstrate the state's capacity to imprison serious offend-ers rather than prosecute large numbers of tax violators. Argentina has failed to achieve this goal. I argue that where there are a large number of tax evaders, the enforcement of a penal threat becomes less effective.

I also present data on administrative penalties in Chile, where taxpayers found noncompliant are very likely to be sanctioned (that is, where impu-nity is low among those whose fraud is detected). In Argentina, on the other hand, the perceived certainty that penalties will be imposed for tax fraud is lower. In short, I show that regardless of the type and the administration of penalties, sanctions are effective to the extent that they curtail impunity.[5]

---

5. For example, a specialized NGO has recently reported that a case of corruption in Argentina lingers in court for an average of fourteen years. Moreover, as of mid-2007, there were no individuals in Argentina incarcerated for corruption (*Clarin*, July 22, 2007). This, of course, reduces the effectiveness of sanctions.

SANCTIONS POLICY IN CHILE AND ARGENTINA

Closure of Businesses

An example of how a similar measure can have divergent effects in different compliance environments is provided by the temporary closure of businesses. This penalty is administered for violating several tax rules, particularly for failing to issue invoices. Although closures do not carry the stigma associated with criminality, a few days' closure is typically costly for the business affected. Closures require posting clearly marked signs on the premises, which affect a business's reputation in the neighborhood and also punish it financially by reducing business activity and helping competitors. Temporary closures are generally perceived as a very severe punishment, particularly by small- and medium-level taxpayers. This tactic was used significantly in the 1990s in Chile and Argentina, as shown in table 4.1.

In Argentina, there were no significant administrative changes to account for the deterioration of compliance in 1993.[6] Taxpayers engaged in less blatant evasion and relied on more sophisticated noncompliance strategies after they recognized the TA's increased sanctioning capacities. It appears that an increase in the perceived risk of detection led to the adoption of precautionary measures.[7] Conversely, in Chile, business closures are still being used and have not changed significantly throughout the period.[8] In addition, whereas in Argentina the number of inspections increased during the early 1990s, in Chile that number remained constant. Moreover, inspectors in Chile monitor only a small percentage of targeted businesses.[9] This suggests that in Chile a moderate threat of sanction has yielded good compliance effects, whereas in Argentina strong threats have yielded poor results.

6. Between 1991 and 1994, the number of inspections remained constant, but the number of closures started to decline from 1993 onward.

7. The DGI's more active enforcement in the early 1990s initially created the image of a better and more efficient tax agency, as taxpayers' reports confirm. In a July 1994 survey, 67 percent of respondents agreed with the statement, "People today pay more taxes than before." When respondents were asked why this was happening, the main explanation given was the DGI's improved mechanisms of control (Mora y Araujo 1994).

8. I present an in-depth analysis of this measure in chapter 5.

9. Reported by Jorge Trujillo, deputy director of the audits department of SII. Interview held in Santiago, Chile, August 2, 1996. Since 1990, approximately two hundred part-time inspectors have been allocated to the duties of invoicing and other formalities-control operations. For Argentina, see Durán and Gómez Sabaini 1995 and the interview with Horacio Castagnola (July 27, 1996).

TABLE 4.1 Closure of Businesses in Chile and Argentina, 1991–1994

Year	Chile	Argentina
1991	—	8,157
1992	11,246	17,739
1993	8,905	15,253
1994	9,110	10,965

SOURCES: For Argentina, SARC/SELECCIO 1998. For Chile, SII 1996.
NOTE: By 1995, the number of inspectors and closures in Argentina decreased due to legal challenges, whereas in Chile the measure is still used and an average of nine thousand businesses a year are closed.

The Penal Track: Argentina's Tax-Crime Law

The collapse of Argentina's economy and the hyperinflation of the late 1980s contributed to a new political learning. Fiscal and inflationary deficits were no longer considered a viable funding source. In February 1990, Argentina's Congress enacted the Tax-Criminal Law (TCL; Ley Penal Tributaria), a bill (no. 23771) that was part of an overall restructuring of the country's tax policy and administration. Legislators, at the onset of Carlos Menem's government and at the peak of the hyperinflation spiral, facilitated the creation of a new instrument to fight tax evasion (Eaton 2002). The goal was to emulate similar penalties in more developed countries (Tanzi and Shome 1993). The 1990 Tax-Criminal Law (TCL) introduced a new legal understanding of tax violations. The legal conceptualization of *tax* was transformed into a property or good under both criminal tutelage (*bien penal tutelado*) under the public treasurer's jurisdiction (*jurisdicción de la hacienda pública*). Most tax noncompliance, particularly tax evasion, ceased to be defined as a simple misdemeanor (*contravenciones*) and became a felony (*delitos penales*). The punishment for serious tax evasion was made more severe. Because prison sentences carry the social burden of stigma and might negatively affect social status (Braithwaite 1989; Grasmick and Bursick 1990), the TCL was expected to deter evasion, at least in its most blatant form. The bill simplified the mechanism for conviction in order to expedite the certainty of the imposition of sanctions.

The TCL established a specific mechanism for prosecution and adjudication. After certain types of tax evasion were detected, the TA had to file charges in federal criminal court. A new specialized court district was created for Buenos Aires, the economic crime tribunal (*fuero penal económico*), which handled 40 percent of the 8,565 cases filed between

1990 and 1995. For the rest of the country, cases were handled by regular federal criminal courts.

As a civil-code country, Argentina follows the judicial structure of the "instructing judge." This role of the judge is to initiate discovery and safeguard due process during that phase.[10] In the lower penal courts, judges investigate and evaluate the merits and evidence of cases to decide whether to elevate the case for trial before a higher court.[11] By virtue of this role, judges become an active part of the investigation: they coordinate and lead the investigation, and they guarantee due process. Every ruling, however, can be appealed to higher courts. A very important feature of the civil-law tradition that affected the outcome of the TCL is that the district attorneys have a very narrow discretion over the selection of cases.[12]

Table 4.2 describes the status and fiscal claims of the different cases between 1990 and 1995. A provision of the TCL established that within thirty days after formal charges were filed, the TA has to submit a technical report (*informe técnico*). This report must include the substantive evidence or the grounds for the alleged criminal tax violations. This provision was conceived as a mechanism to expedite the process, but it constrained the tax agency's ability to thoroughly investigate cases.[13] At the discovery phase, the prosecution had no discretionary power to decide which cases had strong legal merits. Thus, all decisions to proceed with criminal charges relied on the tax agency's criminal tax division, which decided, on the direct orders of the TA's general director, which cases to press. This process suffered from a lack of clear guidelines regarding which cases merited criminal prosecution. These decisions varied according to political and personal considerations, and lacked institutional coordination. The tension generated by the policy of filing a large number of criminal cases, and the constraints imposed by the time limits for supplying evidence, diminished the effectiveness of the law and severely reduced the conviction rate.

10. In the common-law tradition, judges refrain from prosecutorial duties.

11. Following a 1992 reform, and for the first time in Argentinean legal history, all criminal trials (tax-evasion cases included) became oral.

12. Criminal court has an attached prosecutor (who reports to, and is appointed by, the attorney general's office). The prosecutor acts as the legal representative of the state. The instructing judge carries out the investigation based on the evidence from different sources, including the TA. The prosecutor has a more active role at the trial phase. In that stage, judges become a third party, more in line with their role in the common law.

13. In the United States, for instance, an IRS criminal investigation takes an average of eighteen months before a final Criminal Investigation Department (CID) decision on whether to recommend the filing of criminal charges. In Chile, this process takes more than ten months.

TABLE 4.2 Criminal Cases Filed by Argentine TA and Court Resolutions, 1990–1995

Nature of Adjudication	Number of Cases (Total = 8565)	Fiscal Claim (Total = $1.367 billion)
Article XIV (Plea Bargain)	1,116	$56,530,898
Convictions	53	$5,754,303
Law No. 24587 (New Minimum)	3,659	$68,775,361
Acquittals	1,698	$173,973,854
Total Adjudication	6,524 (64%)	$305,034,416 (22%)

SOURCE: DGI 1996.

Another provision also hindered the TCL's long-term deterrent effect. According to Article XIV of the law, taxpayers had the prerogative to pay tax debts and fines in exchange for the dismissal of criminal charges. This clause could only be invoked for first-time offenses. Table 4.2 shows that many offenders took advantage of this plea-bargain strategy, which partly explains the low conviction rate of the TCL. Although the clause was originally conceived as a mechanism to increase tax collection by fostering fast court settlements, it actually created an incentive for tax evasion, because taxpayers being prosecuted for the first time always had recourse to a settlement. As the odds of being detected were already low, Article XIV eliminated the most efficient deterrent threat. A leading attorney, who worked both as a prosecutor and later as a defense lawyer for major corporations, suggested that for large taxpayers Article XIV was a viable last resort.[14]

A famous case illustrates Article XIV's damaging effects. In 1993, the head of the fiscal-auditing division, Jose Luis Peña, announced that a well-known and powerful entrepreneur, Francisco Macri, was being investigated for alleged tax evasion in excess of three hundred million dollars. In 1994, the director of internal revenues, Carlos Tacchi, ordered the filing of criminal charges against Macri. The defendant's lawyers succeeded in delaying the case, and the TA failed to prove the total alleged evasion beyond any doubt. Because Macri was proved to be delinquent only in the amount of five million dollars, Macri's attorneys, relying on Article XIV, agreed to a settlement in exchange for the dropping of all criminal charges against their client. This case was a victory for the defense. Had Mr. Macri been jailed, however, the deterrent effect of the

14. Interview with Pablo Medrano, former tax prosecutor and current tax-law practitioner, Buenos Aires, June 27, 1996.

law might have been more pronounced. As Wheeler and others (1988) state, sanctions against white-collar offenders are not proportional to the damage inflicted, particularly compared to the sentences handed down to common criminal offenders. For white-collar offenders, the penal process becomes the punishment. Article XIV saved Macri from the stigma and shame that would have attended a conviction and jail sentence.

By 1995, the TCL's serious limitations became noticeable as the TA attempted to collect small claims through the criminal venue. Like any other criminal charge, tax fraud requires hard evidence to ensure conviction. When the TA began attempting to prosecute small-scale cases of tax fraud, it found that the money it could recover from tax evaders was insignificant compared to the total cost of handling their cases. A new law (no. 24587) raised the minimum amount of unpaid tax money required for an evasion to be considered a crime. More than 20 percent of all cases, which represented less than 5 percent of total tax claims, were automatically converted into civil violations, and payment programs were arranged.

Although 64 percent of the 8,565 cases for the 1990–95 period were adjudicated, only 53 (less than 1 percent) resulted in criminal convictions. Moreover, as table 4.2 shows, the first three categories combined (4,828 cases), all of which had a favorable outcome for the state, account for 50 percent of the cases but only 8 percent (approximately $131 million) of the funds that the TA claimed were owed. In addition, 20 percent of cases were dismissed or their defendants acquitted (either on technical grounds or for lack of evidence). The ratio of the state's favorable decisions against acquittals (the first two categories against the fourth) was approximately 30 percent, accounting for only 25 percent of the taxes that the state claimed were owed. In comparison, the U.S. TA has a 90 percent conviction rate, Britain's averages 93 percent, and Chile's rate exceeds 80 percent.

Argentina's TCL failed for several reasons. First, there was a *lack of clear guidelines for prosecutions.* No uniform and clear goal for criminal investigations and prosecutions was established. In the United States (Roth, Scholz, and Witte 1989) and in Britain (Cook 1989), the IRS and the Inland Revenue have clear internal guidelines for the selection of cases, usually going after "the big, the bad, and the heinous" (Croall 1992). Argentina's criminal-tax division was pressured to file charges without a serious evaluation of the evidence or the financial worthiness of cases. Argentina's tax administration conceived the criminal venue as an instrument of fast collection. Such untargeted reliance on criminal charges diluted the severity of the punishment effect. In fact, the TA replaced the criminal threat with a plea-bargain strategy.

Second, *institutional weaknesses* hampered the TCL. Argentina's tax administration lacked the institutional capacity to process large numbers of cases. It failed also to coordinate with other state agencies (prosecutors, courts, other regulatory bodies) to investigate potential criminal cases. The TA failed to provide conclusive evidence for indictments and convictions. In Chile and the United States, at least two different departments within the tax administration are involved in the process of evaluating the evidence and strength of cases. Once the evidence has been weighed, it is sent for an additional evaluation by the district attorney's office. This filtering process ensures high rates of conviction and an efficient allocation of resources.

A third problem was *the legal system's inability to handle tax evasion as a criminal offense.* The judicial establishment and the legal tradition have not perceived tax evasion as a highly punishable form of fraud but rather as a violation in the realm of regulatory law. Thus, legal officers resisted the criminalization of tax fraud. They were trained to work on felonies, particularly violent crimes, and judges consistently extended the burden of proof that the TA had to meet beyond the strict provisions of the law. In a personal interview, a well-known tax judge asked me, "Why should I punish relatively small tax evaders when I cannot imprison the big fish?"[15] In addition, judges appointed for the economic-crime courts did not have any experience or expertise in economic and financial transactions.[16] The TCL became a typical case of failed legal reforms wherein, as Kahan (2000) suggests, "hard shoves" were watered down due to institutional resistance and law enforcement's reluctance to attack behavior embraced by a broad section of the community.

Given the lack of a strong administrative structure and a clear criminal policy, a weak and unprepared judicial system, and institutional resistance, the TCL was ineffective in improving collection and the conviction of tax evaders. In the end, these technical and institutional limitations resulted from a structural problem: noncompliance environments have inherently greater impunity rates, which are difficult to reverse by penal threats. The guidelines for a successful criminal prosecution policy must

15. Interview with judge Julio Cruciani, Buenos Aires, July 24, 1996.
16. Not a single course in basic accounting or tax-related topics was provided for judges and clerks of the new economic-crime jurisdiction (*fuero penal económico*).

be reconciled with the culture and norms of a given society. Argentina has failed because it has attempted to reverse an adverse equilibrium with a misguided policy. Unless the probabilities of detecting noncompliance are significantly raised, the effects of severe punishment quickly vanish. The impact on the deterrent capability of the TCL and the effect on tax compliance became all too predictable.

The Administrative Track

Sanctions are effective to the extent that they are enforceable. Severe sanctions raise the stakes for both the offenders and the TA, and higher stakes lead to less predictable outcomes. In order to secure high rates of conviction and enhance deterrence, tax administrations are better off applying more lenient punishment with a higher probability of conviction. Only exemplary or very clear-cut cases of fraud should be pursued through the penal venue. In the long run, the administrative or civil sanction serves better the deterrent image of the TA. That is the case in Chile.

During the 1990s, SII filed fewer than one hundred criminal charges per year; it imposed the overwhelming number of its sanctions through administrative procedures or in civil courts. Sanctions for noncompliance in Chile can be imposed for different types of tax misbehavior. Four types of sanctions (derived from different types of tax misconduct) account for 98 percent of administrative punishment: First, there are *closures* imposed for failure to issue invoices or other formal misconduct (*denuncios*). If detected, taxpayers who fail to issue invoices, or violate other formal regulations, are punished with monetary sanctions (for first-time offenders) and closures (for repeat offenders). Second, there are *fines and new assessments derived from internal reviews.* SII reviews information on tax returns, and when differences are found, it submits an adjustment and fines the taxpayers concerned. This review covers delays or other formal tax-filing misconduct. The third form of sanctions is fines and assessments derived from audits or *audit adjustment.* Audits that detect noncompliance trigger a demand to pay the difference, in addition to applicable fines. Finally, there are *civil and penal charges* for major tax violations. As a result of different information processes within SII, taxpayers who are found to have committed tax misconduct or fraud, made false declarations, submitted false reimbursement requests, or incorrectly applied tax credits are subject to a wide range of civil and penal charges.

One of the salient features of the tax court system in Chile is that the first stage of justice is within the tax administration. It is an administrative proceeding in which the head of the tax jurisdiction is also the judge of first claims (*juez tributario*, or tax judge). This system was formally introduced in the tax code of 1960, though it had been used earlier.[17] The system has been challenged by different civil organizations because it defies the principle of impartiality. SII becomes the prosecutor and the judge (*juez y parte*) of the suit, and thus fails to fulfill the most basic third-party role of the judicial system. Although SII is indeed the prosecutor and judge in the first instance, all decisions can be appealed to civil, appellate, and circuit courts, or even the Supreme Court. In fact, many cases advance through different jurisdictions. The majority of cases, however, are decided at the first stage. Only taxpayers who have resources to confront SII, those who feel they have a legitimate claim, and those who believe they can very likely win their case pursue the appeal venue.

Most cases are solved expeditiously, the discretion of judges is very narrow, and appeals account for only a small fraction of cases. Table 4.3 presents data for cases initiated in 1995 and 1997. Most tax-administration enforcement actions are never appealed. In the case of minor violations, taxpayers usually abide by the TA's rulings. The larger the pecuniary fines imposed by the TA, the more likely it is that its decisions will be appealed. The first stage within the administration rejects two-thirds of the taxpayers' claims.

Less than 20 percent of cases rejected by the tax judge are appealed in civil courts. Among those, close to 50 percent are rejected by courts of appeal, and another 50 percent benefit from partially or totally favorable rulings for the accused taxpayers. Among the rejected, less than one-third are appealed to the Supreme Court, although close to 70 percent of the lower courts' rulings are upheld. In sum, the odds that taxpayers will succeed in appealing a TA ruling are small. Therefore, taxpayers refrain from pursuing legal recourse as a tactic to delay or reduce tax payments and fines. But the fact that a number of decisions are indeed reversed also signals to tax judges within the TA that appellate courts exercise a considerable degree of control over their decisions.

This system of judicial control over the TA accounts for the small but steady rate of taxpayer claims accepted by tax judges. Table 4.4 summarizes the cases resolved by these judges at first instance for the two larger

---

17. Today, other state agencies also have a judicial first instance within the organization.

TABLE 4.3 Tax Cases Administered by Different Instances in Chile, 1995 and 1997

	1995		1997	
	% at Stage	% of Amount	% at Stage	% of Amount
Tax Judge				
Cases Initiated	(n = 372,212)		(n = 447,366)	
Plea Bargain	9.8		7.2	
Claims	1.6		1.0	
No Claims	88.6		91.8	
Claims	(n = 5,947)		(n = 4,582)	
Accepted	18.6	0.1	22.2	6.4
Rejected	65.6	93.1	65.7	75.1
Partly Accepted	6.4	6.7	9.4	18.4
No Information	9.4	0.1	2.7	0.1
Total	100	100	100	100
Appeal Courts				
Claims	(n = 776)		(n = 699)	
Claims Accepted	19.1	36.5	15.8	4.5
Rejected	48.1	43.3	40.5	39.3
Partly Accepted	23.3	17.8	17.2	2.5
No Information	9.5	2.4	28.5	53.7
Total	100	100	100	100
Supreme Court	(n = 86)		(n = 37)	
Accepted	23.2	10.1	18.9	0
Rejected	50.1	69.5	68.6	100
Partly Accepted	11.6	16.3	5.4	0
No Information	15.1	4.1	8.1	0
Total	100	100	100	100

SOURCE: SII 2001b.

NOTE: In 1995, there were still 69 cases in process at the tax-judge phase and 259 cases in appeal. For 1997, there were 26 cases in process at the first stage and 196 at the second.

SII acts, closures of businesses and tax assessments. These include 80 percent of cases. The acceptance rate of claims by tax judges is approximately 20 percent. The more serious the dispute, the smaller the rejection rate (and the larger the partial acceptance of the claim). *Denuncios* are minor violations that are hard to argue. On the other hand, assessments of tax liabilities are more aggressively disputed. Although the majority of cases are rejected, some claims are partially readjusted and others are solved to the mutual satisfaction of the TA and the accused. Table 4.4 also shows the remarkable stability of results throughout the years, particularly compared to Argentina.

TABLE 4.4 Type of Judicial Resolution of Two Types of Tax Violations, 1996–1999

	Denuncios					Assessments				
	Rejected	Accepted	Partly Accepted	No Information	Total	Rejected	Accepted	Partly Accepted	No Information	Total
1996	77.6%	21.9%	0.6%	0%	3,409	46.8%	17.7%	25.6%	9.8%	1,190
1997	77.4%	22.0%	0.5%	0%	2,723	44.3%	20.7%	28.2%	6.7%	1,297
1998	77.1%	21.9%	0.3%	0.7%	2,491	48.0%	20.1%	24.5%	7.4%	1,326
1999	75.4%	23.7%	0.4%	0.4%	2,628	42.1%	28.1%	29.3%	0.5%	1,453

SOURCE: SII 2001b.

The administrative track, particularly the internal tax judge, is a successful weapon in enhancing the Chilean TA's image as an effective policing agent. Instead of clogging the courts with minor tax disputes, only major cases advance through the system. In fact, the administrative track has become a filtering system that makes the outcome of most cases very predictable and quick to enforce. This enhances deterrence by making the imposition of sanctions more certain, and it reduces impunity, giving taxpayers confidence that they're not suckers. Although both Argentina and Chile handle most cases through the civil venue, the difference between the two countries lies in the efficacy of the tax judge in Chile, where the certainty of imposition and the minimization of delay tactics make sanctions very predictable.

The Effects on Compliance

The effects of the criminal law in Argentina have been meager. The low rates of severe punishment clearly did not increase taxpayers' perception of the threat of punishment for tax fraud. In a 1994 survey, 67 percent of taxpayers reported that they were likely or very likely to continue filing taxes inaccurately (Mora y Araujo 1994). There are no incentives to escape free riding. In Chile, on the other hand, taxpayers perceive that the likelihood of being punished is high and that tax evasion is risky. Seventy-four percent of taxpayers said that SII is effective in sanctioning tax misconduct (Mori 1998).

Legislation itself is insufficient to enhance compliance because severe punishment is effective only when taxpayers internalize its threat. This is achieved when cheaters are caught cheating and sanctions are rendered—that is, when the TA detects serious tax evasion, no corrupt strategy bails taxpayers out, and tribunals are efficient and capable of convicting noncompliers. Certainty of detection, and particularly a high probability that punishment will be imposed, must accompany severe sanctions. None of these conditions exists in Argentina. The detection capabilities of AFIP have not significantly improved, and the courts have been very inefficient in processing large numbers of cases. Constrained by fiscal deficits, the TA adopted a strategy of settling cases, thereby forfeiting the criminal threat; it preferred to collect quick revenue rather than submit to a long trial. In Chile, the TA has adopted rigid standards. Because detected noncompliance is swiftly punished with mandatory fines and sanctions, tax judges have little discretion. Room for plea-bargaining at this level is very limited. For this strategy to work, detection must be likely. The level of tax misconduct shows that many taxpayers remain undeterred by sanctions (since, after all, the certainty of detection can never be absolute). In comparison to Argentines, however, Chileans believe that most taxpayers comply and that tax evasion is very risky.

Another important factor that tends to encourage noncompliance is tax pardons, which promote impunity. Tax amnesties have a long-term effect on perceptions of the severity of sanctions and therefore on tax compliance. Argentina enacted more than twenty-five tax amnesties and pardons between 1971 and 1995 (Calello 1992; *Clarin*, July 26, 1996), whereas Chile did not have any significant tax pardons. Only deferred-payment accommodation is allowed in Chile; no owed taxes are forfeited. Research on tax amnesties has not been conclusive regarding their impact on tax compliance (Alm, McKee, and Beck 1990; Alm and Beck 1993); studies have been based on one-time amnesties, which were followed by additional government enforcement, and these did not include "periodic and recurrent amnesties." Argentina's repeated tax pardons and weak enforcement predispose taxpayers to "wait for the next round" rather than report their entire tax liability. Taxpayers perceive amnesties as rewards for noncompliance. Chile does not face this problem: taxpayers cannot expect to be bailed out by a legal tax pardon.

Thus, we can conclude that the threat of criminal prosecution might have some positive impact on compliance when it is plausible and efficiently administered. On the other hand, civil administrative sanctions remain a very effective threat, particularly substantial yet affordable pecuniary fines. Tax administrations that allocate considerable resources to detecting and swiftly punishing tax violators stand a better chance of enhancing deterrence and overall performance because they drastically reduce the rate of impunity. The case of Chile shows that a stable administration, limited individual discretion, and strict adherence to rules pay off.

TAXPAYERS' PERCEPTIONS OF THE LIKELIHOOD OF
SEVERE PUNISHMENT

In order to assess the effectiveness of a severe sanctions policy, it is necessary to gauge taxpayers' perceptions. Surveys in both Argentina and Chile provide an estimation of these perceptions. Table 4.5 presents means for questions in survey 1 in Argentina and survey 6 in Chile. Respondents were asked two questions to assess their attitudinal estimates of the se-

TABLE 4.5 Perceptions of the Severity of Sanctions

	Argentina	Chile
THREAT	2.16	1.81
SANCTION	2.49	2.21
PUNISHMENT	2.23	2.89
SEVERITY	2.20	2.01

SOURCES: Surveys 1 and 6.

NOTE: Scale: 1 = strongly agree, 4 = strongly disagree. Questions found in the text. All values in table are means. Valid n for Argentina = 541; for Chile = 528.

verity of sanctions. The first (THREAT) measures their level of agreement with the sentence, "Generally, DGI (for Argentina) or SII (for Chile) generates fear among taxpayers." Taxpayers in both countries believe that the TA is capable of generating fear: 23 percent of the sample disagreed with the statement in Argentina and only 15 percent in Chile.

A second question described a situation to which respondents were asked to react (variable SANCTION): "Taxpayers are tempted to evade taxes but decide not to do so because they have heard about the sanctions with which the government punishes tax evaders." In Argentina, 49 percent disagreed or strongly disagreed with the statement, whereas in Chile less than 30 percent disagreed. This question coincides with another variable, PUNISHMENT, for which respondents were asked to react to the following sentence: "In fact, nobody or almost no one who evades taxes is being actually punished or fined." In Argentina, 60 percent of respondents agreed or strongly agreed with that sentence, and a correlation coefficient of −0.11 on SANCTION and PUNISHMENT at a significant level of 0.05 denotes a moderate association between responses to these two questions. In Chile, only 25 percent of respondents agreed with the statement. Most Chileans believe that sanctions and punishment are indeed imposed. This evidence supports the previous assertion that coordination games require shared values between participants: thus, the makeup of conditional cooperation is found in Chile, whereas in Argentina cheaters believe that the enforcer fails to fulfill the role of guarantor of cooperation.

To test perceptions of the severity of punishment, a fourth question (SEVERITY) asked respondents to agree or disagree with the following statement: "The punishment or fines applied by the TA to a firm or business like yours are very severe." In the United States (Yankelovich 1984; Kinsey 1987), as well as in Britain (Levy 1987), most surveys indicate that taxpayers estimate fines and sanctions as severe. Although Argentine and Chilean taxpayers fit with this trend, more taxpayers in Chile (78 percent) agreed with the statement than in Argentina (67 percent). Chileans perceive that sanctions are more plausible and more severe than do Argentines.

Assessments of perceptions should be based on individuals' reactions to hypothetical situations to enhance the validity of individuals' reporting of their views. Two major problems are crucial in tax-evasion surveys: impression management and awareness behavior.[18] Thus, the attitudinal questions mentioned above must be interpreted with caution, because their validity might be problematic. Experimental approaches partly overcome problems of data validity and enable better measurement. In surveys 1 and 4, several questions were preceded by standard assurances of anonymity.[19] Taxpayers were asked to make choices about hypothetical situations, engaging in thinking processes applicable to real tax experiences. The goal was to assess taxpayers' estimation of criminal-prosecution probabilities given certain simulated circumstances.

Survey 1 introduced cases involving premeditated tax evasion. Typically, the interviewer presented a case wherein an average taxpayer made various fraudulent transactions. Several questions then asked the respondent to estimate the probability that these violations would be detected and that the taxpayer would take such risks (see chap. 3). Following these questions, respondents were asked, "What is the probability (from 0 to 100 percent) that AFIP will file criminal charges against this taxpayer?" The average probability reported was 44.08 percent (sd 34.07). Only 25 percent of respondents estimated such likelihood at higher than 70 percent. Taxpayers perceived that the chances of criminal prosecution for blatant noncompliance were not particularly high, although the variance in their responses is considerable.

Survey 4 replicated this question, but the wording was changed somewhat. Whereas in the first survey taxpayers might have thought that AFIP had detected the violation, survey 4 explicitly established the fact. A mean of 40.16 (sd 30.25) suggests that taxpayers' perception of the likelihood that criminal charges would be filed diminished slightly when they were told that the TA had detected the violation. The question wording does not appear to have had an impact. The sample of survey 4 overwhelmingly includes recently audited taxpayers; the control group of non-audited

18. People act to gain social approval and shape an image according to an expected ideal (impression management), and sometimes cognition of an act becomes real by virtue of an induced question (awareness behavior).

19. Unfortunately, these questions were not replicated in Chile for several reasons, including technical and legal restrictions.

taxpayers scored a mean of 45.01, however, which is very similar to the mean in the general population of survey 1. (The mean for recently audited taxpayers in survey 4 was 37.96.) Also, among the recently audited tax-payers, only 22 percent of the sample estimated the likelihood of criminal prosecution at higher than 50 percent. Socio-demographic variables do not account for the differences either in attitudes or perceptions. Age, gender, or size of firm do not deviate significantly from the mean (survey 4). Only a small difference was found between audited and non-audited taxpayers.

THE ROOTS OF CRIMINAL RISK PERCEPTIONS

The evidence from surveys clearly indicates that Argentine taxpayers be-lieve that the likelihood of severe punishment for tax fraud is low. Deter-rence theory predicts that punishment would be seen as severe only to the extent that taxpayers perceive the certainty of detection to be high. I estimated a regression model for the purpose of testing this hypothesis. The dependent variable (TAXCRIME) is the taxpayer's estimation of the probability that the TA will pursue criminal charges in response to a se-rious tax violation. The independent variables of the model are the fol-lowing: *age,* because the older the taxpayer is, the more likely he or she is to be deterred by the punitive capacity of the TA;[20] a dummy variable, *construction* (coded 1), reflecting whether the taxpayer belongs to this sector (the results of the previous analysis of means predict the incidence of this effect); *certainty of detection,* a variable composed of two ques-tions that estimate taxpayers' perceptions regarding the probability of the TA detecting two different cases of tax evasion (see chap. 3); and two additional attitudinal variables, *SEVERITY* and *THREAT,* which were de-scribed in the previous section.[21] Table 4.6 summarizes the results.

The first major conclusion we may draw from these results is that the explained variance is unusually high. No other studies (e.g., Klepper and Nagin 1989a, 1989b) report R^2 results higher than 0.24. An explained variance of 32 percent indicates that the predictors (or at least some of

20. In other surveys—in the United States (Kinsey 1992) and Britain (Webley et al. 1991)—this has been highly correlated.

21. Because both attitudinal variables are correlated at 0.12, multicollinearity prob-lems could be raised. Moreover, cautious interpretations should be made about perceptions regressed by attitudinal variables. The collinearity test, however, rejects multicollinearity problems.

TABLE 4.6 Regression Analysis of Perceptions of the Likelihood of Criminal Prosecution for Tax Fraud

| Model | Unstandardized Coefficients | | Standardized Coefficients | T | Sig. | Collinearity Statistics | |
	B	Std. Error	Beta			Tolerance	VIF
(Constant)	32.935	8.371	—	3.934	.000	—	—
Severity of Punishment	-3.90	1.90	-.083	-2.04	.041	.980	1.020
Fear of DGI	-5.626	2.161	-.105	-2.603	.010	.975	1.026
Certainty of Detection	7.529	.602	.514	12.512	.000	.947	1.056
Construction Dummy	-4.215	3.293	-.052	-1.280	.201	.962	1.040
Age	1.991	1.728	.046	1.153	.250	.991	1.009

SOURCE: Survey 1.

NOTE: R = .565, R^2 = .320, adjusted R^2 = .312, standard error of the estimate = 28.19.

them) partly account for individuals' estimations of the likelihood of severe penal prosecution. Second, the explained variance is accounted for
overwhelmingly by the certainty of detection. Thirdly, neither the construction dummy variable nor age are statistically significant; only the
feelings of fear that DGI generates are significant (PUNISHMENT and
THREAT are moderately correlated to perceived severity). These results
clearly support the deterrence hypothesis. In Argentina, taxpayers are not
deterred by the severity of the TA's criminal prosecution; their estimates
of the probability of being detected by the tax agency are very low.

As I pointed out above, Klepper and Nagin's study (1989a, 1989b)
states that when taxpayers estimate the probability of detection as high,
their subjective perception of the likelihood of criminal prosecution becomes nonzero. In order to test this proposition, the sample was divided
between those who estimated the detection capacity (CAPDET) at 75 percent or higher (only 47 cases) and the vast majority, who estimated it at
a level lower than 75 percent (451 cases). As a measure of comparison,
table 4.7 includes a control sample of those who estimated the detection capabilities at lower than 25 percent. The mean of taxpayers who
believe that the detection is very likely (a very small subsample) estimate
the probability of severe punishment at close to 78 percent. In contrast,
those who estimate the probability of detection as unlikely believe the
likelihood that the TA will criminally prosecute an offender who has committed a serious tax violation is 22 percent.[22]

In the analysis of survey 4, the variable DETECTVAT estimates the respondents' perception of the TA's detection capabilities for a simulated
tax-evasion case (a transaction that led to a ten-thousand-dollar evasion;
see chap. 3). The variable PROSECUTE estimates the taxpayers' assessment of the likelihood of criminal prosecution, similar to questions in
survey 1. The correlation coefficient between these two variables is 0.23
(.01-two tailed). This result denotes that the perceptions regarding the
TA's capacity for detection and the severity of likely punishment are positively correlated. This survey was based on a sample of recently audited
taxpayers (400) and a control group of non-audited taxpayers (150). Although the audited group places the likelihood of penal prosecution at an
average of 38 percent, the non-audited group perceives this likelihood at
an average of 45 percent.

As shown in chapter 3, there is some evidence that the auditing process negatively affects both compliance and perceptions of the likelihood

---

22. It should be remembered that the question asks about the probability of criminal
prosecution *after* the tax authority has already detected violations.

TABLE 4.7 Mean of Prosecution Probabilities Based on Perceived Estimates of the TA's Detection Capabilities

Perceived Capacity of Detection 0–74%	Perceived Capacity of Detection 75–100%	Perceived Capacity of Detection 0–25%	Perceived Capacity of Detection 0–100%
40.41%	77.93%	22.66%	44.08%

SOURCE: Survey 1.

NOTE: Responses to question, "What is the probability the DGI will initiate a criminal prosecution if it detects a large evasion?" Valid n = 498.

of being criminally prosecuted for serious tax violations. Why do audits discourage compliance? Several possible answers come to mind. First, audits that are badly done lead taxpayers to realize that the dog is all bark but no bite. Second, the financial result of audits, either in the form of fines or bribes, reduces the estimated costs of criminal prosecution. Third, because some of the criteria of selection for audits are past history of noncompliance and suspicion of current noncompliance, a random distribution of taxpayers yields a concentration of more aggressive, risk-taking taxpayers in the audited sample; therefore, the sample might overrepresent noncompliers. I argue that the real answer to the question of why audited taxpayers tend to be more noncompliant lies in a combination of the first two alternatives. Poorly conducted audits and a "safe" outcome do not seriously disrupt taxpayers' activities; in fact, they act directly to make taxpayers more likely to believe they will not be severely punished for tax misconduct in the future. The third hypothesis seems a less likely answer because the direction of causality appears to be the opposite: the personal tax experience might cause one to adopt an aggressive or conservative approach to taxes, not vice versa. Although this point will be further developed in the following chapters, an analysis of means for the data on penal prosecution renders some support to this proposition.

A set of questions in survey 4 asked respondents to report how they would file their taxes in a given situation (see table 3.14). Each respondent was asked to pretend that he or she were a physician who had evaded paying ten thousand pesos one year and had to make choices the following year based on changes in withholding levels. Refunds could be claimed ranging from five thousand pesos to fifteen thousand pesos. Claiming a refund of five thousand pesos would represent total compliance with the law, whereas claiming fifteen thousand pesos would represent an evasion of ten thousand pesos, equal to that of the previous year. Chapter 3 contains a thorough explanation of the questions. I divided the sam-

TABLE 4.8 Mean of Criminal-Prosecution Probabilities Estimated by
Risk-Aversion Level

	Conservatives	Risk Takers	Total
Audited	39%	36%	38%
Not Audited	43%	52%	45%
Total	40%	40%	40%

SOURCE: Survey 4.
NOTE: Valid n = 522.

ple into two groups: those who reported that they would claim refunds
of up to ten thousand pesos and those who reported that they would
claim refunds for more than that. I called the first group "conservatives"
(although clearly there are tax violators in this group), and I called the
second group "risk takers." As table 4.8 shows, there is a 4 percent difference between audited and non-audited taxpayers in their estimates of
the likelihood of penal prosecution among the risk averse but a remarkable 16 percent difference among the group of risk takers. Previous tax
experience and encounters with TA enforcement appear to strongly alter
natural estimates of the level of risk of penal prosecution.

This chapter has established a clear correlation between weak tax enforcement and low estimates of the likelihood of suffering from severe
sanctions. In this way, it has corroborated some of the main hypotheses
of deterrence theory. In Argentina, severe punishment, and particularly
criminal threat, has failed to enhance compliance, because it has not
relied on policies that improve standards of detection capacities or, more
important, sanction imposition.

SUMMARY

Tax systems generally avoid reliance on criminal venues for punishing
evasion. Despite the social and legal reluctance to criminalize and prosecute many forms of tax evasion, states are interested in penalizing selective cases as an instrument of general deterrence. The severity of criminal
punishment has a powerful effect on compliance only if there is a high
probability that cheaters will be caught and punished—or, to put it another way, only if impunity is low. Tax agencies generally aim to pursue
criminal prosecutions that have the potential to result in substantial sanctions that will be noticeable in the community. Criminal investigations of
athletes, celebrities, and other well-known personalities are of high priority because they discourage general taxpayers from taking the risks of tax

noncompliance. Such investigations signal to potential cooperators that the Leviathan is keeping its part of the bargain.

The analysis of survey data in this chapter confirms that Argentine taxpayers have not internalized the perception that blatant tax evasion is likely to be punished severely. Conversely, Chilean taxpayers fear sanctions and punishment, and therefore are more likely to obey the law. This chapter has indicated that Argentina has not benefited from a consistent criminal tax policy, that the state lacked the institutional strength to launch a campaign to enhance taxpayers' compliance behavior, and that the court system has failed to develop a reasonable level of efficiency in prosecuting violations of tax law. In other words, the criminalization of tax evasion in Argentina has failed at the enforcement level. The large number of tax evaders further contributes to the sense of impunity from prosecution. The failure of TCL shows that to improve compliance, criminal punishment should target selective cases; its implementation as a replacement for surveillance and administrative sanctions has a damaging impact on tax compliance.

Chile has adopted a different strategy. Tax fraud is pursued in the Chilean court system only rarely, and these prosecutions have a largely symbolic purpose. SII, however, has been very effective in enforcing legal rules through the administrative and civil domain. This policy has diminished the structural advantage of defendants, placed the burden of proof on taxpayers, and fostered an image of an effective and severe administration. This image—that is, taxpayers' perception of the severe threat of sanctions for tax fraud—has allowed the TA to administer its resources more efficiently and target evaders within a "smaller crowd" of cheaters: the smaller the crowd of cheaters, the greater the effectiveness of tax administrations. Sanctions and punishment policies, therefore, should serve to shrink that crowd of cheaters, thereby feeding the virtuous circle of compliance.

In assurance games, the threat of severe sanctions serves as an incentive for everybody to cooperate. If such an equilibrium is to be reached, sanctions must be perceived by their targets as likely to be imposed. That this is the case in Chile explains the relative success of general deterrence in that country. I argue, then, that general deterrence largely depends on the administration of sanctions in a way that is prone to be successful under a compliance equilibrium. Conversely, impunity, which results from structural factors in a noncompliance equilibrium such as that of Argentina, undermines general deterrence. The next chapter will explore whether individual deterrence can compensate for such deficiencies.

5

SPECIFIC DETERRENCE AND ITS EFFECTS
ON INDIVIDUAL COMPLIANCE

Carniábamos noche a noche
alguna res en el pago;
y dejando allí el resago
alzaba en ancas el cuero,
que se lo vendía a algún pulpero
por yerba, tabaco y trago.

¡Ah! ¡Viejo más comerciante
en mi vida lo he encontrado!
Con ese cuero robao
El arreglaba el pastel,
Y allí entre el pulpero y él
Se estendía el certificao

[We killed night after night
some errant cow in the fields
and leaving there what the rest
we picked up the leather
which he later sold to some shopkeeper
for yerba, tobacco, and booze.

Ah! A more tricky old man
I have never in my life encountered.
As to the stolen leather,
the matter was quickly fixed,
since right there and between him and the shopkeeper
the fake document was extended.]

— JOSÉ HERNÁNDEZ, *Martín Fierro* (1878); translation mine

Tax administrations spend large amounts of their resources in monitoring and controlling tax evasion. Is it worth it? What is the optimal level of enforcement that tax administrations must exert? Does the actual enforcement of tax laws determine the level of individual compliance with taxes? What is the role of institutional enforcement in enhancing compliance? In the previous chapter, I analyzed cross-sectional official and survey data to test the propositions of deterrence theory for Argentina and Chile. I have shown that government agencies have limited impact on reducing tax evasion when the norm of compliance is weak. General deterrence works under favorable equilibria, but severe sanctions cannot compensate for deficiencies in detecting illegal behaviors under adverse equilibria. Tax administrations, however, have a variety of powerful direct enforcement measures, such as audits and checkups of individual income reports, that can induce taxpayers to modify entrenched non-compliance behavior. We must determine whether deterrence can still be effective if enough cheaters are targeted for audits and surveillance. In short, there is a need to examine whether direct law enforcement over law violators can transform noncompliance into compliance equilibria, and whether individual or specific deterrence can contribute to fostering norm-abiding societies. This question is central for any theory of governance because it tests the boundaries of state actions and the real possibilities of social transformation by government policies and administration agencies.

In this chapter, I turn to tax-return information filed by taxpayers to address the question of how direct TA enforcement affects individual compliance. By analyzing comparable data, I elucidate the influence that tax agencies have on taxpayers' future behavior. I analyze here for the first time the post-enforcement individual compliance level by comparing the impact of audits and closures of businesses in Argentina and Chile, as well as the compliance level of taxpayers subject to the new compulsory use of cash-register machines in Argentina. Most studies of tax compliance have relied on self-reports or aggregate information, rarely depending on individual tax information. Here, I use actual tax-return data to test the effect of enforcement on compliance. I find that in both Argentina and Chile the effects of enforcement are overestimated. Taxpayers who have previously cheated on taxes generally continue to do so. In Chile, the scale of noncompliance is lower, allowing the TA to be more effective in targeting tax evaders. The effect of enforcement on generating deterrence, however, is meager.

This chapter's investigation also elucidates the limitations of specific deterrence in the tax field. Once the tipping point of the compliance equilibrium is passed, cheaters will continue to cheat (because enforcement cannot reverse the equilibrium), whereas rational taxpayers profit from noncompliance. When most taxpayers cheat, individual deterrence does not generate the incentives necessary for taxpayers who have encountered enforcement to reverse course. This is particularly relevant in Argentina, where the overwhelming majority of taxpayers targeted by the enforcement measures of the TA continued cheating afterward.

I begin by briefly summarizing propositions about compliance behavior as it relates to individual deterrence. From there, I present the data, hypotheses, and methods. In the following two sections, I describe the findings using descriptive statistical analyses, and present the results of a multivariate analysis, to explain the changing rate of individual compliance. The final section summarizes the findings and discusses them in the context of the general argument of this book.

THEORY

According to deterrence theory, the reasons for compliance are instrumental: taxpayers comply because the benefits of doing so outweigh the costs. Therefore, when individuals have contact with authorities, they are only interested in securing a favorable outcome. If the results of enforcement contacts are perceived as severe, those contacts might deter future noncompliance. Conversely, enforcement contacts that fail to detect or severely punish noncompliance might have a diminished deterrent effect. As we have seen, deterrence can be specific or general. The threat of incarceration, for instance, might have a specific-deterrent effect on a single law violator, but it also has a general-deterrent effect on a larger group by sending a message regarding the potential risk of breaking the law.[1] In this sense, audits and other enforcement measures can be specific and general at the same time.

Many theories of law abidance emphasize the importance of trust, moral obligation, sense of duty, and procedural fairness in influencing individual behavior, rather than focusing on sheer self-interest (Scholz 2003; Tyler 1990; Braithwaite 1989). At times, such theories argue, people obey the law (regardless of the outcome) if they feel that their voices can be heard, if they perceive the laws that affect them to be moral, and if they perceive the authorities that enforce the laws to be legitimate. According to the theory of procedural fairness, individuals' contact with law enforcement will yield law abidance if this contact is perceived to be fair. An in-depth study of this dimension for Argentina and Chile is undertaken in the next chapter.

In the present chapter, I address enforcement's individual deterrent effect on tax behavior. Deterrence and procedural-fairness perspectives on compliance have largely studied enforcement contacts in cases of violent or property crimes.[2] Here, I study their effect for the more elusive field of white-collar crime. Although some studies have been conducted on the effects of audits on taxpayers' own reports of the likelihood that

1. See Blumstein and Cohen (1987), Paternoster (1987), and Roth, Scholz, and Witte (1989) for discussion on this topic.
2. According to different model specifications, studies found partial or full support for both theories. See Paternoster and Simpson 1996.

they will evade tax law in the future (Andreoni, Erard, and Feinstein, 1998; Erard 1992; Scholz 1998), to my knowledge there are no studies that actually measure tax compliance based on tax-return information. Such research has theoretical and practical implications. First, it tests the propositions of specific-deterrence theory using official data under a time-series design. Second, because there is a need to understand tax decisions in a field in which individual behavior rarely becomes public, this study allows for pure and uncontaminated measures of personal utility. Finally, tax administrations could use such an approach to empirically test the effects of tax enforcement on tax behavior.

HYPOTHESES AND DATA

Appendix 1 specifies the characteristics of the information provided by the VAT and income-tax-return data that I collected for this analysis. Surveys could not, unfortunately, complement the audit or closure-of-business samples.[3] My hypotheses are as follows.

First, deterrence theory establishes that an anticipated punishment is subjectively perceived, based on partial information and the experience effect. In this sense, my first hypothesis is that an individual's future level of compliance will reflect that person's perceptions of the severity of the sanctions likely to be imposed. If noncompliance is found prior to an individual's contact with the TA, and if no changes are found after enforcement, we may assume that the enforcement measures did little to change the subject's behavior. I hypothesize that changes in tax behavior are determined by the effectiveness of tax enforcement. Therefore, *the more severe the penalties and sanctions, and the more effectively they are administered, the greater the likelihood that they will deter future noncompliance.*

Second, taxpayers wish to avoid the costs of sanctions. Taxpayers who have been audited or controlled by other measures are therefore likely to better comply with tax law. Thus, *individuals who have been subject to enforcement will exhibit improved compliance compared to those who have not been prosecuted.*

Third, enforcement is costly for tax administrators. Ideally, new reve-

---

3. Ideally, self-reported data could be matched with respondents' tax returns and the enforcement information generated by the TA; due to legal impediments, however, I was not permitted to assemble this database.

nues raised through additional assessments, penalties, and fines neutralize the cost of enforcement. Therefore, *the larger the enforcement apparatus, the more tax revenues will be raised.*

Fourth, crime scholars have established that rule breaking is highly correlated with opportunities. The tax literature has presented persuasive evidence that structural opportunity is associated with tax evasion.[4] Therefore, structural opportunities affect the effectiveness of enforcement contacts. *The greater the opportunity to hide income from the authorities, the less impact that enforcement contact will have on future tax behavior.*

Fifth, the theory of procedural fairness holds that beliefs, attitudes, and compliance are weakly affected by the contents of the law; they are more influenced by the social processes through which individuals internalize their duties and obligations. Thus, enforcement contact may have a significant effect on future behavior, regardless of the outcome of that contact. Therefore, *the expectation of a favorable outcome will not have a particular effect on future behavior.* If the analysis of the data rejects this hypothesis, perceived procedural fairness may account for some effects on future behavior.

Lastly, taxpayers react to policies and enforcement. They seek to maximize benefits by adjusting to changes in a given equilibrium. The perceived effectiveness of a tax administration will determine the extent of changes in future tax behavior. *The stronger the effect of institutional efficacy, the more drastic the changes in compliance after enforcement will be.*

DATA AND METHOD

Because the VAT is the pillar of the tax system, and because it is the tax most thoroughly audited, I have chosen to compare VAT compliance.[5] I use a well-developed methodology of comparison, the debit/credit ratio (or d/c ratio). This is a proxy to the ratio of sales over purchases for a selected period of time. *Debits* are the total VAT *charged* by taxpayers

4. In the United States, close to three-quarters of the total income that has to be reported on tax returns is matched to information provided by third parties.

5. Measuring VAT compliance is more cumbersome than measuring compliance with the income tax. Studies of individual compliance are generally based on tax-audit results. For Argentina, however, itemized audit results are unreliable due to corruption, nonprofessional data collection, and the organizational designs of tax-audit strategies (Bergman 2001).

when they sell goods or services. *Credits* are the VAT already *paid* by tax-payers when they purchase goods or services needed for manufacturing, retailing, and so forth. The difference between debits and credits is the taxpayer's net VAT liability.[6] I compare debits and credits, as well as the ratio before and after an enforcement action has taken place.

To control for seasonal and size effects, I test changes in compliance using two different methods. First, I measure the difference between each taxpayer's individual ratio and the debit/credit ratio of the trade or sector to which each taxpayer belongs. In this case, the dependent variable is *the percentage change between the difference in these ratios prior to and after the enforcement action.*[7] A widening of the gap indicates that enforcement has had a negative effect on compliance.[8] Second, I compare the aggregate behavior of the treatment group (those subject to enforce-

6. If the ratio is lower than 1, it means that taxpayers had more credits than debits for a given period: the higher the ratio, the higher the gross profit. Typically, manufacturing industries (which purchase raw materials) have lower debit/credit ratios than services (because the payroll, which is exempted from VAT, is heavier in the service sector). The lower the debit/credit ratio, the more likely it becomes that tax evasion is taking place. But the type of industry and the size of firms both matter. For example, a service firm (a bank or an insurance company) with a debit/credit ratio lower than 1.5 would be considered "high risk"; a car manufacturer, food-processing firm, or construction company with the same debit/credit ratio might be considered very profitable. Compliance analysis must account for sector and size of the firm.

7. The debit/credit ratio for the sector is based on the total debits divided by the total credits of every trade for any given period. This information is compiled by adding the debits and credits for each activity code (of which there are more than eight thousand) in which taxpayers have registered. Once the ratio for each taxpayer ratio is calculated, it is compared to the debit/credit ratio for the given activity code. Because the debit/credit ratio will reflect the state of affairs of the activity code or sector, the distance between the individual ratios and the activity-code ratio provides a measure of compliance. There are two problems, however, with this classification. First, taxpayers remain registered under one activity, even if they diversify activities. Therefore, debits and credits for one activity code may reflect the sales and purchases of taxpayers who have changed activities. Second, the debit/credit ratio is biased by the decisive weight of large taxpayers. To neutralize this bias, a better comparison could be made between the mode values for each activity code; such data, however, was unavailable. I contend that the results are still valid, for two reasons. First, this methodology compares the period prior to and following enforcement. Because there was no change in code classification between periods, the distance between an individual and the sector would not be significantly altered by the fact that the activity-code d/c ratio is "noisy" (even if a given taxpayer does not technically belong to a given sector). What is being measured is not the activity code but the relation or distance between an individual and a fixed number of taxpayers. Second, for this same reason, a small taxpayer whose d/c ratio is different than the activity-code d/c ratio will be expected to maintain the same distance in any given period.

8. It should be remembered that taxpayers were selected for enforcement because they had lower d/c ratios than the median for the activity code. Thus, a reduction of the gap means that their d/c ratio has moved closer to the median, and thus that they have become less noncompliant with respect to their industry.

ment) to the aggregate behavior of a control group of taxpayers, who were not audited or sanctioned by the TA and who share similar characteristics with the treatment group.[9] In the Argentine audit sample, I excluded 350 cases due to incomplete information or because they belonged to the largest category of taxpayers.[10] In Chile, I excluded 125 cases for similar reasons. For the closure-of-business sample, I measure the compliance of the treatment group using a non-sanctioned control group in both countries. For the sample of cash registers in Argentina, I do not compare this data with a control group because the incorporation of machines was universal for each activity-code category (industry), and because there were no similar control groups. I compare reported debits and credits prior to and after the cash registers were installed. Because the goal of this policy was to increase the taxpayers' reported sales (debits), I tested the effect of this measure by analyzing changes in tax returns' debits and credits.

In addition to the compiled tax information, socio-demographic data were collected only for the sole-proprietor category in Argentina (34 percent of the sample). I did this because the TA does not keep accurate information on corporations (66 percent of the sample). For Chile, the information is somewhat richer and includes data on corporations as well as sole proprietors. I also collected additional information on previous enforcement contacts. The process of collecting audit and sanction information has been confirmed through a subsample verification and by cross-checking with other sources of internal information.

One final methodological note: comparing VAT returns over short periods could pose several problems. Ideally, periods of comparison should be at least a year in length to neutralize seasonal and fiscal credit biases.[11] That data is available for Chile but, unfortunately, not for Argentina. To overcome these problems, I took two steps. First, I estimated two sets of comparisons, one that included at least the d/c ratio average for four months and another that included eight months, depending on the data.

9. Each case of a taxpayer against whom enforcement actions have been taken has been matched to a "twin," non-enforced taxpayer. The "twin" case shares the same location, the same trade or activity code, and the same level of tax payments.

10. A major segment of the two thousand largest taxpayers of the country are routinely audited on a rotating basis. Those largest taxpayers included in the original sample were excluded from the analysis.

11. Some sectors accumulate credits over a long period and generate debits (sales) in short periods. For example, an apartment construction company accumulates credits while purchasing building materials throughout months and years. Then it sells all the apartments in one month, generating large debits. Because VAT is filed monthly, in that particular month the d/c ratio for that company would be unusually high.

Second, I compared pre- and post-enforcement periods for the same filing months. By comparing identical periods for different years, I have controlled for possible seasonal effects.

RESULTS

Audits

The most puzzling result is that, on average, audits do not affect the level of future individual compliance. On the contrary, the gap between pre- and post-audit compliance for certain groups widened. On average, non-audited taxpayers displayed better compliance than audited taxpayers after enforcement. Figure 5.1 describes the median of the d/c ratio for the samples of both countries in the period prior to, during, and after audits.[12] Each line indicates the ratio of the audited group with respect to the non-audited control group in each country. For example, the median of the d/c ratio of VAT for Chile in the period prior to auditing was 90 percent of the median for the non-audited group over the same period; for the period during the audits it was 104 percent; and it decreased to 89 percent for the period after the audits. Prior to audits, in both Chile and Argentina, the d/c ratio of audited taxpayers was smaller (less than 100 percent) than that of the control group. Compliance increased slightly during audits and returned to previous levels, or even decreased, after audits were closed. Given that taxpayers are selected for auditing on the basis of a presumption of tax evasion, larger-than-average noncompliance should be expected among the audited group prior to auditing. Therefore, the smaller median of 10 percent in Chile and 17 percent in Argentina (as compared to their respective control groups) supports the noncompliance selection bias of the audit departments.

Several tax-administration officials contend that taxpayers refrain from misreporting sales during audits, thus yielding an increase in compliance in that period.[13] We tested the officials' hypothesis and could not find substantial support for it. Reported sales among audited individuals did not increase significantly during audits compared to those of non-audited

12. I present here the median, although the mean curve is similar for figure 5.1.

13. If such an assumption is correct, it might indicate that the actual level of compliance during audits should be considered the compliance base for the audited group. In other words, the median of compliance for tax evaders (the audited-sanctioned group) should be at least 8 percent higher in Chile and 2 percent higher in Argentina.

Fig. 5.1 Audit and VAT Compliance (Median of d/c Ratio)

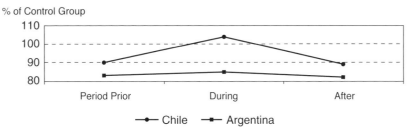

% of Control Group

SOURCE: My own elaboration based on audit tax return data, AFIP 1999, and SII 2002.

taxpayers. In fact, 53 percent of sanctioned Argentines and 57 percent of sanctioned Chileans actually reduced reported sales during the audit period. As will be discussed below, evasion strategies appear to have included fake purchases.

Tables 5.1A–C and 5.2 report the median of several distributions of the net balance paid (debits minus credits) for both countries across different samples.[14] The first column reports the difference of two distributions: the median net balance paid in the post-audit period minus the median net balance for the period before auditing. The second and third columns are not strictly the same distributions, although they yield similar results. The second column is the median of the distribution for the difference in net VAT payment of each group. The third column is the median of the distribution for the percentage change of the difference in contributions with respect to the periods before audits. These differences between non-audited and audited groups are presented for the entire Chilean and Argentine samples (tables 5.1A and 5.2). Although in Argentina 98 percent of the sample was found in noncompliance, in Chile only 62 percent of audited taxpayers were sanctioned. Therefore, I present for Chile two additional tables, one that compares audited sanctioned and non-sanctioned taxpayers (5.1B), and another for sanctioned taxpayers with respect to the non-audited control group (5.1C).

These results show that the gap between both samples is noticeable, and in all cases the differences between groups are statistically significant at different levels. Audited groups consistently decreased their net payments to the tax authority more than did the control group (see first column of tables 5.1A–C and 5.2). The trend is very clear in all distributions. The median of sanctioned taxpayers decreases in all cases, signaling that, in the aggregate, audited taxpayers do not pay more taxes after

14. I report pesos for both countries. At the time of data collection, the conversion rate for Argentina was 1 peso = US$1, whereas in Chile it was 550 pesos = US$1.

TABLE 5.1A Chile: Median of Debits Minus Credits Between Post- and
Pre-enforcement Periods for Audited and Non-audited Taxpayers

	Net Difference After-Before ($)	Median of Difference ($)	Median of Difference (%)
Non-audited, n = 763	−93,083	0	−39
Audited, n = 722	−385,485	−86,576	−56
Difference	−292,402	−86,576*	−17**

SOURCES: My own elaboration based on audit tax-return data; SII 2001a.
*Statistically significant at 90 percent level.
**Statistically significant at 95 percent level.

TABLE 5.1B Chile: Median of Debits Minus Credits Between Post- and
Pre-enforcement Periods for Non-sanctioned and Sanctioned Taxpayers

	Net Difference After-Before ($)	Median of Difference ($)	Median of Difference (%)
Non-sanctioned, n = 357	−88,160	8,196	−52
Sanctioned, n = 367	−781,381	−321,011	−74
Difference	−693,221	−329,207*	−22**

SOURCES: My own elaboration based on audit tax-return data; SII 2001a.
*Statistically significant at 95 percent level.
**Statistically significant at 99 percent level.

TABLE 5.1C Chile: Median of Debits Minus Credits Between Post- and
Pre-enforcement Periods for Non-audited and Sanctioned Taxpayers

	Net Difference After-Before ($)	Median of Difference ($)	Median of Difference (%)
Non-audited, n = 763	−93,083	0	−39
Sanctioned, n = 406	−781,381	−321,011	−74
Difference	−688,298	−321,011*	−34*

SOURCES: My own elaboration based on audit tax-return data; AFIP 1999; SII 2001a.
*Statistically significant at 99 percent level.

enforcement actions have been taken against them. These results signal,
however, that for certain taxpayers, audits might increase post-audit
compliance. In Chile (table 5.1B), previously compliant taxpayers (those
audited taxpayers not assessed with additional liabilities) paid considerably more than sanctioned taxpayers, contributing to the better overall
compliance trend.[15]

15. I assume that there is no perfect compliance. It appears that most taxpayers cheat;
the difference is in the scale of noncompliance. Those who were not sanctioned appear to
have been small-scale cheaters.

TABLE 5.2 Argentina: Median of Debits Minus Credits Between Post- and
Pre-enforcement Periods for Audited and Non-audited Taxpayers

	Net Difference After-Before($)	Median of Difference ($)	Median of Difference (%)
Non-audited, n = 1227	−1,049	−84	−08
Audited, n = 1,025	−3,464	−597	−20
Difference	−2,415	−513*	−12*

SOURCES: My own elaboration based on audit tax-return data; AFIP 1999; SII 2001a.
*Statistically significant at 99 percent level.

A closer analysis of credits and debits in Chile yields another meaningful result: between 1998 and 2000, reported credits (purchases) grew
more than did reported debits (sales). The median debit of the sanctioned
group fell more (−3.6 percent) than did that of the non-audited group
(−1.4 percent), and the median credit (0.57 percent) grew more than it
did for the control group (0.29 percent). In the aggregate, the trend was
for sanctioned taxpayers to report lower sales and more purchases than
taxpayers in the control group. In other words, by reducing reported sales
and increasing reported purchases, the Chilean sanctioned group appeared
to show a moderate drop in compliance after enforcement.

To illegally reduce tax dues (as mentioned above), taxpayers can either
manipulate sales to diminish their reported debits or artificially increase
credits by reporting fake or bogus purchases, which carries the risk of
severe sanctions.[16] What appears to explain better compliance during the
audit period is the reduction of reported purchases (credits). In Argentina, 65 percent of those who were sanctioned or audited decreased their
reported purchases during audits (compared to 48 percent of the control
group), thus yielding a higher d/c ratio (between 3 and 9 percent; see fig.
5.1). Once audits had been completed, however, many of these taxpayers might have felt safer reporting fake invoices, assuming that another
enforcement action in the near future was unlikely. Because tax balances
in VAT are carried forward, taxpayer purchases can be reported in subsequent months in order to reduce the net debit-credit balance.[17] This is

16. An entire industry of fake invoices exists. Taxpayers may use "advertisement purchases," "research and development endeavors," "representation expenses," and so forth
to justify fiscal credits and thus reduce their tax dues. Because those expenses never materialize, the claims are obviously fraudulent. This is very difficult to prove, however, and
therefore such fraudulent claims are rarely detected. Taxpayers need only an invoice to
prove any kind of expense, and there are many companies and individuals willing to take
the risk of selling (for a price much lower than face value) a fake invoice.

17. Also, if a taxpayer has overpaid in one month, tax liabilities can be deducted in the
following months.

presumably what happened in the post-audit period, which would account for the decrease in the d/c ratio immediately after audits.

Other independent research supports these findings. A study by Fundación Mediterranea has found that the ratio between the fiscal credits reported by taxpayers and the potential fiscal credit derived from the analysis of national accounts increased from 1.34 in 1997 to 1.47 in 2001 (Argañaraz 2004). The use of fake invoices became the favorite strategy of tax evasion in Argentina. (Indications from personal interviews with tax officials in Chile suggest that this practice is also widely used there.) This finding supports Martinez Vazquez and Rider's claim (2003) that taxpayers take advantage and shift among different opportunities to defy full compliance. It seems that in the late 1990s, "inflated credits" became the most suitable evasion strategy.

Finally, the total amount of fines and additional taxes levied in audits accounts for 54 percent of the difference in net VAT payments between the pre-audit and post-audit periods. In other words, the total reduction in the VAT contributions of the enforced group (adjusted by the control groups) is almost twice as large as the revenues collected in fines and additional assessments. The net effect of audits is puzzling. Had the audits not taken place, and had the compliance trend continued at the rate of pre-audit period, the net revenues from these taxpayers would have been greater. Clearly, taxpayers assessed with additional taxes and fines made up for their losses later with even greater noncompliance.[18] The level of post-audit noncompliance and assessed taxes and penalties are positively correlated for both countries (r = 0.28), indicating that the larger the fine, the greater the post-audit noncompliance.[19] In short, penalties have the undesired effect of reducing compliance.

Several additional initial conclusions can be drawn. Although the trend in the two countries is similar, post-audit noncompliance in Chile is somewhat moderate compared to that in Argentina. Also, it appears that the larger impact of audits is on those who are audited but not sanctioned—that is, on the more compliant taxpayers. This suggests that audit policies are more effective among those who take the threat seriously and who are more deterred by the tax administration. It appears that the

18. This is particularly relevant for Argentina. I estimated the AFIP's lost revenues as a result of the increased subsequent noncompliance as equal to three months of tax dues for the entire sample. In other words, the new net revenues raised by the tax agency through audits are in fact wiped out within ninety days following the audit as a result of post-audit noncompliance.

19. The data also indicates that smaller businesses, on average, engage in subsequent noncompliance on a larger scale.

higher the level of their tax evasion, the less likely that evading taxpayers will reduce their noncompliance due to an audit.

Closure of Businesses

As mentioned in the last chapter, tax administrations have what they consider a strong weapon against tax evasion: the temporary closure of businesses. In this section, I analyze whether taxpayers sanctioned with business closures do indeed change their previous tax-evasion practices. I estimate the effect of business closure by comparing pre- and post-closure tax information for both Chile and Argentina. For Argentina, I analyze the four months following the closure compared to the same four months of the previous year. For Chile, I have compiled data for a longer period, comparing tax information from a year prior to the closure (1998) to the year after the closure (2000). As opposed to Argentina, first-time violators in Chile can choose to pay a fine and be exempted from the closure. In cases of subsequent violation, however, no more appeals are allowed and shutdowns become mandatory. These and other minor differences invite a separate study.

For both countries, the aggregate compliance results of the treatment group are compared to the control group that shares similar characteristics (see the above "Audits" section for explanation). In Argentina, the closure group includes all businesses effectively closed during the second half of 1998. The sample of both groups is 1,375. For Chile, I include all businesses effectively closed in the second semester of 1999. The sample for Chile is 9,142 cases, 4,594 of which were sanctioned and 4,548 of which are a control group. Among the sanctioned, 2,955 were closed, whereas 1,693 first-time offenders benefited from a warning and fine.

Tables 5.3 and 5.4 report total change for Argentina in absolute terms, as well as the percentage change between the period prior to and after the closure of businesses. The effect was completely different for the treatment and control groups. Whereas total debits and net amounts due for the non-sanctioned group increased moderately, the total debits and net amounts due clearly diminished among sanctioned taxpayers. Moreover, as the subsample of small taxpayers demonstrates, the size of the firm does not explain the difference in post-sanction behavior.[20]

I estimated the percentage change for each case, as shown in the histogram of figure 5.2. Fifty-six percent of sanctioned taxpayers reduced

20. Retailers with reported total sales of less than one million dollars a year were considered small taxpayers.

TABLE 5.3 Changes in Tax Dues After Business Closures for Argentina

		Tax-Dues Changes	
		All	Small
Control	Sum	$120,000	$225,000
	Mean	2%	8%
Closed	Sum	-$411,000	-$171,000
	Mean	-10%	-6.4%

SOURCE: Closure-of-business tax-return data; SII 2001a.
NOTE: With respect to a similar period prior to enforcement. Valid n = 1,231.

TABLE 5.4 Mean of Debits for Argentine Businesses Closed by the TA

	Previous Debits	Subsequent Debits	Difference	
Control, Mean (n = 274)	$32,570	$31,930	-$640	-2%
Closed, Mean (n = 359)	$19,092	$18,258	-$834	-4.3%

SOURCE: Closure-of-business tax-return data; SII 2001a.
NOTE: Valid n = 1,233.

Fig. 5.2 Percentage of Individual Compliance Variation After Enforcement

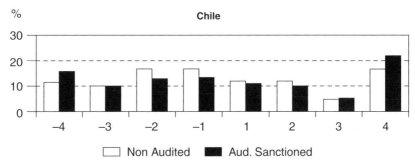

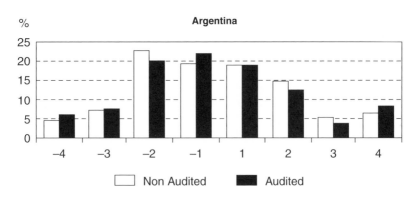

reported sales in the later period, compared to 60 percent of the non-sanctioned group. The distributions (sanctioned and non-sanctioned) are similar, which supports the assertion that closures have little effect on post-compliance behavior.

In order to assess the immediate impact of closures, I plotted a limited analysis of two-month debit periods for sanctioned taxpayers. This analysis is based on four- or six-month periods for the previous year, which coincide with the months that immediately follow the closures. Period –1 refers to the two months previous to the closure (when a business is notified of the future sanction), and period 1 refers to the second and third months following the closure (a month was skipped to neutralize the effect of lower debits that resulted from the closure). Seven two-month periods of information are reported. Periods –4, –3, and –2 represent the months prior to closure. Periods 1, 2, and 3 refer to the two-month periods of tax returns after the closure. Figure 5.3 displays the results.

I draw three conclusions from figure 5.3. First, the large-taxpayer debit line follows the rest of the taxpayer curve at a different level of Y (debit); therefore, the size of a business does not show a significant effect on the average behavior of sanctioned taxpayers. Second, closures do not positively affect the amount of debits reported after a closure. On the contrary, in the months immediately following closures, sanctioned taxpayers reported lower debits than they had in the immediately previous months. Third, a compensation effect appears to be present. After initially reducing their reporting behavior in periods 1 and 2 (to recuperate via tax evasion the losses from closures), taxpayers increased those behaviors slightly in period 3.

Fig. 5.3 Bimonthly Sales Before and After Sanctions (Pre- and Post-closures)

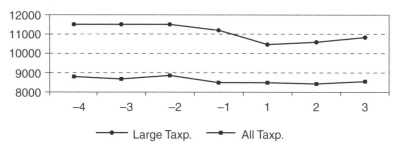

SOURCE: Closure of business tax return data. DGI 1999.
NOTE: Valid n = 1,233.

TABLE 5.5 Median of Percentage Change and Net Payment Change Based on
Types of Sanction in Chile (2000 compared to 1998)

	97-10* Closure	97-10 Fine	Control
	Median	Median	Median
Debit	4.04%	10.06%	–7.92%
Credit	4.48%	8.86%	–7.45%
Net Payment**	–0.007	–0.015	0.006

SOURCE: Closure-of-business tax-return data; SII 2002.

*Sales without issuing invoices. This is the most recurrent type of violation, covering more than 91 percent of the cases.

**In millions of pesos.

The evidence presented thus far allows us to conclude that temporary closures have no positive impact on tax-reporting behavior in Argentina. Table 5.5 describes the aggregate results for Chile and presents the median percentage change with respect to the pre-enforcement period for the control and sanctioned groups (both first timers and those who had previously been sanctioned). The median debits and credits reported by the control group decreased, whereas the sanctioned group reported higher debits (sales) but also higher credits (purchases). Both the mean and the median of net payments is higher for the control group than for the sanctioned group, meaning that the trend among sanctioned taxpayers after enforcement is, as in Argentina, to pay less than the nonsanctioned. The same trend is found for the differences between types of sanctions. The median of taxpayers who have been sanctioned more heavily with closures shows a smaller difference for the control group than for the fined group. This might illustrate a higher willingness among more lightly sanctioned taxpayers to risk and cheat. The increase in their reported debits is greater, as is their increase in reported credits; presumably, they used fake invoices to reduce their net payments. This trend, however, should be more carefully analyzed.

Table 5.6 analyzes the same changes in tax reports based on the size of businesses. I only include the micro-, small- and medium-sized businesses (93 percent of the sample). The control group has a more stable pattern than the other groups, particularly in the critical reporting of VAT credits. Regardless of the size of the firm, non-sanctioned taxpayers reduce purchases at a median rate of 7 percent. Also, net payments to the TA increased moderately for the control group, whereas they decreased in all the sanctioned-group categories. The variability of the medium size in the sample is due to the small number of cases in that category (1–2:

TABLE 5.6 Median of Percentage and Net Payment Change for Repeatedly Sanctioned Taxpayers in Chile (2000 compared to 1998)

	Number of Closures	Medium	Small	Micro
Debits	Fined Only	13.65%	4.97%	15.22%
	1–2	13.6%	4.81%	3.29%
	+3	20.6%	3.21%	1.47%
	Control	–3.59%	–4.03%	–8.29%
Credits	Fined Only	22.59%	2.06%	16.64%
	1–2	–4.02%	5.50%	3.89%
	+3	24.97%	1.1%	–.22%
	Control	–7.10%	–7.15%	–7.49%
Net Payment*	Fined Only	–.90	–.04	–.002
	1–2	.03	–.04	–.004
	+3	–1.06	–.03	–.002
	Control	.16	.16	.005

SOURCE: Closure-of-business tax-return data; SII 2001a.
*In millions of pesos.

forty-seven cases; +3: twenty cases). For the other two categories, the harsher penalties after more than three sanctions appear to have had a moderate impact on compliance. For the small and micro businesses, debits, credits, and net payments reported were closer to the medians of the control group. In other words, the threat of additional detection appears to have moderated evasion practices.

Considering the evidence for the two countries together, it would seem that individual taxpayers generally remain undeterred after business closure. The Chilean sample, which allows us to control for repeat violators, shows that sanctions have a moderate effect on these taxpayers; the evidence is far from conclusive enough, however, to allow us to assert that repeated enforcement enhances better compliance. Both in Argentina and in Chile, taxpayers reduce their reported net payments after business closures. Although debits sometimes increase, credits increase as well, neutralizing any improvements in compliance. This evidence suggests that taxpayers manipulate VAT compliance via credits, presumably by the use of fake invoices. Even though there is a similar trend in both countries, taxpayers in Chile appear to reduce their revenues by smaller amounts than those in Argentina. In other words, though they show the same patterns of behavior, Argentine taxpayers appear to cheat more aggressively than do Chileans. This may be because the closure of businesses in Chile is a long-standing practice and consequently instills better deterrence. Finally, aggregate behavior does not predict individual decisions. There is considerable individual variation, indicating that enforcement has some impact on certain taxpayers. This variation should be analyzed using other statistical instruments.

Cash Registers

Since 1998, most retailers in Argentina have legally been required to use new cash registers.[21] These machines are equipped with a memory chip that TA auditors can review during inspections to check total sales entered over more than a year. Whereas audits and closures are standard enforcement measures, cash register requirements grow out of a different philosophy about how to make taxpayers comply with the law, one in which authorities pursue better compliance by enacting legal requirements that reduce taxpayers' range of "free action and decisions." Withholding is the most widely known among this family of measures, but in fact thousands of regulations are in force that are designed to improve compliance. Invoice-issuing requirements, compulsory payment of large invoices by check, and reporting requirements for banks and brokers are examples of measures that lead taxpayers to perceive that enforcement is likely to occur if they evade the law. The enactment of this regulatory philosophy is in fact a consequence of a weak deterrence environment: the more that tax authorities rely on regulatory requirements, the weaker their enforcement capacities. In essence, cash-register regulation results from the TA's inability to induce taxpayers to comply with invoicing procedures and submit accurate reports of sales.

To assess initial compliance with this new requirement, I analyze the data using measures of central tendency. The main question that I test is whether the size and type of firm affects the degree of future compliance. Table 5.7 presents the percentage change in sales within each interval after new cash registers were introduced. The last row shows that the median rate of change in reported sales is weakly and positively correlated with the size of the firm. The median change suggests that the larger the firm, the more likely it is to report higher sales. Even in category IV, however, 45 percent of businesses reported lower sales after installing the cash registers than they had a year before. If we assume a normal distribution in variation among each category, it seems remarkable that many of the larger firms have been unaffected by the cash-register measure. This might be because these firms were in compliance before cash regis-

---

21. I thank Rafael Levy, with whom I initially analyzed this section's data.

TABLE 5.7 Total Number and Median of Changes in Reported Sales
Following Introduction of New Cash Registers

Intervals Change Ranges (%)	Category I (n = 6,511)	Category II (n = 3,351)	Category III (n = 960)	Category IV (n = 1,045)
Up to –50	3.2	2.6	4.2	3.3
–50 to –11	35.0	30.8	29.9	23.4
–10–0	17.5	20.3	19.7	18.5
0–10	12.2	14.5	16.0	16.6
11–49	20.6	23.1	21.8	29.1
50+	11.5	8.8	8.4	9.2
Median of Changes	–3.3	–0.3	–0.4	4.0

SOURCE: Cash-register tax-return sample, 1999; SII 2001a.

NOTE: I: Very small firm (less than $12,000 of monthly sales); II: small firm ($12,001–$24,000); III: medium-sized business ($24,001–$45,000); IV: large business ($45,001+). Valid n = 10,867.

ters were introduced—and thus the sales reduction is due to a normal downturn in the business cycle—or because these taxpayers were undeterred by the new regulation.[22]

The expectation of tax officials was that businesses with several cash registers would become more compliant with the new machines in place.[23] The larger the retailer, the more complex its accounting and the more difficult it would be to artificially manipulate sales. As table 5.8 shows, results for this measure were mixed. The median of changes in reported sales, credits, and debits indeed reflects that there is a positive association between the number of new registers installed and the percentage of change: the more cash registers installed in a business, the greater the percentage change in reporting. Nonetheless, as the last column shows, even in cases where more than ten cash registers were installed, 40 percent of taxpayers reported lower sales than they had a year before.

Figure 5.4 clearly shows the association of higher sales with the installation of cash registers. As shown by the credit curve, however, taxpayers who reported higher sales increased their reported credits by the same proportion. This indicates that either the rise in reported sales resulted from a natural increase in business (thus, credits would rise as well) or credits were artificially inflated to compensate for higher reported sales (by the use of fake invoices). If this is the case, the cash registers had

22. Since the introduction of this system, new computer "entrepreneurs" have been found in Argentina who alter (for a fee) the information of cash registers. Although this is a fraudulent behavior, it appeared to be widespread in certain industries (e.g., restaurants and small supermarkets). See *Clarin*, June 22, 2003.

23. In numerous interviews conducted during the period, I was informed that this was the goal of the policy.

TABLE 5.8 Mean Rate of Variations by Number of Cashiers

No. of Cash Registers per Taxpayer	Sales (Mean)	Debits (Mean)	Credits (Mean)	% of Taxpayers Who Increased Sales
1	−0.91	−1.71	−6.26	—
2	6.33	4.64	0.11	—
3–5	7.61	6.81	4.15	43
6–9	11.89	11.66	7.70	56
10+	12.70	14.21	9.92	60

SOURCE: Cash-register tax-return sample, 1999; SII 2001a.
NOTE: Valid n = 10,768.

a perverse consequence: by forcing taxpayers to report sales accurately, they opened the door to yet another evasion strategy. The data is insufficient, however, to ascertain which of the two alternatives is more likely.

Taken together, the data shows that the cash-register measure did not disrupt previous tax behavior, as many taxpayers did not increase their compliance. Large taxpayers, on average, reported higher sales; many of the large firms, however, decreased their tax-debit reports as well. It appears that large taxpayers' increases in reported sales point mainly to the natural growth in market share (as the similar increase in credits suggests) rather than to any improvement in taxpayer compliance behavior.

Review of Hypotheses

A preliminary analysis of the data fails to support the first hypothesis, that sanctions have a positive effect on individual compliance. In Argentina and Chile, no association was found between future compliance and penalties imposed following audits or business closures. On the contrary, the analysis shows that the larger the fine imposed, the bolder the future noncompliance of the fined individual. No association was found between the number of days of business closure and an increase in subsequent reported sales. The univariate analysis is conclusive in asserting that sanctions, not being controlled by other variables, cannot account for subsequent compliance. Rather, it points in the other direction: taxpayers tend to compensate for revenues lost to sanctions through subsequent noncompliance. The second hypothesis is also rejected: not only do taxpayers not improve their compliance after enforcement measures are taken against them, but they appear to recuperate the losses of enforcement with additional noncompliance. The third hypothesis, too, could not be supported. I have shown that the net income from additional

Fig. 5.4 Variation Rate of Business Sales by Number of Cashiers

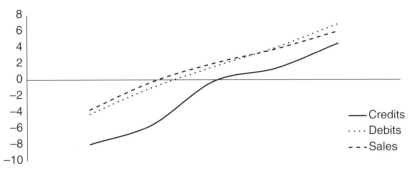

assessments and penalties raised by tax agencies is wiped out by further noncompliance following enforcement.

Conversely, the fourth hypothesis found partial support in the aggregate data. Results from the cash-register sample demonstrate that *the more numerous the opportunities to hide income from authorities, the smaller the impact of enforcement contact in changing subsequent tax behavior.* Because taxpayers who run family-type operations can control how many times they click the machines to register a sale, the measure was totally ineffective in these small businesses. Although taxpayers with more complex operations tended to increase reported sales after installing the cash registers, some larger businesses found other ways to evade taxes without altering reported sales. This conclusion could also be applied to closures and audits. The tendency of sanctioned taxpayers to further decrease their level of compliance clearly demonstrates that taxpayers were undeterred by the prospect of future enforcement actions being taken against them. The larger the firm, however, the less likely this trend is to apply. By definition, larger firms have fewer opportunities to evade VAT (at least in reported sales and debits), and consequently they display better compliance.

The fifth hypothesis could not be fully tested with this data because measuring for fairness requires perception or attitudinal data. But we could estimate compliance using a measure of the favorable or unfavorable outcome of enforcement measures. If audits with little financial cost yield similar subsequent compliance to that of non-audited taxpayers, then no association can be established between enforcement and future behavior. The data does not show that the favorable or unfavorable outcome of audits affects compliance.

MULTIVARIATE ANALYSIS

Thus far, I have analyzed data using aggregate behavior. I have suggested, however, that taxpayers react differently—and, consequently, the effect of enforcement differs from one taxpayer to the next. In this section, I present results of regression models to test the determinants of individual compliance. I test changes in individual compliance behavior after audits.

The dependent variable is the percentage of change in tax reports, measured by the net payment to the agency before and after audits—that is, the dependent variable measures how much taxpayers increased or decreased their net VAT payments after audits were completed. The independent variables include the following:

(1) Assessments (*Ln_Assessment*). This variable measures the log of the additional assessments resulting from audits. Additional assessments include fines and penalties. This variable tests the effect of pecuniary charges due to audits on subsequent compliance with taxation law.

(2) Size of the firm (*Size*). This is a continuous variable that accounts for the size of firms. It is the log of debits (a proxy for sales) for the period before audits.

(3) *Region*. This is a dummy variable where 1 = interior and 0 = metropolitan area (Greater Santiago for Chile, Greater Buenos Aires for Argentina).

(4) Difference in sales (*Dif_Sales*). This variable measures the percentage of increase in debits to control for larger tax payments due to natural increases in sales.

(5) Negative previous balance (*D_balance*). This is a dummy variable signaling that a taxpayer in the period prior to audit did not pay VAT because it carried a balance in his favor. This control variable is very important for VAT analysis; although taxpayers who accumulate balances of already paid VAT do not have to pay taxes, they are still in compliance. This variable also assumes a strong association with the dependent variable, because it is very unlikely that taxpayers with a negative previous balance will continue to have negative payments for extended periods. Net tax payments are expected to improve significantly for this group.

(6) *No-Compliance*. This is a dummy variable only relevant for Chile, where a large segment of those audited are not charged with additional assessments (1 = charged, 0 = no additional charges).

I present results for several models (two for Argentina and four for Chile) estimated by ordinary least squares (OLS). For both nations, all

TABLE 5.9 Regression Models for Changes in Tax Contributions in Argentina

	Model 1			Model 2		
	Coef.	Std. Error	t	Coef.	Std. Error	t
Ln_Assesment	−6.51	1.61	−4.04	−7.24	1.52	−4.77
Size_da	6.58	1.80	3.65	9.36	1.73	5.42
Region	17.90	5.48	3.27	13.84	5.16	2.68
Dif_sales	—	—	—	6.69	1.47	4.55
D_Balance	—	—	—	90.87	11.96	7.6
_cons	−33.69	22.76	−1.48	−61.95	21.64	−2.86
Number of Observations	724			724		
R-squared	0.044			0.1587		
Root MSE	72.183			67.809		

SOURCES: My own elaboration based on audit tax-return data, AFIP 1999.

eligible cases were included. Model 1 for each country tests the effect of audit assessment on future contributions, including two basic controls: size of the firm and region. Model 2 includes two relevant variables for VAT compliance: the difference in sales between periods and the status of carrying a previous VAT negative balance. Model 3 adds the control of those who were found in noncompliance. This case is only relevant for Chile, where 62 percent of the sample were found in noncompliance but the rest were in full compliance; in Argentina, on the other hand, only 2 percent of cases resulted in no additional assessments, and therefore there are not enough cases to control for full compliance. I introduce a dummy variable where 1 = found in noncompliance.[24] Given these results, I estimate a fourth model for Chile, which includes only those taxpayers found in noncompliance. This last model allows for a better comparison with the second model for Argentina. Tables 5.9 and 5.10 report the results of the analysis.

An initial and steady result across the models indicates that firms in rural areas and the provinces in both countries increase their level of tax payments after audits. Also, the larger the firm, the higher the individual percentage increases in its VAT payments will be. As expected, a previous negative balance is positively associated with an increase in tax payment. Also, for both countries the difference in sales is statistically significant. Leaving other variables constant, each percentage increase in reported

24. The mean of future contributions for the noncomplier group is −10.22 percent, whereas for the compliers it is 0.5 percent. Moreover, the 95 percent confidence interval was −22.1 percent and 1.8 percent, revealing that most noncompliers reduce contributions after audits; the interval for the compliers group is −11.5 and 12.3 percent.

TABLE 5.10 Regression Models for Changes in Tax Contributions in Chile

	Model 1			Model 2			Model 3			Model 4		
	Coef.	Std. Error	t	Coef.	Std. Error	t	Coef.	Std. Error	t	Coef.	Std. Error	t
Ln_Assesment	-0.58	0.63	-0.92	0.15	0.62	0.25	-6.56	2.96	-2.21	-6.89	3.11	-2.22
Size_da	1.09	2.25	0.49	3.12	2.19	1.43	4.07	2.22	1.84	6.43	3.38	1.9
Region	0.84	0.43	1.96	0.83	0.41	2.03	0.82	0.41	2	1.34	0.56	2.4
Dif_sales	—	—	—	2.98	1.35	2.2	2.73	1.35	2.02	3.40	1.51	2.25
D_Balance	—	—	—	65.48	11.14	5.88	64.41	11.11	5.8	69.12	17.87	3.87
No-Compliance	—	—	—	—	—	—	-99.98	43.22	2.31	—	—	—
_cons	-23.78	34.66	0.69	-74.79	34.31	2.18	8.79	49.73	0.18	-24.20	59.63	0.41
Number of Observations	568			568			568			304		
R-squared	0.009			0.0834			0.0921			0.125		
Root MSE	108.91			104.93			104.53			106.8		

SOURCES: My own elaboration based on audit tax-return data; SII 2001a.

sales is associated in Argentina with a 6.7 percent increase in net tax payments and in Chile with a 2.7 percent increase. The coefficient suggests that the increase in sales explains compliance better in Argentina than it does in Chile.

The most important finding, however, describes the effect of assessments on future compliance. The coefficient is stable for both models in Argentina, whereas it dramatically changes in Chile for the last two models. In Argentina, every log-unit increase of assessments due to audits yields significantly lower tax contributions afterward. In Chile, the effect of assessments appears inconsistent, because in models 1 and 2 there is a good portion of compliers, which neutralizes the effect. Once these observations are controlled for (with the dummy no compliance in model 3), the results appear to be robust. A fourth model, which only includes cases of noncompliance, shows similar coefficients to the third model. Moreover, the coefficients of the fourth model in Chile are very similar to those for Argentina—namely every log unit of additional assessment yields a reduction of 6–7 percent in tax contributions after audits for both countries. Holding constant all other variables, the higher the additional assessment, the lower the future tax payments will be.

In this sense, the models support the previous section's analysis: a compensation effect appears to be present. These models also predict that higher penalties and fines will yield a decrease in the percentage of tax payments as a result of audits. Conversely, given the drastic change in the coefficients for Chile, many of those who were found in compliance appear to have increased their VAT payments, even controlling for other effects. In short, for taxpayers who take higher noncompliance risks, enforcement does not deter future compliance behavior, whereas moderate tax evaders or fully compliant individuals in Chile appear to be more deterred by personal enforcement.

Finally, a very important finding from this section's analysis is that entrenched cheaters appear to behave similarly, irrespective of the social environment in which they live. Model 2 for Argentina and model 4 for Chile render similar results despite the difference in the tax compliance trends of these two countries.

SUMMARY

In this chapter, I have provided evidence to reject the deterrence-theory hypothesis that tax enforcement in Chile and Argentina directly improves individual compliance. The evidence indicates that several types of enforcement measures did not improve specific deterrence. On the contrary, the results signal that sanctions have the perverse effect of increasing tax evasion (to a large extent in Argentina and to some degree also in Chile). In comparable studies conducted in the United States, the results have been mixed (Beron, Tauchen, and Witte, 1992).

Why should enforcement in two different tax environments, like those of Chile and Argentina, show these peculiar results? One of the most plausible responses is that enforcement does not affect specific deterrence, but that it does affect general deterrence. The threat of punishment is credible among those who are not targeted by enforcement officials. Among unshakable cheaters, once audits or other enforcement actions have occurred, the threat of enforcement is no longer perceived as severe. Many studies have provided compelling evidence that the high risk of detection discourages noncompliance. My evidence suggests that there was no high risk of detection among audited taxpayers, and that those who were sanctioned appeared undeterred by the threat of subsequent sanctions. Many studies suggest that audits have little specific deterrent value (Erard 1992; Mason and Kinsey 1996). This chapter not only supports that assertion but also provides additional proof that audits, under certain conditions, negatively affect the accuracy of subsequent tax reporting.

Chile's superior compliance levels notwithstanding, individual enforcement did not encourage better law abidance in either country; Chilean cheaters are no more likely to be deterred by enforcement than Argentine cheaters are. Conversely, taxpayers who have previously complied and had enforcement actions taken against them take seriously the threats of audits. The assessment coefficients for Chile in the regression models 1 and 2 of table 5.10 suggest that compliers neutralize the perverse effect of audits shown both in models 3 and 4 and those models for Argentina. As shown in table 5.1B, audited compliers in Chile increase their subsequent tax payments. This conclusion, however, says nothing about the large majority of taxpayers who never come into contact with enforcement. In short, cheaters might always be cheaters; in a world of legalists they might be circumscribed into a small target group. The improved after-audit compliance of the non-sanctioned in Chile shows that compliers take enforcement seriously. No similar findings seem to apply to Argentina.

Taking the evidence of chapters 4 and 5 together, we may conclude that in compliance equilibria, enforcement measures serve general deterrence better than they serve specific deterrence. Here, cheaters might continue to cheat, but the majority of honest taxpayers perceive the tax administration as capable of posing a credible threat; more important, the honest majority will believe that compliance within the community is widespread. Conversely, in a tragedy-of-the-commons situation (i.e., non-compliance equilibria), enforcement fails to enhance specific deterrence and very likely fails to achieve general deterrence as well. The "commoners" (taxpayers) are forced to add cattle (engage in tax evasion) to keep the same level of operation (as all their competitors do the same); moreover, as the evidence suggests, they cheat even more after enforcement actions are taken against them. Unless everybody stops evading at once, there is no coordinated solution that makes individual compliance a valuable strategy. Enforcement is effective when it targets a small group of free riders or monitors the majority of taxpayers. Therefore, the scale of tax evasion matters.

Does enforcement enhance compliance? The answer seems rather simple: it depends on the particular social context and on the given individual. In better-compliance environments, enforcement might enhance general deterrence; in societies where cheating is the norm, enforcement fails to foster improved individual compliance. In the United States and the Netherlands (Webley et al. 1991), studies have found that taxpayers cheat on taxes far less than is rational given their chances of being punished, even though taxpayers accurately estimate their odds of being formally sanctioned. Why is there so much honest reporting, and why don't cheaters cheat more? Individuals may refrain from tax evasion if they hold certain values and adhere to a norm of conforming to authority. The evidence for Chile shows that cheaters continue to cheat moderately, whereas compliers are more deterred by the TA. The data for Argentina shows that tax compliance is based overwhelmingly on perceptions of the likelihood of being punished for noncompliance. Therefore, not only does the effectiveness of the enforcement matter but so does the setting, the culture, and the social norms, which are largely shaped by the context and type of equilibrium. The next two chapters examine the structural dimensions of cultural and normative effects on compliance behavior.

6

THE ROLE OF TRUST, RECIPROCITY, AND
SOLIDARITY IN TAX COMPLIANCE

Over the last two decades, many studies have investigated the challenges posed by the logic of collective action, whereby the incentives for individuals to cooperate diminish as the number of participants rises (Olson 1965; Hardin 1982). One of the most promising approaches to these challenges emphasizes social norms as a solution to collective-action problems. Different studies have focused on trust, fairness, and reciprocity as the norms that overcome rational egoistic impulses, resolve problems of information, and help to coordinate superior outcomes (Kahan 2001; Ostrom 2000; Fehr and Schmidt 1999).[1] This chapter undertakes the task of testing the effects of these norms in the field of taxation, where the scale of the problem is large. In particular, using survey data I examine the association of levels of trust, perceived fairness, and reciprocity with conditional cooperation in taxation. I then study some of the determinants of individuals' disposition to contribute to fund social programs to alleviate poverty—a clear sign of social solidarity.

Because general deterrence has a limited effect on enhancing wider compliance, there is a need to examine how societies overcome the individual's temptation to free ride and violate the law. In the following pages, I test the effect of norms and culture in fostering compliance. Moreover, I extend the deterrence paradigm, showing that enforcement might be very effective under cultures of compliance. In short, this chapter explores how norms and culture resolve a critical piece of the tax compliance puzzle.

Given the inherent problem of scale that the taxation problem poses, standard solutions of cooperation, based on communication among players, become irrelevant. I contend that legal culture partly resolves the problem of size in collective-action problems because it enables the best learning mechanisms for adaptation to the contextual environment in

---

1. See also Hardin 1995 for examples of norms that can lead to disastrous outcomes.

which people live. Conditional, passive cooperators draw from culture to best estimate whether to comply, whether to invest in horizontal enforcement costs, and whether to invest in upholding legal behavior. Culture provides individuals with the necessary cues about the extent of trust, fairness, and reciprocity in large communities. By assessing the importance of legitimacy, trust, and fairness in taxation, I draw particular attention to the process of taxpayer-information gathering.

The first section studies the sociological dimensions of compliance and the social role of culture in taxation. I then move on to examine the effects of equity, trust, fairness, and legitimacy in tax compliance in Chile and Argentina. Using multivariate analysis, the third section elucidates the factors that explain the individual's willingness to contribute to social solidarity in both countries.

THE SOCIOLOGICAL DIMENSIONS OF TAX COMPLIANCE

Several years ago, I asked a well-known economist to venture an explanation for the disparity in compliance between Argentina and Chile. After thinking briefly, he said, "Well, I do not have a definite answer; however, it seems to me that the fact that a large wave of Italian immigrants arrived to Argentina, and Germans migrated to Chile, has something to do with it."[2] Although I find this answer clearly flawed, it calls for other explanations of compliance that exceed the strict microeconomic or macroeconomic analysis. Sociological interpretations are not "default" explanations; rather, they must be actively incorporated into different models of economic behavior.

Deviating from Norms

A starting assumption of my research is that the decision making of taxpayers is generally the outcome of routine rather than estimations of costs and benefits. People adopt routine and "automated" decisions because such decisions have previously provided some material or psychological rewards (Steenbergen, McGraw, and Scholz 1992; Webley et al. 1991). These decisions trigger a process of differential reinforcement through which taxpayers learn what works and what does not. Thus, norms and behaviors are subject to a continuous process of exchange and negotiation with social, tax, and legal environments. The predisposition to

2. Interview with Rudiger Dornbush, Washington, D.C, February 24, 1999.

comply or evade taxes is based on individual levels of self-control, previous experience, opportunity, and social learning.

Several contributions from the field of deviance studies provide useful insights into how perceptions are formed. People engage in accepted behaviors through a process of *imitation and differential reinforcement*, which evolves into standardized practices and a legal culture (Akers 1977). Tax behaviors derive from the same principle. Compliance environments generate reinforcement (rewards or punishments), which leads to the internalization of tax behaviors. When impunity rewards noncompliance decisions, it triggers citizens' noncompliant disposition. Conversely, tax compliant attitudes result from social learning that rewards legal behaviors. This fosters automatic tax compliance decisions, often irrespective of the material costs of compliance.

Individual self-restraint also explains why people refrain from deviating from rules. According to control theory, violators of the law show an invariant personal disregard for future costs in favor of immediate benefits.[3] In social environments where histories of noncompliance produce high individual payoffs, people tend to value immediate pleasures and disregard future potential costs (because sanctions are not imposed effectively). This mechanism partly explains the formation of discount rates. The culture of noncompliance in Argentina thrives because such noncompliance has paid off. Taxpayers in Chile are not more rational than those in Argentina, but they tend, on average, to be more cautious.

Rules and social norms are effective to the extent that they are enforceable—that is, to the extent that they inflict costs on those who violate them. Ultimately, tax behavior results from institutionalized behavior. Whether tax decisions are the outcome of the perceived benefits of norms (March and Olsen 1989) or the distributional consequences of their application (Knight 1992), compliance with institutionalized patterns of behavior results from the acceptance and application by individuals of standard patterns, which are determined by the social perceptions of norms and the effective mobilization of resources.

Tax Culture

Economists and tax administrators involved in the tax reforms of the 1990s have claimed that those failures resulted from a "mysterious" and

---

3. People who dismiss the future costs of certain acts disregard the effect of sanctions because they value the pleasures of immediate gratification. See Gottfredson and Hirschi 1990 for a discussion of control theory and its application to white-collar offenses.

"uncontrolled" variable not related to economic causes. Political and cultural factors have been used to explain the limited success of the reforms. I interviewed four general directors of AFIP and numerous policy makers and tax analysts in Argentina. They all seem to agree that a culture of tax evasion partly explains the failure of different programs, although no one could specifically describe this "culture." Because the normative dimension of tax compliance is inherent to the tax system, I contend that a given tax culture is not a mysterious or default variable. A normative approach to tax behavior is the by-product of a complex socialization process in which deterrence, enforcement, and legitimacy intertwine to produce numerous outcomes. Culture strongly affects the way that taxpayers perceive benefits and costs, as well as gains and losses.

In chapter 1 and appendix B, I propose a framework whereby taxpayers develop propensities to comply on the basis of the environment in which they live, which affects their discount rates. I also present a road map to signal mechanisms of norm creation and norm maintenance, all tied to the enforcement and values of norms. I will further develop an endurance and imitation mechanism in chapter 7. All these mechanisms are instrumental to resolving the most daunting problem in taxation, which is how to convince taxpayers that they are not being suckered—that their contribution is critical for the provision of public goods, and that others are not free riding on their costly compliance. Finding a solution to this problem is the critical component that allows the idea of contingent consent to function.

What puts tax compliance in the assurance-game context is precisely the warranties taxpayers have that others reciprocate their compliant behavior. This classical solution to collective-action problems has flourished over the last few decades.[4] The structure of information gathering, however, is vastly different from that modeled in the standard laboratory games or field studies conducted on relatively small-scale groups; with such a large number of players, personal communication is impossible, thereby producing less desirable outcomes.[5] Moreover, given the private nature of tax filing, the incentive to free ride increases, making the signaling of cooperation less practical.[6] I argue that the basic individual

4. See Ostrom 2001 for a good review of the literature.
5. Laboratory experiments rarely exceed hundreds of participants. Studies in the field of common-pool resources, such those reported by Ostrom (1990), ranged from a few hundred to a maximum of fifteen thousand. Tax compliance involves one hundred million people in the United States and several million elsewhere.
6. Eric Posner (2000) claims that social norms are vehicles for signaling cooperation between individuals. By abiding with the norm, cooperators signal to others that they belong

motivation to comply—or rather the lesser motivation to aggressively cheat—draws on perceptions of what others do. The most trusted source for information about the general population's level of taxation-law abidance, then, is the tax culture.

Because the structure of consent in collective games creates large incentives to free ride, taxpayers' basic approach will be to cheat on their taxes. This is predicted by rational-choice theory and has been found to be the dominant strategy in a noncompliance environment. What requires better explanation is why people abide by rules in the absence of real threats of punishment. Kahan (2001) suggests that humans are moved by reciprocity and trust considerations that override the calculations of Homo economicus, but he does not show how these considerations operate or are upheld in large-scale settings. But ignoring the structural difference in how reciprocity works between small-to-medium-sized cooperation groups and very large groups is taking an unwarranted leap of faith.

I contend that trust, reciprocity, and fairness do create the incentives for refraining from aggressive tax evasion. They become inhibitors to crossing from passive cooperation to active defection. In compliance cultures, most taxpayers cheat a little and believe that others behave similarly. They feel comfortable with full compliance or marginal tax evasion because they believe that others do not exploit them. Therefore, they do not spend large amounts of resources, time, and energy in finding or coming up with evasion schemes that can significantly reduce their tax burden. What greatly undermines compliance equilibria is the discovery of many aggressive cheaters, which generates incentives for otherwise-compliant taxpayers to emulate the behavior of the greedy, particularly in large groups and when decisions are made privately. In short, culture provides the social validation to convince both legalists that they are not suckers in compliance environments, and cheaters that they are making the right choices in noncompliance equilibria.

This argument is consistent with other perspectives that emphasize the importance of trust and norms for tax compliance. Taxpayers rely on these values and norms to constrain decisions that rely on subconscious and sometimes far from rational criteria (Scholz and Pinney 1995; Scholz and Lubell 1998; see Steenbergen, McGraw, and Scholz 1992 on how personal attitudes toward taxes are affected by others). Consistent with heuristic and social-mechanism explanations, taxpayers draw on shared

---

to the group and are willing to engage in cooperative endeavors. Although this approach has limitations (see Bergman 2003), it nonetheless shows that social norms are central for resolving large-scale communication problems in social dilemmas.

values and beliefs to decide what is best for them. Two leading factors affect the way that taxpayers incorporate compliance behavior: the effect of tax enforcement and the perceived legitimacy and fairness of laws. Hence, tax compliance is explained by the effect of culture (the incorporation of morals, values, and beliefs) *and* by subjective estimations of the state's capacity to enforce tax laws. I call for the dynamic integration of both effects.

Tax Culture and the Limits of Enforcement: An Example and Evidence

Most multinational-organization and tax officials assume that successful enforcement mechanisms will yield similar results in different countries. The following example shows the limitations of this approach. Let us assume that in country A 10 percent of the population does not obey a given law and the other 90 percent are successfully deterred by governmental enforcement (E). In country B, 50 percent do not obey the same law. Assuming that other factors are held constant, the standard policy recommendation for country B will be to increase enforcement (E) fivefold to achieve compliance similar to that in country A. This policy would very likely fail, however, because it does not account for the imitation effects of noncompliance. In country A, the probability that a law-abiding citizen will meet a cheater and imitate his or her behavior is 10 percent, or one in ten,[7] whereas in country B it is 50 percent, or one in two. As the simulation in appendix C shows, if there is no enforcement and only imitation is at work, 19 percent of country A will be cheaters at t2 (the original 10 percent plus another 9 percent of the remaining 90 percent), whereas 75 percent of country B will be cheaters. Hence, (E) for country A prevents the extra 9 percent from crossing into noncompliance, but a large share of 5(E) in country B must be allocated just to prevent the further deterioration of compliance.[8] Only a small fraction of the significant fivefold increase in enforcement resources produces a reduction of noncompliance, and this enforcement does not bring country B anywhere near the equilibrium in country A. Precise estimates of necessary enforcement levels will depend on the characteristics of the given law and many other contextual considerations, but the failure to

---

7. In fact, this probability is unknown and depends on factors such as networks, trades, frequency of contacts, and so forth. For the sake of this argument, let us assume that one citizen meets only one other citizen randomly.

8. To achieve similar results, the increase of (E) for country B will not resemble a linear, but rather some exponential, function.

account for the damaging effects of noncompliance cultures explains the often-frustrating results of replicating the enforcement policies of other countries. The enforcement needed to reverse a climate of illegality is so large and incremental that it partly explains the resilience and stability of noncompliance equilibria. It also explains why attempting to reverse equilibria based purely on enforcement will likely fail.

In chapters 1 and 4, I argued that under a compliance equilibrium, enforcement becomes more effective and taxpayers perceive it more severely. Conversely, when tax administrators need to diversify resources and monitor larger groups of taxpayers, effective enforcement is diluted and citizens' perception that the TA is doing a poor job grows stronger. The evidence of chapter 5 is very conclusive: poorly performed audits that fail to detect underreported income diminish citizens' perception of the likelihood of future detection. Vicious circles of noncompliance are hard to break. Tax audits in Argentina fail to detect a significant share of noncompliance. In survey 4, 75 percent of respondents whose returns were assessed with additional tax liabilities reported that audits found only a small or a very small fraction of their total noncompliance. Moreover, in the same survey these taxpayers estimated the probability of detection for underreporting income by one hundred thousand pesos at 42 percent, whereas a control group of non-audited taxpayers estimated the same underreporting at 57 percent.

The implication is clear: noncompliance decisions continually rewarded by the absence of effective sanctions, as they are in Argentina, lead to a noncompliant attitude in which citizens give little weight to the threat of punishment. Conversely, a tax compliant attitude results from social learning that rewards legal behavior. Because in Argentina the rewards of noncompliance exceed its associated costs, a general culture of noncompliance thrives. Here, cheaters imitate other cheaters. Conversely, in Chile a tax culture developed from a strong centralist state with higher levels of legitimacy. Individuals therefore perceive that tax laws must be obeyed. Similar levels of enforcement consequently achieve better results in Chile than in Argentina.

This difference stems from a distorted perception among Chilean taxpayers, who have usually overestimated SII's detection capabilities, whereas in Argentina taxpayers accurately perceive AFIP's shortcomings. Public-opinion surveys support this finding. In Chile in 1992, only 28 percent of those surveyed agreed with the sentence, "In this country it is easy to evade taxes," and just 48 percent agreed that "there are people who evade taxes and are proud of it."[9] In Argentina, 81 percent said that is easy or very easy to evade taxes (survey 4).[10] The evidence suggests that Chile and Argentina diverge in the normative dimension of taxation and that such disparities are associated with differences in perceptions of the TA's enforcement capacities.

THE SOCIAL ENVIRONMENT OF COMPLIANCE DECISIONS IN ARGENTINA AND CHILE

This section examines how the social or environmental dimension of compliance affects taxpayers in Argentina and Chile. I examine the value of equity in taxation, the "state of trust and legitimacy," the norm of fairness, and duty and moral obligations to comply with taxes; I also consider how these norms affect individuals' processes of information gathering about taxes in both countries. I describe the values, norms, and beliefs related to taxation, and I show their strong association with the respective levels of compliance.

Equity in Taxation

In traditional tax research, the framework for the assurance game is the exchange equity between taxpayers' contributions and the state's delivery of public goods.[11] One problem with this approach is that taxes are compulsory, whereas exclusion from the benefits of public goods in modern states is difficult, posing questions about voluntary cooperation on the one hand and the encouragement of free riding on the other (Bates 1989). Moreover, given individual disparities in perceptions of the value of public goods and the variance in contributions within a population, it is unclear how best to describe where exchange equity is firmly established.

Players will play the assurance game voluntarily because they value the good that such cooperation produces; they might, however, accept a compulsory solution only to the extent that the value of goods is unambiguously higher than the contributions they are asked to make.[12] This

9. Reported in Etcheberry 1993.
10. See also survey responses in table 1.1.
11. See Steinmo 1993 for an excellent study of the problems of taxation and provision of public goods.
12. See appendix B for a formal analysis of equity and taxation.

assumes that taxpayers consciously accept that the provision of goods makes a society better and that the sharing of the burden is superior to the private provision of a good. Given that the subsidizing and redistribution of goods is inherent to the tax game, however, compulsion is not only necessary to ensure universal participation but also provides warranties that both the rich and the poor will pay and be equally committed (Bird, Martinez-Vazquez, and Torgler 2006).[13] This yields two important considerations: Assurance games in taxation cannot be conceived only as a pure exchange equity; they require enforcement to ensure that the better-off pay their taxes. Also, when goods can be efficiently provided by private consumption, the incentive to escape from cooperation dramatically increases, even in cases where people might highly value the provision of public goods. (The multivariate analysis at the end of this chapter will support this assertion.)

A compliance equilibrium generates the virtuous circles of compulsory but effective contributions to the collective because most taxpayers value public goods more highly than do the taxpayers in a noncompliance equilibrium. In many Latin American states, taxpayers contend that they refrain from paying taxes because of the poor quality of state services, which elicits vicious circles of noncompliance. Although causality remains problematic, the correlation between satisfaction with public goods and voluntary compliance is strong. In the comparison between Argentina and Chile shown in table 6.1, the level of strong satisfaction in both countries is small (lower in Argentina), but strong feelings of dissatisfaction are far less common in Chile than they are in Argentina.

When people in Argentina were asked where they thought their taxes ended up, 44 percent said, "They are being stolen by the politicians," whereas only 15 percent said that this money was channeled to "fund social programs" (survey 1). When they were asked, "How satisfied are you with the government's use of public funds?" 92 percent said that they were very dissatisfied. In another illustrative example, respondents were asked to react to the following statement: "Tax revenues are used to support needier people." Only 12 percent of Argentine respondents agreed, whereas in Chile 46 percent agreed. In the United States, only 16 percent of people disagreed or totally disagreed with a similar statement (Harris 1987). In response to the statement, "I am ready to pay more

13. What is clearly missing in many Latin American countries is precisely the commitment of the middle and upper-middle classes to the provisions of public goods. Many of these citizens opt to invest heavily in the private supply of valuable goods, such as personal security and education for their children.

TABLE 6.1 Satisfaction with Services Provided by the State

	Public Services*		Education		Internal Security	
	Argentina	Chile	Argentina	Chile	Argentina	Chile
Very Satisfied	8%	—	12%	18%	5%	16%
Very Unsatisfied	60%	—	58%	21%	62%	12%

SOURCES: Surveys 1 and 6.
NOTE: Values of response were "very satisfied," "somewhat satisfied," "somewhat unsatisfied," and "very unsatisfied." I report here the two extremes.
*Obras y Servicios Públicos.

taxes if they are channeled to benefit the poor," 76 percent of Chileans agreed or totally agreed (survey 5).

It is still unclear whether such correlations are mechanisms that help to reduce cognitive dissonance (Argentina) or approval behavior (Chile), but perceived equity in Chile is considerably higher than in Argentina. Conditional cooperation can only operate where the norm of fairness is widely embraced and where the government reciprocates the costly contributions of citizens. These are necessary but not sufficient conditions to ensure tax compliance.

Trust and Legitimacy

Tax evasion is the outcome of a lack of trust. The threat of credible enforcement reduces mistrust among players and leads to cooperative solutions; the inability to reach an assurance-game equilibrium results in a prisoner's dilemma solution because players remain uncertain regarding the preferences of others. The social configuration of trust should therefore be examined to understand how tax evasion became widespread in cultures where noncompliance thrives.[14]

Trust in the tax system has a profound effect on the construction of norms and beliefs. Levi (1988) has persuasively demonstrated that only when channels of trust between governments and taxpayers are solidly established are significant revenues raised and tax evasion reduced. Kahan (2001) considers trust the basic social norm that enhances cooperation and facilitates voluntary tax compliance in a "high-trust" equilibrium. Hardin (1992; 2001) stresses that the capacity to trust depends greatly on the social environment in which individuals are raised and socialized.

14. A large literature on trust has emerged from the works of Coleman (1990), Gambetta (1988), and Putnam (1993). I will only refer here to trust in the context of tax evasion. For good reviews of the literature on trust, see Levi 1998 and Hardin 2001.

An environment of mistrust, such as that of Argentina, undermines the possibilities of building contingent consent.

Trust is enhanced by the trustworthiness of conditional cooperators and institutions.[15] In his seminal work on this topic, Coleman (1988) equated trust to a credit slip that someone is willing to give others to engage in cooperative endeavors. In the same vein, it could be said that, being a form of credit, trust will be granted to the extent that there is a high probability that the debt will be repaid. Societies that have institutions that make contracts valid—that is, societies in which debts are repaid—stand a better chance of enhancing conditional cooperation. In short, trust depends on the trustworthiness of the trustee and the plausibility that sanctions will be imposed when the terms of the contract have been breached.[16]

The results of several studies (Scholz and Pinney 1995; Scholz and Lubell 1998) suggest that there is at least a strong association between high levels of trust and a willingness to abide by tax laws. Where the trustworthiness of social institutions is high more citizens have a sense of obligation to comply with laws, and tax compliance is lower. Causation, however, remains unclear.

Compliance also depends on the capacity of rulers to establish an enduring social contract. Ceteris paribus, fragmented and unstable societies will have greater difficulty enhancing compliance than will more stable and legitimate systems. During the first years of the Concertación government (starting in 1990), for example, Chile enjoyed better tax compliance than it had under General Pinochet in the 1980s (see figs. 2.1 and 2.2). This was partly due to the greater legitimacy of the new democratic government. Players are prone to accept cooperative solutions when they are socialized in a trustworthy environment. In this sense, democracy is conducive to compliance with tax laws, not only because states can deter taxpayers more efficiently but also because democracy is based on social exchanges of the sort necessary to foster trust in citizens (Bird et al. 2006). As Scholz (2003) hypothesized, democracies develop the range of controls on which citizens can draw to better adapt to implicit tax-contract

---

15. The concept of encapsulated trust developed by Hardin (2001) denotes a disposition of person A to trust B to do X, or, in other words, the disposition to engage in conditional cooperation to achieve a desired result. This can be translated into a tax compliance schema whereby taxpayer A will trust taxpayer B to honor his share. If he does not believe that B will comply, A will not trust others and will refrain from compliance.

16. For a full discussion, see Bergman (2009).

TABLE 6.2 Independent Measures of Trust in Argentina and Chile

	Argentina	Chile
Trust in the Police*	77%	48%
Trust in Legal System*	84%	39%
Trust in Banks*	85%	59%
Whom Do I Trust: Government Employee**	3%	19%
Whom Do I Trust: A Police Officer**	7%	23%
Whom Do I Trust: Family Member**	69%	54%
Interpersonal Trust***	18%	24%

SOURCE: Own estimation based on 2003 survey data.
*Percentage of valid responders who report to have little or no trust.
**Percentage of valid multiple and open responses that mentioned trusted individuals or figures.
***Response to the standard question that asks whether most people could be trusted.

obligations. Democracies are better positioned than authoritarian regimes to enhance trust and thus make conditional cooperation feasible.

Climates of trust and trustworthiness are very different in Chile and Argentina, as table 6.2 indicates, and they independently contribute to the divergent compliance behavior found in these two countries. Several surveys not linked to tax behavior provide independent measures of the levels of trust and trustworthiness that foster these different environments. Moreover, by measuring trust, we can indirectly gauge whether the bedrock is in place on which conditional cooperation may be built.

Corruption also undermines trust (Rose-Ackerman 1999). In developed countries, taxpayers often complain about the size and intrusiveness of the tax authority; surveys conducted in the United States and Britain, however, found no major complaints about corruption or the mishandling of tax revenues. In Chile, most taxpayers believe that tax officials cannot be bribed and that social spending is properly handled (see table 6.3). On the other hand, in Argentina corruption and lawbreakers' impunity from prosecution are clearly among the public's major grievances. Bribing tax officials in Argentina is not perceived by citizens of that country to be a particularly risky behavior. Given the similarity of the survey design and administration used in these countries, the differences between Chile and Argentina described above are dramatic. Other surveys confirm that corruption has become one of Argentina's major problems. In survey 1, 36 percent of respondents answered that corruption was the number one problem in the country, whereas 29 percent selected unemployment; 85 percent of respondents said that corruption was among Argentina's top three major problems. When people were

TABLE 6.3 Opinions About Corrupt Officials

Country	Bribe an Auditor (1)		Easy "Arrangement" (2)		Honest Officials (3)	
	Argentina	Chile	Argentina	Chile	Argentina	Chile
Agree	24%	80%	53%	16%	42%	75%
Disagree	72%	17%	42%	81%	52%	21%

SOURCES: Surveys 1 and 6.

NOTE: Valid percentage results. Totals do not add up to 100 due to nonresponse. "Agree" includes "strongly agree" and "agree." "Disagree" includes "strongly disagree" and "disagree."

(1) "People believe that if a taxpayer tries to bribe a (DGI or SII) auditor, the taxpayer will most likely end up getting in trouble."

(2) "People think that it is quite easy to find a 'settlement or deal' with tax inspectors."

(3) "Generally, DGI or SII employees are honest officials."

asked where tax money ends up, 44 percent said that that some of the revenues were being stolen by politicians.[17] In Chile, respondents identified unemployment, poverty, and education as major problems. No respondents mentioned corruption as one of the nation's top two problems (survey 6).

In addition to corruption, tax policy and inequity might undermine trust if taxpayers perceive that taxes are too high and enforcement is unfair. For instance, in many U.S. surveys more than 60 percent of taxpayers report that they pay far more than their reasonable share in taxes.[18] The data for Chile and Argentina also shows this trend; the scale of discontent in Argentina, however, is remarkable. An overwhelming 86 percent of Argentines disagreed with the statement, "The TA serves (or treats) taxpayers on an equal basis." The results in Chile, where 51 percent disagree, are more consistent with those for the United States. In response to the statement, "The tax policy in this country is just and fair," only 13 percent of those surveyed agreed in Argentina, whereas 46 percent agreed in Chile.[19]

---

17. Twenty-nine percent said that foreign debt is being paid with the tax receipts, and only 15 percent said that the first use of the money is to finance social programs.

18. See Harris 1987, Yankelevich and White 1984, and Kinsey 1987. Sixty-five percent of taxpayers believed that their income-tax burden was "too high" (reported by Fennell and Fennell 2003, n6).

19. Surveys attempt to measure tax fairness with questions about the tax burden. Taxpayers tend to estimate their own tax burden as high, irrespective of the level of their income. This is also the case in Argentina and Chile. To the statement, "The tax burden is excessive for people in a similar economic situation to me," 81 percent agreed in Argentina, and 67 percent agreed in Chile.

Law Abidance and Procedural Fairness

Scholars in social psychology contend that people will obey laws, irrespective of the impact that these laws might have on their own lives, if they perceive the laws' content and administration to be fair (Tyler 1990, 2008; Braithwaite 1984). Consequently, these scholars argue, individuals' allegiance to authority and the perceived legitimacy of an administration affect compliance decisions. To the extent that authorities conduct and enforce policies fairly, respecting the individual voice, they develop greater governmental legitimacy. Procedural justice creates stronger incentives to comply, even when compliance is costly. Building on the norm of reciprocity, people want fair, respectful, and dignified treatment from authorities (Cialdini 1989), and they are more concerned about whether their views are heard by authorities than about whether their views affect the decisions made (Tyler 1990).[20] Extending procedural-fairness research to tax compliance, however, is difficult due to several limitations. First, tax compliance is a private matter, based on limited contact with authorities, and rarely made public. Second, research on reciprocity usually relates to specific and simple quid-pro-quo acts. Notwithstanding these constraints, perceptions of procedural fairness can potentially create an even more powerful incentive to comply.[21]

Chapters 3 and 4 (see also table 6.5) provide evidence that Chilean taxpayers perceive tax officials as fair and balanced, regardless of whether they have been audited and regardless of the outcome of those audits. In Argentina, distributional justice—that is, the material outcome of an enforcement action—was more important in developing individual perceptions of the TA's fairness. The data in table 6.3 about corruption provides additional indirect support that Argentines and Chileans have different perceptions of fairness in taxation. These two cases indicate that in compliance equilibria, individuals weigh procedural-justice considerations positively, whereas in noncompliance equilibria material outcomes dominate individual perceptions. The breakdown of the basic tax contract undermines the possibilities of procedural fairness; hence, for cheaters only material justice (the perceived favorable result of audits) matters.

20. See also Bardach and Kagan 1982 and Braithwaite 1984 on individual responsiveness to regulatory agencies, and Merry 1990 on the importance of voice regardless of the outcome of judicial processes.

21. As Scholz (2003, 177) states, "Procedural justice provides an alternative means of evaluating whether institutions are performing to expectations, and hence provides an additional contingency in deciding whether or not to fulfill related obligations."

TABLE 6.4 Responses to Questions About Law Abidance, Duty, and Justification in Taxation

	Argentina	Chile
Abidance by Unjust Laws (1)	1.9 (.55)	—
Abidance by Bad Laws (2)	2.1 (.71)	1.7 (.51)
Justifying Disobedience (3)	2.6 (.65)	2.8 (.68)
Duty (4)	1.6 (.54)	1.5 (.54)
Justification of Tax Evasion (5)	3.3 (6.1)	3.6 (.51)
Full Compliance (6)	1.5 (.72)	—

SOURCES: Surveys 1 and 6.

NOTE: All values presented in table are means, followed by sd in parentheses. Valid percentage results. Scale 1 = strongly agree, 2 = agree, 3 = disagree, and 4 = strongly disagree.

(1) "People should obey the laws, even when a citizen would consider them unjust."

(2) "I always try to obey the laws even when I think these laws are bad."

(3) "Disobeying the law is sometimes justified."

(4) "I consider that it is a duty to contribute to the country with my taxes."

(5) "Tax money always ends up in the hands of the less needed people; therefore it's justifiable to avoid paying taxes."

(6) "People should pay their taxes entirely and then punish the politicians in the elections."

Cheating on taxes, however, does not necessarily imply an open challenge to the duty of complying with taxation law. Tax evasion is not equivalent to the open defiance of authority but rather a subtle exit strategy. Table 6.4 shows that the responses of those surveyed to questions about law abidance, duty, and justification in taxation do not vary significantly, as cheaters do not make their decisions public and do not justify their acts.

The most positive effect that procedural justice can have on compliance operates through personal experience. Because the majority of people have only limited contact with authorities, they develop perceptions indirectly through their contact (lack thereof) with a generalized normative commitment to comply. In countries where procedural fairness is weak, the ground for a social norm of reciprocity is fragile. Argentina has historically faced many difficulties in enhancing tax compliance, particularly because reciprocity has rarely been fostered. Tax evasion in Argentina cannot be explained as a rational disobedience or as open defiance of the system. Former U.S. Supreme Court Judge Holmes's maxim that "taxes are the price we pay for a civilized society" is an idea certainly shared by Argentines and Chileans. Nonetheless, tax evasion is rampant in Argentina. The gap between Argentines' reported acceptance of that idea and their actual avoidance of taxes is correlated with Argentina's poor procedural justice and a lack of trust.

Personal acknowledgement of the fairness of a taxation process, along with the creation of a forum in which the taxpayer's voice may be heard, might have a positive impact on the perceived fairness of the taxation system. Tax compliance can be enhanced by audits and by the tax agency's responsiveness in other contacts (which affect taxpayers' normative commitment to comply; Smith 1992; Kinsey 1992). There is less clear evidence, however, regarding how perceptions of responsiveness and procedural fairness are formed. The private nature of filing taxes, in which there is seldom a voice to be heard, dwarfs any compliance effects that might be attributed to attitudes toward the tax agency (Lempert 1992). Tax behavior is embedded in a sea of complex state-citizen interactions and exchanges that inhibit a proper evaluation of the isolated effect of tax contacts.

In Argentina and Chile, people believe that their tax administration treats them somewhat unfairly because of the scrutiny and intrusiveness of its actions. In Argentina, 78 percent of those surveyed agreed with the statement, "DGI (the TA) treats honest taxpayers as if they have done something wrong." Taxpayers' satisfaction regarding their contact with authorities is also negatively correlated with their intentions to become more compliant. (Survey 4 in Argentina produced a weak but statistically significant correlation, r −0.15, and for Chile, r −0.11.) The more that taxpayers are satisfied with the outcome of audits, the less likely they are to fully comply with their taxes, particularly in Argentina.

Sources of Information

Given that rational imitation and contagion are valuable mechanisms in the adoption of strategic actions related to compliance with taxes, sources of tax information have a direct impact on the benefits that taxpayers may receive for undertaking steps to reduce their tax burden (Mazur and Nagin 1989); further, they may also affect the formation of attitudes and beliefs about the tax system. People assign different weights to messages according to their sources. In conditions of uncertainty, taxpayers seek information and opinions from others in similar positions, and they tend to rely on similar networks to gather useful information about the tax administration's enforcement methods. In seeking information from peers, individuals may encounter less disapproval of their tax cheating than they would from a family member. In similar situations, peers and interrelated businesses might share information on how to cheat. On the other hand, family and society are primarily concerned with normative issues.

TABLE 6.5 Effects of Audits

	Audited		Noncompliance*	
	Argentina	Chile	Argentina	Chile
Do you consider the results of the audit fair (*justo*)?	84%	55%	83%	55%
Are you satisfied with the economic outcome of the audit?	78%	79%	70%	52%
Would you change little or anything in your future tax planning?	86%	64%	80%	51%

SOURCES: Surveys 4 and 6.
*Audited taxpayers who have been assessed additional fines and taxes as a result of the audit.

Stalans and colleagues (1991) found that communication with family members regarding tax noncompliance increases tax cheaters' sense of guilt, whereas similar communication with coworkers decreases guilt. They also found that mass-media communication does not affect individuals' perceptions of the likelihood that the TA will detect more tax evasion than it has in the past. These findings have two important implications: first, mass-media campaigns apparently do not work to instill fear of detection in taxpayers; and second, diverse sources and decision contexts (structural opportunity) directly affect individual tax decisions.

Table 6.6 indicates that the majority of taxpayers share at least some information with their colleagues and peers. Peer networks appear to be a good source of information, and their impact cannot be underestimated. There is some variation among each population but no major differences across countries. In both Argentina and Chile, less than a third of the sample shares no information with peers, and a significantly cumulative 60–67 percent report that they exchange information on what the tax agency is unable to detect, while 70–72 percent share at least some information regarding what the TA is indeed capable of detecting. Such a widespread exchange of information may have fostered informal networks of sharing tax-noncompliance practices. These networks partially explain the ability of taxpayers to rapidly adjust to changing environments and shield their noncompliance from detection.[22]

22. An interesting caveat is the role of accountants in providing valuable information. Only 6 percent in Argentina and 7 percent in Chile said that no information was provided by accountants regarding what can trigger an audit, and just 10 percent in Argentina and 17 percent in Chile did not receive any information about the detection capabilities of AFIP or SII.

TABLE 6.6 Shared Information Among Taxpayers

Shared Information	Tax Preparation		"Audit Triggers"		Inability to Detect		Detection Capability	
	Arg.	Chile	Arg.	Chile	Arg.	Chile	Arg.	Chile
Very Much	19%	17%	13%	12%	10%	6%	11%	16%
Quite a Bit	26%	27%	26%	32%	23%	14%	27%	26%
A Little	28%	29%	35%	30%	35%	40%	34%	28%
Nothing	28%	26%	27%	25%	33%	40%	28%	28%

SOURCES: Surveys 1 and 6.

NOTE: Question: "How much have you talked [or chatted: *ha charlado*] with your colleagues or peers about the following issues: (a) How to prepare tax returns? (b) What are the things that make the TA decide to launch an audit? (c) What are the things the TA is unable to detect? and (d) What is the TA capable of detecting?" The answer options for these closed-ended questions were, in Spanish, (a) "Mucho," (b) "Bastante," (c) "Poco," and, (d) "Nada." Valid n for Argentina = 530, for Chile = 514.

Notwithstanding the similarity of the results for Chile and Argentina, the implications of information networks differ according to the compliance equilibrium. Where most taxpayers are compliant, shared information relates to the efficacy of the TA and the cautious decisions of taxpayers. Conversely, in a noncompliance environment, shared information relates to "safe" tax-evasion practices. In short, shared information produces different outcomes depending on the type of equilibrium, which reinforces the perceptions, values, and beliefs of the compliance environment.

Moral Obligation and Duty

Moral obligation affects the citizen's sense of duty to obey the law. The higher the level of moral obligation, the more likely taxpayers will be to feel compelled to abide by the law. Conversely, lower levels of moral obligation negatively affect feelings of duty. The literature on voting behavior has shown how the costs incurred by going to the polls (against the minimal individual benefits of this act) are neutralized by the citizen's sense of duty, which in turn biases perceptions and provides nonmaterial rewards. Scholz and Pinney (1995) have extended this research to tax compliance and found that the sense of duty to pay taxes biases taxpayers' subjective perceptions of the risk of getting caught. Taxpayers who feel no obligation to pay taxes tend to perceive the risk of detection as being lower than those who report a strong commitment to obeying tax laws; those law-abiding taxpayers tend to overestimate the TA's detection capacity, making them less likely to take risks.

Respondents in Chile and Argentina were asked to measure their sense of obligation and duty to pay taxes using this question, "Based on your personal opinions of what is right and wrong, do you feel a moral obligation to comply while you prepare and/or file your tax return?"[23] On a scale of 1 to 5 (1 = very high moral obligation, 5 = none), the mean for Argentina was 2.56. Only 19 percent of those surveyed reported feeling a very low or no moral obligation, whereas only 17 percent reported feeling a very high moral obligation to comply with tax laws. In Chile, the moral commitment to pay taxes is much higher, with a mean of 1.71 (sd 0.78). Eighty-nine percent of respondents said that they feel a very high or high sense of moral obligation, and only 1.5 percent said that they feel none at all. In survey 4 in Argentina, respondents were asked to rate the same question on a scale from 0 to 10 (0 = none, 10 = very high), and the mean in this case was 6.75 (sd 2.26). The differences in taxpayers' sense of moral obligation in the two countries are significant: in Chile, there is clearly a stronger sense of moral obligation to comply with tax laws.

The social commitment to tax abidance may affect compliance by causing taxpayers to overestimate the TA's capabilities of detecting noncompliance. A positive correlation was found between individuals' perceptions of the detection capability of their TA and their sense of moral obligation to comply with tax law (r 0.28 in Argentina and r 0.32 in Chile). Although causality cannot be determined, following cognitive heuristics it can be said that morally obligated taxpayers frame their tax decisions by inaccurately estimating detection probabilities, even after controlling for many other variables, such as structural opportunity and socio-demographic effects (Carroll 1992). Past tax experience and measures of tax duty are also associated (r 0.33).

Taxpayers in Argentina do not report a strong sense of moral obligation to be honest in filing their tax returns. The survey evidence, however, shows two dimensions of tax behavior. On the one hand, there is an implicit support of the system's legitimacy and a willingness to abide by the rules (the acceptance in principle of a social contract; see table 6.4); on the other hand, there is an extensive practice of tax noncompliance. Because neither country has a structural-legitimacy problem, tax evasion should be understood as a problem of free riding rather than anarchy. Argentines pay lip service to the tax contract but fail to abide by its rules, which enables, potentially, a coordinated solution to the collective problem (because Argentines do not reject or actively defy the legitimacy

23. The question was slightly changed from the U.S. standard surveys to adjust for wording and cultural interpretations.

of taxation). Though Argentina lacks the conditions for conditional co-operation, tax compliance in Argentina may be more attainable than in, say, Haiti, Nigeria, or Indonesia.

Social Norms and Sanctions

The violation of norms imposes costs (material or psychological) that are inversely related to the norms' legitimacy (Ullman-Margolit 1977). The standard costs of violating legal norms are fines, penalties, or even imprisonment, whereas the costs of violating social norms include guilt, shame, and social embarrassment. A measure of the latter can indirectly shed light on the legitimacy of norms and the ability of groups to inflict social costs on deviants.

The normative climates for taxpayer compliance in Argentina and Chile are remarkably different. In a 1998 survey in Chile, 79 percent of those surveyed agreed or strongly agreed with the sentence, "The lack of integrity among certain taxpayers is not an excuse for others to avoid paying taxes," and 72 percent believed that fellow Chileans were honest in filing their taxes (Mori 1998). Conversely, respondents in a 1994 survey in Argentina (Mora y Araujo 1994) were asked to choose between two sentences: (a) "There is no justification for not paying taxes"; or (b) "Sometimes there are reasons for not paying taxes." Only 27 percent chose (a), while 73 percent chose (b). In another question, respondents were presented with the following situation: "Suppose that one of your friends has proof that someone is evading taxes and asks you for advice. Would you recommend that he/she report this tax evader to the authorities?" Only 47 percent of valid responses were affirmative.

In surveys 1 and 6, I replicated, with minimal adjustments, questions from surveys administered in the United States about guilt and social sanctions. Respondents in Argentina and Chile were asked how likely they would be to feel a sense of guilt if they misreported their taxes carelessly or deliberately. Table 6.7 reports the results. Although in Argentina the population was fairly evenly divided, in Chile the projected sense of guilt in both cases was much higher. In Argentina, less than 40 percent reported that they would feel a sense of guilt for deliberately under-reporting taxes, whereas in Chile 74 percent reported that they would feel a sense of guilt.

In addition, respondents were asked to estimate the social sanctions associated with tax noncompliance: would they likely feel socially condemned if it became known that they had intentionally underreported

TABLE 6.7 Feelings of Guilt for Underreporting Taxes

	Deliberate		Careless	
	Argentina	Chile	Argentina	Chile
Very Much	16%	37%	10%	25%
Quite a Bit	23%	37%	20%	42%
Some	24%	15%	22%	15%
Little	21%	5%	22%	9%
None	16%	4%	26%	6%

SOURCES: Surveys 1 and 6.

NOTE: Questions: "(a) I would like you to imagine yourself in a situation in which you had deliberately not paid the taxes prescribed by law. How likely is it you will feel guilt [in Spanish, for Argentina, the words used were *cargo de culpa*] for not abiding by the tax law in its entirety? (b) I would like you to imagine yourself in a situation in which you had carelessly not paid the taxes prescribed by law. How likely is it you will feel guilt for not abiding by the tax law in its entirety?" Valid n for Argentina = 523, for Chile = 511.

their tax dues? As table 6.8 indicates, in Argentina respondents reported that there is no social sanction for tax evasion: tax cheating is widely accepted, and therefore social sanctions have a very limited effect in inhibiting tax evasion. In Chile, social sanctions are reported to be much higher. Only 24 percent of Chileans reported that they would feel no social sanction as a result of tax evasion. This response has important consequences for horizontal enforcement. Where the norm is widely upheld and social sanction is high, people are willing to incur the costs of making others comply. Thus we may conclude that horizontal enforcement of tax abidance, at least potentially, is much stronger in Chile.

Summary

Although tax compliance itself is not a social norm, trust and fairness are, and breaching them is a serious violation of the social contract. Informal mechanisms of horizontal enforcement are effective to the extent that they can produce feelings of shame and guilt. The cost of breaking norms is measured by the subjective feeling of being shunned or ostracized by the group. Social sanctions for tax noncompliance are weak in Argentina but very strong in Chile; most taxpayers in Argentina do not feel as socially compelled to abide by the tax laws as do taxpayers in Chile.

This section presented cross-sectional data in support of the strong association between compliance and social norms. Trust, fairness, and reciprocity are necessary for conditional cooperation to evolve. A compliance equilibrium has the virtuous effect of fostering norms that allow for the cultural transmission of an initial predisposition to comply. These

TABLE 6.8 Perceived Likelihood of Social Sanctions for Cheating on Taxes

	Argentina	Chile
Very Likely	4%	32%
Quite Likely	6%	17%
Likely	11%	25%
Unlikely	30%	9%
Very Unlikely	49%	15%

SOURCE: Surveys 1 and 6.

NOTE: Question: "What is the likelihood that you will lose the respect of people you know or who are important to you [in Spanish: *pierdan el respeto*] if they find out that you have cheated on your taxes?" Valid n for Argentina = 523, for Chile =504.

attributes, however, are grounded in individual perceptions of the likelihood that contracts will be upheld, that cheaters will be punished, and that the state will abide by its commitments. Therefore, fostering a culture of compliance requires at some early stage the successful enforcement of emerging norms.

COMPLIANCE AND PUBLIC GOODS:
A MULTIVARIATE COMPARATIVE ANALYSIS

Thus far, I have presented descriptive statistics in order to depict trends and individual perceptions in the tax field in Chile and Argentina. In this section, I control for various effects in my analysis of the survey data to measure the magnitude of these effects on compliance. Using a survey of 1,200 respondents conducted in Chile in 1998 (Mori 1998) and survey 1 from Argentina, I am able to empirically compare the relationships among taxpayer behavior, individual perceptions, and satisfaction with social policy in Argentina and Chile. This comparison is critical for testing propositions about exchange equity, fairness, and reciprocity in taxation for both countries. I trace the attitudinal and normative dimensions of taxpayers in an attempt to determine how satisfaction with social policy affects willingness to comply with the law.

Because the questionnaire and designs for surveys 1 and 5 are not identical, the comparison is based on a country-by-country assessment of the data. In both surveys, respondents were randomly selected from the tax administration's active taxpayer register. Given the differences in survey administration, what I test is the *reported willingness of taxpayers to comply with tax law in order to fund social policies*. In other words, respondents were asked to react to statements about how much they are willing to pay in taxes (or comply with current tax laws) to fund social programs. As stated in the previous section, conditional cooperators might overcome resistance to redistribution when they share common goals and believe that their contributions help make a world more valuable than one without public goods.

The dependent variable for Chile is the response to the statement, "I am ready to pay more taxes if they will be channeled to benefit the poor" (DVCHILE, 1 = totally disagree, 4 = totally agree; mean = 2.96). No identical question was asked in Argentina; however, the level of agreement with the statement, "I consider it a duty to comply with my taxes in order to fund social programs" serves as a proxy (DVARGEN, 1 = totally agree, 5 = totally disagree; mean = 2.57). Independent variables were selected from the surveys and tax-administration information (size of firm, number of employees, etc.). Based on demographics and attitudinal questions, new variables were constructed. I then estimated an OLS (ordinary least squares) multiple regression model for each country.

According to contingent-consent theory, trust in institutions and perceptions of the fairness of the system affect the commitment to comply. On the other hand, deterrence theory states that reported willingness to comply will greatly depend on perceptions of the likelihood of detection and sanctions—that is, in the case of taxation, interaction with the tax administration and personal assessments of the chances of getting caught are tied to individuals' decisions about whether to comply. To test these two theories, the models include measures of deterrence as well as legitimacy and trust, along with demographic controls. Inhibitors of norm violations, such as social sanctions, guilt, and shame, are included only for Argentina.

Results

Table 6.9 presents the results of a regression model used to determine reported willingness to increase the personal tax burden to alleviate poverty. I found that in Chile, attitudes and opinions about honesty correlate with the dependent variable. Rendering support to the theory of conditional cooperation and the horizontal tax-equity proposition, the analysis indicates that the more taxpayers believe in the honesty of others, the greater will be their willingness to increase their own tax share. The stronger they disapprove of cheating under any circumstances, the greater their readiness to pay more. These coefficients are significant at p = .05.

TABLE 6.9 Determinants on Reported Willingness to Increase the Tax Burden in Chile (OLS)

	B	Std. Error	t(p)
Constant	3.50	.247	14.23 (.000)
Attitudes			
Honesty	0.079	.046	1.718 (.086)
Justification to Cheat (a)	−.130	.032	−4.045 (.000)
Justification to Cheat (b)	−0.086	.032	−2.668 (.008)
Integrity	−.143	.037	−3.903 (.000)
Public Service			
Efficiency (Dummy)	.162	.075	2.165 (.031)
Trust and Approval (Factor)	−.163	.032	−5.052 (.000)
Recipient of Health Service (Dummy)	0.080	.066	1.216 (.224)
Personal Taxation			
Evasion Difficulty	−0.060	.029	−2.022 (.044)
Perception of Detection	−0.036	.042	−.847 (.398)
Recently Audited (Dummy)	.188	.059	3.192 (.001)
Tax Burden	0.084	.041	2.050 (.041)
Evaluation of Tax Administration	−0.056	.040	−1.390 (.165)
Demographics			
Age	−0.051	.024	−2.098 (.042)
Male (Dummy)	.131	.066	1.968 (.049)

SOURCE: Mori 1998 (P values in parentheses).

NOTE: R^2 = 0.127, adjusted R^2 = 0.11, standard error of the estimate = .75, n = 703.

The most robust finding, however, is the strong association between trust in government and satisfaction with DVCHILE. Trust has been factorized from ten questions about respondents' opinion of ten public offices. As predicted by legitimacy and consent theory, trust in public offices and satisfaction with their performance is associated with reported willingness to pay. Conversely, a dummy variable that identifies recipients of benefits from public health institutions shows no impact on reporting behavior.[24]

Information about personal contacts with SII and estimations of risk and detection are mixed. A dummy variable for those who had been audited in the past five years has the most significant coefficient, showing that those who have been audited are more willing than the group as a whole to increase their tax burden. This is intriguing because taxpayers are selected for audits on the basis of suspicion of tax evasion: why

24. Unfortunately, no other services related to social rights were included in the questionnaire.

should potential tax cheaters report higher levels of commitment after being audited? Two other results show that subjective estimations of the difficulties of tax evasion are moderately associated with a diminished willingness to pay, and Chilean perceptions of their own tax burden moderately affect readiness to increase tax dues. Contradicting, in part, the propositions of deterrence theory, the regression found no effect related to the survey respondents' subjective estimates of sii's detection capacity. On the other hand, males and younger taxpayers are more likely to agree to pay more; these coefficients are only marginally significant, however, at a 0.05 level.

The model for Chile, then, supports an association between individuals' perceptions of the legitimacy of taxation and their commitment to alleviate poverty through taxation. It presents mixed results for other controls, such as gender and age. The tax agency's effectiveness does not affect individuals' decisions to pay more; having contact with sii, however, correlates with the highest willingness to increase the tax burden.

Table 6.10 presents the results of a regression model measuring willingness to comply with tax laws in Argentina. Satisfaction has been factorized from four variables related to satisfaction with education, public services, public security, and health. Tolerance of evasion is also a factor extracted from five questions on how acceptable respondents perceived certain illegal transactions to be. Finally, a third factor, detection, is extracted from several measures of responses regarding the likelihood that tax fraud will be detected.[25] Age has been coded in ranges. Because measures of income were unavailable, I report the number of employees as a proxy. In addition, for Argentina, questions about social sanctions and guilt were asked and included in the model.

In comparison to Chile, the goodness of fit for the Argentine model is higher. The first model, which excludes the unmeasured variables in Chile, also fits well, and all relevant coefficients remain statistically significant. Although many attitudinal variables were included, no severe collinearity was found.[26] The results demonstrate that satisfaction with public service has a strong positive effect on willingness to comply with tax law in Argentina. Tolerance is also strongly associated with the expected inverse direction: the greater the willingness to comply, the lower the tolerance for tax evasion. On the other hand, as in Chile, perceptions of the likelihood of tax fraud being detected do not affect the reported readiness to comply. Age also has an effect, as younger taxpayers are less

25. All factors have been rotated (Varimax) and standardized for regression analysis.
26. None of the independent variables' bivariate correlations exceeded 0.20.

TABLE 6.10 OLS Regression for the Effects of Attitudes and Tax Experience
in Argentina, Controlled for Age and Gender

	Model 1			Model 2		
	B	Std. Error	t (p)	B	Std. Error	t (p)
Constant	3.462	.257	13.48 (.000)	1.900	.330	5.93 (.000)
Satisfaction (Factor)	.186	.055	3.40 (.001)	.173	.052	3.32 (.001)
Tolerance (Factor)	−.349	.055	−6.39 (.000)	−.211	.054	−3.91 (.000)
Audited (Dummy)	−.079	.119	−.66 (.509)	−.030	.112	−.24 (.808)
Detection (Factor)	.086	.056	1.54 (.123)	.030	.054	.59 (.555)
No. of Employees	−.126	.074	−1.70 (.091)	−.164	.071	−2.32 .(021)
Age	−.256	.071	−3.58 (.000)	−.234	.067	−3.47 (.001)
Male (Dummy)	.190	.139	1.37 (.170)	.175	.130	1.34 (.179)
Guilt				.289	.044	6.61 (.000)
Social Sanction				.144	.053	2.72 (.007)

SOURCE: Survey 1 (P values in parentheses).
NOTE: Model 1: R^2 = 0.145, adjusted R^2 = 0.132, standard error of the estimate = 1.16,
n = 468. Model 2: R^2 = 0.260, adjusted R^2 = 0.245, std. error estimate = 1.08, n = 457.

willing to contribute. Guilt and social sanctions exercise the most significant effects on reported willingness to comply. Consistent with similar
findings in the field (Grasmick and Bursik 1990; Kinsey, Grasmick, and
Smith 1991), measures of social and inner morality have a positive effect
on support for the idea of contributing tax monies for social solidarity. In
fact, for Argentina, the lack of a social norm in favor of tax compliance,
and consequently the lack of guilt experienced as a result of violating tax
laws, partly explains the low reported willingness to comply.

Discussion

Similar surveys in two countries measure different social approaches to
compliance and social commitment to citizenship. Chile differs from Argentina not only in its compliance rate but also in the population's reported
willingness to abide by the rules. Measures of social solidarity are stronger
in Chile than in Argentina.

Both models found a strong association between satisfaction with
public institutions and willingness to comply with tax law or even to
increase the individual tax share. In fact, for Argentina the results can
be interpreted inversely: it is the lack of satisfaction and the low trust in
public institutions that largely explain the low levels of solidarity. Social
enforcement of upheld norms is very weak; therefore, guilt and shame do

not operate as inhibitors of law violation. In Chile, confidence in public institutions generates public trust in the agencies' capacity for fostering social solidarity. A larger commitment to alleviating poverty is then enhanced by a feeling of trust.

Demographic controls are weakly correlated to social solidarity. Age appears to be more closely associated with commitments to comply, but gender unexpectedly was not found to be significant.[27] The measure for income is weak, and the data does not allow for a definite answer. Measures of personal tax history and perception of detection and sanctions appear to have little effect on social commitments to foster citizenship. Results for Chile are mixed and signal that being audited contributes to a higher willingness to comply, which rejects the alternative hypothesis that it is precisely the noncompliant taxpayers who are less likely to report higher solidarity. Other results are not sufficiently robust to draw firm conclusions.

For both countries, measures of deterrence were not correlated with the variables for trust, social sanction, or satisfaction.[28] This indicates that willingness to comply is not biased by the subjective perception of the likelihood of detection. In short, the perception of institutional performance is not associated with and does not influence the perceived detection capabilities of tax administrations, thereby giving the contingent-consent theory an independent effect.

This analysis proves that trust and perceptions of institutional performance are among the most consistent variables that explain reported commitment to comply with tax law. Social norms of solidarity and sentiments of guilt and shame are effective inhibitors of free-riding behavior. In societies where these inhibitors are weak, compliance will also be weaker. It would be misleading, however, to assume that subjective perceptions of detection and sanction are ineffective in enhancing compliance. This model only studies taxpayers' reported willingness to comply; it does not test taxpayers' actual compliance behavior. Although many studies have found a causal link among beliefs, values, and tax abidance,

---

27. This finding is intriguing. Men in Chile tend to be willing to pay more for fighting poverty than are women. This is perhaps explained by the sampling characteristics. Women were almost exclusively drawn from managerial positions in large companies (and thus tended to be very young and career-oriented), whereas men were more representative of the entire population. Thus, some validity concerns require additional tests to draw firm conclusions about this finding. In Argentina, however, where the sample is more representative, the trend is in the expected direction (i.e., males feel less duty to pay for the sake of social solidarity), although the coefficient is not statistically significant.

28. No correlation was higher than 0.11.

there is substantial evidence that without an effective tax administration, tax compliance diminishes substantially. This study proves that social variables have an additional effect on conformity to rules.

SUMMARY

This chapter has shown that the perverse effect of unfairness and lack of trust in Argentina inhibits the emergence of cooperative solutions and enhances motivations for tax evasion, whereas trust in governance in Chile correlates with better compliance. In this chapter, I have described an association between the normative and cultural dimensions of collective attitudes and the level of tax compliance, and I have shown how different legal cultures in Argentina and Chile affect the dispositions of taxpayers to comply. The next chapter will integrate these dimensions into a single model of compliance. There is more than a simple correlation, I will argue, between weak enforcement and cooperation with tax law: weak enforcement ultimately fosters the culture of "dodging the system," whereas strong enforcement facilitates the emergence of conditional cooperation.

7

SOCIAL MECHANISMS IN TAX EVASION
AND TAX COMPLIANCE

This chapter integrates the previous chapter's discussion of social values and norms into a dynamic model of compliance that includes monetary utilities, as well as imitation and contagion effects, into the calculus of how people make tax decisions. Relying on the results of an experimental study conducted in both Chile and Argentina, I examine the mechanisms that shape the social construction of perceptions, and I show that taxpayers make decisions in a milieu that constrains their choices. The cultural embeddedness of their decisions must be incorporated into rational-choice theory to successfully account for divergences in compliance behavior.

The goal of this chapter is less to draw out the Chile and Argentina contrast than to uncover the general logic of decision making in tax compliance. The experimental study described here centers around social mechanisms in simulated situations rather than on the effects of the social environment of both countries on taxpayers' decisions (studied in chapters 3–6). In the following pages, I hope to demonstrate not only that the environment influences taxpayers but also to make evident *how* their environment influences them.

I have stated throughout the book that although taxpayers abide by the rules because they are afraid of punishment, they do not optimize every single decision they make. What remains to be explored is the process by which taxpayers *do* make decisions. How do legalist or non-compliant environments emerge and develop? Does lack of enforcement foster a cheating culture, or is it the other way around? Is enforcement effective because it thrives in a legalist culture, or is the credible threat of the state what shapes norms and values of law abidance? To address these questions and test them empirically, there is a need for longitudinal rather than cross-sectional data. The lack of longitudinal survey and official return information makes it impossible to test the questions in a conventional way. Therefore, I conducted a quasi-experiment wherein I replicated tax behavior at different rounds in an attempt to observe variation in individual behavior over time.[1] This experiment illustrates how early enforcement shapes a compliance culture and how imitation and reliance on social norms affect compliance behavior. These results contribute to the analysis of tax compliance decision making by providing a set of causal mechanisms that link cost-benefit analysis to the ecology of taxation.

I begin by briefly justifying, from a theoretical perspective, the inclusion of ecological factors in studies of tax compliance decision making. In the second part of the chapter, I explain the experiment, present the results, and discuss the findings.

HOW DO TAXPAYERS MAKE COMPLIANCE DECISIONS?

Rational taxpayers adjust their behavior according to their personal tax history and changes in the environment; therefore, decisions about tax compliance are strongly influenced by the payoffs of previous tax decisions. We have seen that enforcement does not have a linear effect on compliance. Under compliance environments, strict enforcement appears to yield good general-deterrence but only moderate specific-deterrence effects, whereas poor enforcement yields, in the long run, minimal compliance. Yet taxpayers will play the assurance game if they believe that others will fulfill their respective commitments. The dominant strategy is cooperation because there are shared norms and values regarding mutual behavior. To meet the basic conditions of assurance games, the players must share beliefs regarding the conditions of reciprocity. The effect of enforcement is therefore cumbersome. It is absolutely necessary to foster a culture that facilitates general tax compliance, but enforcement has only a cumulative and incremental effect; people must first trust that everybody else is cooperating before they decide to cooperate themselves.

Cheating and the pursuit of self-interest in taxation can only be reversed if at least one of the following two conditions is met: (1) taxpayers estimate that the likelihood of punishment is very high, and (2) the costs of cheating exceed the benefits. Agents cooperate on the basis of a mutual beneficial recognition of such cooperation (the warranty-game

1. As will be explained later, this was a quasi-experiment in the classical sense, because participants were not randomly selected; rather, they participated voluntarily in response to several incentives. Thus, they were to some extent self-selected, and therefore, assignments to groups were not entirely randomized. In this chapter, I will use the term "experiment" with this self-selection in mind.

TABLE 7.1A Satisfaction with the Use of Public Funds

	Argentina	Chile
Very Satisfied/Somewhat Satisfied	8%	48%
Somewhat Dissatisfied/Very Dissatisfied	92%	52%

SOURCES: Surveys 1 and 6. Estimated based on satisfaction of public services on responses for three questions in Argentina and four in Chile (see table 2.3).
NOTE: See also regression table 6.8 for analysis of these variables on reported commitment to comply. Valid n for Argentina = 451, for Chile = 431.

assumptions). The first condition is straightforward: tax enforcement must be able to negate free-riding incentives. But cooperation also requires individuals to be disposed to enter into social exchanges. Motivations to cheat are not simply temporal preferences; they are deeply rooted in learning experiences, both individual and social, adopted through a set of ideas that bias subjective estimations. How beliefs and social imagery are formed is crucial to the mechanisms that agents rely on to process information, and thus are crucial to the way that players frame and choose tax alternatives.

Tables 7.1A and 7.1B display basic data showing the remarkable differences in how Chileans and Argentines feel about the use of public resources. Chileans tend to be more satisfied than Argentines regarding the public goods provided by the state, and they trust their government more regarding the use of public resources. The underlying assumption that governs this proposition is the horizontal tax-equity principle: people cooperate if they believe that the net gain from their cooperation increases social welfare (see also Scholz and Lubell 1998). The experimental data supports the assertion that taxpayers may find compliance somewhat rewarding if it contributes to the general welfare.

I have stated that social norms are behavior regularities backed by force. They facilitate cooperation among players by providing a common language to participants in large games. When a player only sees aggregate behavior (as in collective-action situations), social norms emerge as a viable tool to teach the collective's expectations for behavior. The more that a taxpayer knows about tax evasion, the more likely that person is to engage in the practice. Argentines' belief that many other taxpayers engage in tax evasion correlates with a very low level of social sanction for the practice. Conversely, in Chile, tax evasion is perceived as more circumscribed, and social sanctions of the practice are higher. In the United States, where social sanctions for tax evasion are also high (Kinsey 1992; Grasmick and Bursik 1990), taxpayers report knowing fewer tax evaders,

TABLE 7.1B Perceptions of Good Use of Tax Revenues

	Argentina	Chile
Strongly Agree	1%	6%
Agree	18%	41%
Disagree	46%	45%
Strongly Disagree	35%	8%

SOURCES: Surveys 1 and 6.

NOTE: Question: "The government uses tax revenues to aid [*ayudar*] needier people." In the United States, only 16 percent disagree or strongly disagree with a similar statement (Harris 1987). Valid n for Argentina = 497, for Chile = 504.

which means a larger social stigma for evasion (Elster 1989). The extent of tax evasion correlates with the strength of norms that facilitate tax compliance. In Argentina, the majority of respondents said that they know many tax evaders, but they refuse to provide information about these people to the authorities; further, they report greater willingness than Chilean respondents to engage in noncompliance themselves. This implies that their strong motivation to evade taxes is grounded in shared beliefs.[2]

The experiment conducted for this chapter tests the effects of the norm of reciprocity on compliance. As shown in table 6.10, the strong association in Argentina between diminished tax compliance and the poor quality of social goods provides partial support for the reciprocity norm. If cooperation requires conditional behavior, it is significant that many taxpayers in Argentina believe that the quality of services provided by the state is poor. This perception does not enhance their willingness to reciprocate. In this chapter's experiment, I examine the conditions under which reciprocity is attained. The underlying assumption is that the norm of fairness is generated by the willingness of individuals to cooperate so long as everybody else (or at least most other people) will engage in similar behavior. This assumption is the bedrock of collective action. Individual defection in situations of universal cooperation might generate a powerful dissonance that compels a free rider to reconsider strategies. The norm of fairness dictates that an individual should follow the collective. Therefore, the erosion of cooperation will rapidly convince an ever-greater number of individuals to defect. Taxpayers will reciprocate with superior compliance, on the other hand, if they believe that the system is fair.

2. Individuals may also learn from government messages that tax evasion is the rule rather than the exception. The more the authorities appeal to morality or civic duty, the more citizens might believe that the effects of norms are vanishing. Therefore, and paradoxically, campaigns to increase compliance may have the opposite effect, because people are more likely to evade paying taxes if they believe many others already do so.

Over the last decade, a growing body of empirical and laboratory research has emerged that studies the dispositions of individuals to reciprocate.[3] Most research shows that people are willing to contribute a share of their endowments for the provision of public goods, but they will reduce future contributions if they believe that the outcome of previous rounds did not warrant those contributions. Contextual factors, communication, and the possibilities of horizontal sanctions affect the level of personal contributions; the longer the period of interaction and the better the perceived honesty of other players, however, the more likely individuals will be to cooperate. The results of the experiment on tax compliance are consistent with this proposition.

Contagion, Imitation, Public Goods, and Enforcement

Imitation, contagion, and epidemic models are abundant in the economic, political, and psychological literature. Surprisingly, very few studies have analyzed these social effects in tax compliance behavior. Since the 1990s, three new studies have tested hypotheses about reciprocity and contagion in taxation. A study conducted by the Australian tax authority has found that taxpayers who were informed about the honesty of others' tax reporting tended to improve their own compliance (Wenzel 2001). Similarly, the Minnesota Department of Revenue sent letters to a random sample of taxpayers stating that the compliance rate with state taxes was at 93 percent; they found that this group of taxpayers subsequently showed modest improvements in compliance (Coleman 1996). Finally, Davis, Hecht, and Perkins (2003) have developed a theoretical model using epidemic logic to explain the convergence of equilibria based on the effect of observing others' behavior. Despite the scant research, I contend that the study of the social effects of imitation, contagion, and epidemic mechanisms could be very fruitful in helping us to unpack the more established and contested assertions about the role of norms in tax compliance.

Contagion and adaptation are rational behaviors. The individual observation of successful past choices, either of one's own or of others, are considered superior choices for given decisions and therefore encourage rational imitation (Hedstrom 1998). People frame tax decisions by imitating collective outcomes, by reciprocating perceived fair treatment, and by accounting for prior experiences. A compliance equilibrium mitigates

---

3. See Davis and Holt 1993 and Ostrom 2000 for a summary of the findings.

individual free-rider or egotistic motivations, whereas a noncompliance equilibrium accelerates and promotes them.

This chapter's experiment tested three mechanisms of compliance behavior: the imitation effect, reciprocity and fairness regarding public goods, and the way that taxpayers overweigh low probabilities of detection.[4] I show how taxpayers adjust their decisions about tax compliance based on the impact of these mechanisms.

Experimental Design

To overcome the limitations of studying tax compliance with cross-sectional data, I developed in appendix C a sequenced simulation, and in chapter 5 I analyzed tax-filing information from periods before and after enforcement actions were taken against taxpayers. These research designs, however, cannot test properly either the individual intentions and motivations of taxpayers or the direct effect of social messages. Therefore, I developed an experimental study that measures compliance over time by manipulating some of these exogenous variables.

Student-subjects of two leading universities in Santiago and Buenos Aires were invited to participate in the study. A total of 262 students (half from each country) attended a thirty-minute session of a game in which they had to make simulated tax decisions. Participation was strictly voluntary, and the experiment was conducted at computer labs at University of Chile and Di Telle University. I conducted sixteen sessions with thirteen to twenty students each. Students read a two-page set of instructions about the game, asked questions to clarify any points about which they were unclear, and then participated in a three-round practice session. Participants were unable to observe other students' decisions.

The experiment consisted of individual voluntary reports of income on which subjects had to pay 30 percent in taxes. Every round, each

4. Even though taxpayers face low odds of detection, they do not adjust based on the objective probabilities of sanction but rather on the perceived enforcement capacities of the tax administration. Thus, they overweigh the probabilities of detection. This overweighing process is greatly enhanced by the effectiveness of previous enforcement. Prior effective controls and audits have a multiplying effect on future compliance, irrespective of the current enforcement capabilities of the state. As will be explained, this is predicted by prospect theory. Here, I describe a mechanism for how this frame is adopted by taxpayers.

participant received an income (expressed in tokens) and paid taxes only on the amount that he or she decided to report. No taxes were paid on non-reported income; a fine was imposed if non-reported income was detected, however, based on a fixed, random audit probability. For example, if income in round n was fifteen tokens and the participant reported ten (for which he or she paid three tokens in taxes), had he or she been randomly selected for audit the non-reported five tokens would have been automatically detected, and penalties and fines would have been applied. There were twenty-seven rounds, but students did not know in advance how many rounds they would be playing. Subjects accumulated virtual tokens and were informed at the end of every round of their net income and the total from previous rounds. At the end of the session, the accumulated tokens were converted at a rate that the students had been told about in advance (it varied slightly for Chile and Argentina based on the exchange rate). On the average, students earned US$10, although their earnings ranged between US$4 and US$16 based on individual performance.

At the beginning of each round, the computer terminals showed a predetermined amount of income (between eight and fifteen tokens). Students had thirty seconds to decide how much of that amount they wished to report. After their decisions were made, the tax was imposed only on the fraction of income that had been reported, and 30 percent of that amount was automatically deducted. In addition, a fixed "participation fee" of three tokens per round was also "charged." At the end of each round, subjects were informed whether they had been selected for audit. In that case, the program also automatically fined noncompliant players the tax for the undeclared portion of the income plus twice that amount. In addition, audits that found tax evasion automatically triggered a review of the two previous rounds and imposed the same sanction rate for underreporting in those rounds.

There were four different types of games. Each game or session had slight differences but kept the same structure: students received roughly the same income, had the same decision time, and so forth. Students did not know what type of game they were playing. In some of the games, each player received messages between rounds regarding compliance rates for the group or about the reimbursement of additional tokens as a reward for the group's supposedly high level of compliance (see table 7.2).

The structure of such games has been tested in several experiments (Alm, Jackson, and McKee 1992; Alm, Sanchez, and de Juan 1995), yielding important lessons regarding the effect of tax rates and sanctions.

TABLE 7.2 Experimental Design

Type of Session	Audit Probability			Compliance Messages			Public Goods		
Control	12%			—			5T	9T	7T***
							22	24	26****
Contagion A**	12%			87%	85%	86%	5T	9T	7T***
				5	10	15	22	24	26****
Contagion B**	12%			55%	53%	54%	5T	9T	7T***
				5	10	15	22	24	26****
High Audit	25%	18%	12%				5T	9T	7T***
	(1–9)	(10–18)	(19–27)*				22	24	26****

*Probability rate applied in these rounds (e.g., 25 percent in rounds 1–9).
**Messages provided after the stated round.
***Number of tokens provided.
****Round in which those tokens were provided.

Therefore, I did not test tax rates or optimal sanctions. I made significant changes to address different audit probabilities, particularly the effect of norms, culture, and contagious effects, as well as the provision of public goods, and I included four variations of the game: a first control group, two contagion groups (A and B), and a fourth group ("high audit"), which faced higher probabilities of being audited. Table 7.2 summarizes the parameters of each game.

Audit Rates

Most players had a one-in-eight chance of being selected for audit in each round. I estimated the audit rate at 12 percent because it represented the best equilibrium point at which there was no dominant strategy for risk-neutral individuals. In the "high-audit" sessions, the probability of being audited in each round began much higher but declined to 12 percent in the last nine rounds. Most players faced three to four audits throughout the game, although the players in the "high-audit" group had a 25 percent chance of being audited in each of the first nine rounds.

Fines

The evidence of previous experiments has shown that fine rates affect compliance: the higher the fine, the better the compliance (Alm, Sanchez, and de Juan 1995). This study did not evaluate the impact of various fine rates. I adopted a flexible yet realistic approach. Instead of fixing a given fine, students were informed in the instructions that audits detecting unreported income would tax that income at the regular rate (30 percent) and impose a fine of twice that amount. They were also audited for two previous rounds when noncompliance was detected, resembling the actual behavior of tax administrations. In this way, taxpayers were rewarded for current compliance and heavily sanctioned for enduring evasion.

Public Goods

I introduced a new mechanism to study the effect of satisfaction with governmental performance: the reimbursement of excess taxes.[5] In the four sessions, I introduced a legend after rounds 22, 24, and 26 saying, "Due to larger compliance and excess of revenues, some of the contributions are reimbursed and distributed among participants. You are due [seven, nine, or five tokens, according to the round]." The study tested the individual level of compliance in subsequent rounds compared to the individual compliance trend of previous rounds.

Imitation Effects

In two sessions (A and B), subjects were presented with the following legend after rounds 5, 10, and 15: "The average compliance for this group has been X." (In table 7.2, the different rates are specified according to the given session, A or B.) All rates were fictitious, but subjects did not have any way to corroborate or deny the information. There were two types of simulated compliance: highly compliant groups (contagion A) and less-compliant groups (contagion B).

Results

The compliance rate for each subject was measured as the proportion of individual income reported in each round with respect to the given income for that particular round. (For example, if the income was twelve tokens and the subject reported nine tokens of income, the subject's compliance rate was 75 percent.) Tables 7.3A and 7.3B present the aggregate compliance results for the two countries. Compliance was slightly higher in Chile, but not as significantly higher as it is in the real world. Gender, consistent with propositions of crime theory, had a stronger impact on

5. Although tax reimbursement is common in the United States and European nations, it is a novel concept in Chile and Argentina, where most taxpayers never get refunds for paid taxes. By returning excess payments to taxpayers, I tested their willingness to reciprocate with future accurate tax reports. Instead of telling them about the public goods that their tax money paid for, in other words, I tested the reciprocity that resulted when actual money was given back to the taxpayer.

TABLE 7.3A Aggregate Compliance Rate by Session

| | Gender | Country | | General Compliance |
		Argentina	Chile	
Contagion A	Male	0.57	0.64	
	Female	0.65	0.59	
				0.61
Contagion B	Male	0.52	0.57	
	Female	0.62	0.65	
				0.59
Control	Male	0.53	0.55	
	Female	0.48	0.58	
				0.53
High Audit	Male	0.58	0.60	
	Female	0.72	0.68	
				0.66

TABLE 7.3B Average Aggregate Compliance Rate by Gender and Country

	Male	Female	Total
Argentina	0.55	0.63	0.58
Chile	0.59	0.64	0.61
Total	0.57	0.63	0.59

compliance than did nationality.[6] Aggregate differences among the sessions were moderate, but the subjects in "high-audit" sessions were more compliant than those in the other sessions due to the higher probability that they would be audited. All treatment sessions (the contagion A, contagion B, and "high-audit" sessions) exhibited higher average compliance than sessions in the control groups.

That average compliance rates in the experiment were similar for Chile and Argentina should not be interpreted as a rejection of my hypothesis, because this experiment does not directly test the compliance cultures in both countries. I expected to find similar compliance rates, because experimental designs are more sensitive to the administration of the experiment than to the broader social environment of each nation. In other words, a country's general culture and social values that are not directly tested in experiments have only a small residual effect (and indeed, this residual effect is apparent in the better aggregate compliance of Chileans). As the literature suggests, hypotheses in experimental designs should be tested by directly manipulating the targeted variables. My study does

6. There is a large literature on the more "controlled" behavior of women in upholding legal and prescribed behavior.

not manipulate variables for Chilean or Argentine culture; it looks only at individual responses to specific messages, to audit and sanction probabilities, and so on. Therefore, to test for the effect of shared values, I introduced a particular measure of contagion effect.

Contagion

Tables 7.4A and 7.4B present some relevant results. I found that the stated average or aggregate compliance level distorted individual compliance decisions, particularly after treatment effects. In order to test for such effects, I estimated the individual average compliance rate for the previous three rounds before treatment was introduced (rounds 10 and 15) and compared that rate to the individual compliance rate after treatment. To the extent that a decrease or increase in compliance is noticeable, the cases were counted as "improving" or "worsening" in their compliance. For contagion A, the threshold was established at 70 percent, and for contagion B it was 54 percent (the average compliance stated in the legend). I excluded both the fully compliant taxpayers (those above 95 percent compliant) and the fully noncompliant (those who were less than 5 percent compliant).[7]

The students who were not subject to treatment followed a random distribution: that is, when no messages or information about compliance for the group were provided, the taxpayers tended to improve or reduce compliance randomly. Contagion A showed a larger reduction in the compliance rate because the cutoff was set at 70 percent compliance, meaning that the random probabilities of becoming less than 70 percent compliant were more than twice the probabilities of becoming more than 70 percent compliant. In the case of contagion B, the distribution of the control group was 50 percent. (The cutoff was 54 percent, meaning that there were almost the same probabilities of improving or reducing compliance.)

When the threshold of compliance was high (contagion A), the results from the treatment group were not very different from those of the control group. Students who were not subject to messages changed their compliance randomly: approximately 50 percent of those who did not comply

---

7. There are several reasons for this. First, I suspect that 100 percent and 0 percent compliance decisions are the result of purely strategic approaches to the game and were not affected by treatment. Second, cases of full compliance and full noncompliance balanced out. Third, these cases are insensitive to administration. Fourth, and perhaps most important, in the real world most taxpayers are neither fully 100 percent compliant nor fully 0 percent compliant.

TABLE 7.4A Number of Previously High-Compliance Taxpayers Who
Improved or Decreased Compliance at Rounds 11 and 16

| | Contagion A (High Compliance) | |
	Control	Treatment
Reduced Compliance	18 (35)	22 (44)
Improved Compliance	45 (89)	48 (83)

NOTE: Numbers in parentheses refer to the total number of observations for that category. For example, out of forty-four observations of the treatment group that had above 70 percent compliance, twenty-two observations reduced below 70 percent in the subsequent round. Out of eighty-three that had below 70 percent compliance, forty-eight improved above 70 percent after treatment.

TABLE 7.4B Number of Previously Low-Compliance Taxpayers Who
Improved or Decreased Compliance at Rounds 11 and 16

| | Contagion B (Low Compliance) | |
	Control	Treatment
Reduced Compliance	31	54
Improved Compliance	32	33

NOTE: Table covers taxpayers whose average compliance prior to treatment was above 54 percent.

at 70 percent shifted into higher compliance, and vice versa. In the treatment group for whom results are displayed in table 7.4A—that is, those who received the message about the compliance level of the group—58 percent of noncompliers improved their compliance, bringing it above 70 percent, and another 15 percent of the group improved their previous compliance rate by at least 10 percent. Although these results show that the messages had only moderate effects, it should be remembered that the compliance level was set to be high, as opposed to the level set for the contagion B group. Nonetheless, among those who were compliers before receiving the message, 72 percent kept their compliance above 70 percent, and only 26 percent who were noncompliers before treatment maintained the same level or a lower level of noncompliance afterward. Despite the fact that the results are only statistically significant to small degree (due to the small number of observations), the trend is clear: messages reporting the better tax compliance of others improve individuals' compliance levels.

The most significant results came from the treatment that exposed subjects to messages about the low compliance level of the larger group: the data shows that more people are sensitive to such messages than to messages about a group's good compliance. For example, whereas 49 percent of the control group in contagion B reduced their compliance in the given rounds, 63 percent of the treatment group became less compliant after learning of the noncompliance of others.[8] Using a binomial distribution, in both cases the independence of the message of compliance is rejected. The likelihood that these results would occur randomly is lower than 1 percent.

The experiment indicates that taxpayers are sensitive to messages about the environment. Many adjust their tax decisions to bring them in line with other taxpayers' behavior. Learning of other taxpayers' superior compliance (contagion A) led cheaters to improve their compliance (at least somewhat), whereas compliers who found out that most people cheat (contagion B) became less compliant. These results are statistically significant at a p level of < .05, even given the small number of cases. Although many participants kept their strategies the same regardless of the administration of the experiment, comparison of treatment groups to the control group shows that treatment had a sizeable effect. Particularly in the contagion B category, an adverse compliance environment affected individual decisions by reducing subsequent compliance rates. The higher that subjects were told that the general compliance rate was, the more likely cheaters were to improve their compliance. The lower the announced compliance rate, conversely, the less likely cheaters were to improve their compliance and the more likely compliers were to begin cheating—or to cheat more—on their taxes.

This study offers the first experimental evidence of imitation effects on tax compliance. Although precise estimation of the extent of these effects is beyond the scope of this book, the study suggests that the magnitude of contagion could be significant, particularly in low-compliance environments. The experiment shows that two out of three taxpayers decrease their compliance—becoming rational imitators—when they are given information that tax evasion is widespread in their environment.

Detection and Sanctions

Compliance rates improve as the detection of fraud becomes more likely. In the real world, under the best-case scenarios, audit rates never exceed 2 percent. Thus, audit rates of 25 percent, or even 12 percent, are highly unrealistic. The evidence of table 7.3A, however, shows the significant effect of increased probabilities of detection on the subjects' behavior. This

---

8. Only 12 percent of this treatment group improved their compliance by more than 10 percent, whereas 45 percent of the control group improved compliance by the same rate.

TABLE 7.5 Average Session Compliance and Audit Rate for Control and
High-Audit Groups

| | Compliance Average | |
Rounds	Control	High Audit
1–9	0.52 (12%)	0.61 (25%)
10–18	0.53 (12%)	0.64 (18%)
19–22	0.59 (12%)	0.67 (12%)
23–27	0.56 (12%)	0.65 (12%)
19–27	0.57 (12%)	0.65 (12%)
1–27	0.54	0.63

NOTE: Numbers in parentheses refer to the audit rate for those particular rounds.

finding is consistent with previous studies of tax compliance (Alm 1992; Andreoni, Erard, and Feinstein 1998). In addition, the experiment shows that stringent enforcement and sanctions explain a large share of compliance, controlling for the probability of audit selection.

Taxpayers who faced stringent enforcement in the past are prone, on average, to exhibit better compliance with taxes. Table 7.5 compares compliance rates of the high-audit and control groups. As the data shows, in the first nine rounds participants in the treatment groups were audited and sanctioned almost twice as often as those in the control group. But in rounds 19 through 27, the audit rate for the treatment groups dropped to be equal to that for the control group in those rounds. The average compliance rate of the high-audit group in rounds 20–27, however, was 14 percent higher than that of the control group, despite the fact that taxpayers faced similar probabilities of detection. As will be shown, the imposition of higher sanctions in previous rounds appears to have yielded higher compliance rates among those who had earlier been heavily punished, providing support to my hypothesis about the coevolution of enforcement and compliance.

These results indicate that early enforcement has a lasting effect. Participants who faced more than four audits complied better than those who faced fewer than three audits. These results are also statistically significant, signaling the long-lasting effect of detection and sanctions. Thus, perceptions of the likelihood of detection and sanction are controlled by the lagged effect of effective administration. That taxpayers believe enforcement is stringent is more important in their decision-making process than any calculations about the actual odds of selection for auditing. It should be remembered that in this experiment audits were by definition very efficient—that is, they detected all noncompliance—whereas in the real world this is hardly the case. More important, there was no impunity in the experiment, because each instance of noncompliance detected was heavily sanctioned.

Compliance averages of the subject groups do not depict a complete picture, however, because they do not account for individual variations. Some people are more deterred by audits and sanctions than others. The temporal proximity of audits might also exercise an effect on compliance: those who have recently been audited might behave differently than those who were audited in the distant past. Although a complete statistical analysis of individual trends is beyond the scope of this book, the regression table 7.6 summarizes the effect of audits and penalties on compliance in later rounds. The results of this regression analysis are very powerful: this model explains a large share of the variance (approximately half). Audits in previous rounds have a strong effect on individual compliance in later rounds, as do the size of penalties. Results are in the expected direction regarding audits (the more audits, the better the compliance) and fines (the higher the fines, the lower the compliance). A very important finding should be stressed: those who have been heavily sanctioned (subject to higher fines) were not as deterred as those who were moderately sanctioned. Due to the characteristics of this game, heavily sanctioned students who were persistent cheaters accumulated higher penalties and pulled the coefficient into the negative (the impact of the independent-variable evader). In other words, whereas enforcement convinced moderate cheaters to improve their compliance, it had the opposite effect on a minority of severe tax cheaters. This, of course, has strong implications for the study of cultural aspects in tax compliance. Enforcement might be effective on those prone to comply or in strong compliance environments, but it yields meager results in situations where cheating is the norm or cheaters are extremely risk-prone.

This model demonstrates that, even controlling for repeat tax evaders, the effect of continued enforcement lasts for many rounds: taxpayers who took enforcement seriously showed improvements in compliance, and those who were heavily fined tried to recuperate their losses by cheating more than they had previously. In short, good enforcement has a lasting effect, particularly among those who are disposed to comply with the law.

Public Goods

I tested measures of fairness and reciprocity by comparing previous rounds of compliance to the average compliance rate after reimbursement. Table 7.7 shows the aggregate level of compliance and the number of partici-

TABLE 7.6 OLS Regression for Individual Average Compliance in Rounds 23–27

	Coefficient	Standard Error	t
Audited 1–18	.058	.011	5.32
Recent Audit	−.065	.038	−1.71
Fine 1–18	−.004	.001	−3.96
Recent Fine	−.010	.002	−4.76
Evader	−.084	.071	−1.17
Male	.038	.040	0.95
Constant	.578	.045	12.64

NOTE: R^2 = 0.4995, adjusted R^2 = 0.4798, root MSE = .19467.

Variables:

Audited 1–18: Number of audits for rounds 1–18.

Recent Audit: Dummy variable for being audited in rounds 20–26; 1 = yes, 0 = no.

Fine 1–18: Total penalties (in tokens) for rounds 1–18.

Recent Fine: Total penalties (in tokens) for recent penalties.

Evader: A dummy to control for subjects who in rounds 1–18 had less than 15 percent average compliance.

Male: Dummy variable for gender; 1= male.

pants who showed improvements compared to previous rounds.[9] I report data for Argentina and Chile to show that similar results in both countries demonstrate that the direct manipulation of the norm of reciprocity is independent of country.

Because all participants were exposed to the public-good treatment, I compare in table 7.8 the increase or decrease of individual compliance after treatment (round 25 against rounds 22–24) with respect to rounds 16–19 (control), which had equal incomes. Based on a binomial distribution, the probability that the results of the treatment effect are random is less than 1 percent, given a random probability of 50 percent, as suggested from rounds 16–19. Therefore, the null hypothesis that public goods have no effect on compliance can be rejected. Even at an expected level of 55 percent improvement, the random probability is less than 3 percent. In short, reimbursement has a clear positive effect on compliance. Tangible goods, expressed in tokens, affected compliance in the expected direction. The number of taxpayers who improved compliance after treatment shows that this magnitude of change was not achieved in any other round. Results are statistically significant at p < .01. We can conclude that individuals reciprocate the perceived gratitude of the

9. I provide information for changes in rounds 25 and 27 because, like the contagion messages, the first treatment is considered informative, as subjects did not know exactly what the message meant yet. It is safe to assume that the second and the third messages were better understood.

TABLE 7.7 Average Compliance Rate After Reimbursement

Country	Average Improvement in Round 25	% of Participants Who Improved Compliance*
Argentina	14.09%	64%
Chile	10.94%	63%
Total	12.56%	63%

NOTE: Improvements with respect to the average compliance of previous three rounds.
*This only includes those who improved compliance by at least 3 percent. Those who kept the same level of compliance as previous rounds were considered not to have improved.

tax system with more honest taxpaying. This test suggests that taxpayers who come into contact with the direct provision of goods by the government will tend to comply better with tax laws.

Discussion

The evidence shows that the framework for understanding how compliance decisions are made must include non-sanction effects in addition to the effects of enforcement. I provide empirical evidence for the explanatory power of culture, which links social variables and individual outcomes. Taxpayers comply better with honest governments that reimburse taxes by providing public goods, and they imitate the behavior of peers, particularly when their peers cheat. In addition, the influence of effective enforcement lasts longer and is greater than any influence exercised by the actual detection and sanctioning capabilities of the tax administration.

These results are consistent with the claims of other studies, which claim that taxpayers rely on trust heuristic mechanisms to decide whether to comply or cheat (Scholz and Pinney 1995; Scholz and Lubell 1998). Most taxpayers remain highly compliant if they have previously been severely sanctioned. Small-scale but resilient tax evaders, on the other hand, remain undeterred by sanctions. Overall, stringent enforcement makes taxpayers believe that fraud is far more likely to be detected than it actually is. Thus, taxpayers rely on their sense of the best possible outcome. They consider authority to be trustworthy in its enforcing capacity.

This result also suggests how it is that taxpayers come to overweigh the likelihood that fraud will be detected—a finding of many studies, following the theory of Tversky and Kahneman (1974, 1981). Here, I show one mechanism whereby this frame is formed: where stringent enforcement has been effective, taxpayers frame the detection of fraud as

TABLE 7.8 Number of Taxpayers Who Improved or Decreased Their
Compliance Rate After Reimbursement

	Round 25 vs. Rounds 22–24	Round 19 vs. Rounds 16–18
Decreased or Maintained	77	103
Improved	122	105

far more likely than is actually probable. Participants in the experiment's high-audit group were more compliant in the latter rounds of the game because they "overweighed" probabilities higher than did participants in the control group, even when they faced similar odds of detection. Sanctions have enduring effects that explain variations between groups.

This chapter's discussion offers important lessons to tax administrations. Where the perceived effectiveness of tax enforcement is weak, taxpayers do not significantly overweigh the probabilities of being detected, and therefore tax evasion is high. New taxes, higher rates, withholding systems, and the like will not increase sustainable voluntary compliance in such a context. Conversely, where taxpayers believe that their TA is effective, that its enforcement is uncompromising, and that it severely imposes punishment on the noncompliant, they are likely to overestimate the likelihood that they will be punished for failing to comply with tax law, thereby becoming more compliant. This partly explains why some countries have better compliance than others even though they share similar taxation and enforcement mechanisms. It also explains why some countries enjoy good compliance rates even though their tax administration might not be as effective as it appears (or might even have lost effectiveness). There is a long lag between when taxpayers learn about the deficiencies of their TA and when they adjust their tendency to overweigh the probability of their TA punishing tax evasion.[10] The stringent enforcement of tax laws at an early stage makes it more likely that taxpayers will judge the laws' violation to be risky, which in turn will set in motion conditions of cooperation.

Instead of focusing on why variations among taxpayers occur, I provide here a partial explanation of how they happen. Taxpayers learn from others what is best and then proceed to apply cost-benefit analysis. This

10. In some countries, tax evasion increased slowly with no apparent cause. Several interpretations were made regarding changes in values, legitimacy, and so forth. In the United States, compliance has been slowly decreasing over the last thirty years. I suggest that some of this decline is also tied to the decrease of taxpayers' overestimation of the IRS's effectiveness: the less stringent enforcement of the IRS over several decades has finally reduced taxpayers' inflated estimates of the likelihood that fraud will be detected.

is also consistent with prospect theory. People first gather relevant information and formulate alternatives according to their own psychological makeup; then their choice is selected among choices that best fit personal decision rules. Taxpayers are affected by peer decisions and they frame alternatives by imitating others.

This also explains how social environments affect compliance. The elusive social-norm, or value-centered, variables become meaningful information tools for individual motivations to comply. There is a process that links values and norms to compliance decisions. People imitate success and incorporate valuable learning to decide what is best. Suckers do not want to be suckers, and they learn how to detach themselves from that fate.

Contagion effects help to address the larger question of how societies become prone to either compliance or noncompliance equilibria, which I answer using a tipping-point argument. Irrespective of the effectiveness of a tax administration and tax policies, noncompliant societies have a more difficult time than compliant societies reversing adverse equilibria. The imitation effect appears to have greater influence on taxpayer decision making than does any true assessment of enforcement capacity. If that is the case, tax administrations will have a difficult time effecting better compliance through deterrence.

In short, contagion and imitation from the environment, responsiveness to a fair ruler, and enduring enforcement effects address some of the mechanisms that explain why similar tax systems have different outcomes. They describe how these processes evolve, why equilibria tend to be stable, and why changes in taxpayers' behavior are only incremental and very seldom significant.

SUMMARY

In this chapter, I have described specific mechanisms that link ascriptive characteristics of social environments to individual decisions about whether to cheat on taxes. Traditional explanations of tax compliance fall short of offering a complete theory; they rely on individual-based data that associates variation in social, economic, and organizational ecology with variation in individual outcome, without showing how this association came about. Here, I describe and exemplify some mechanisms that explain how individual decisions are made. The evidence from the experimental study conducted for this chapter indicates that contagion, responsiveness, and the enduring nature of stringent enforcement affect individual tax decisions. The evidence of chapters 3, 4, and 5 is also consistent with this explanation.

Causal explanations must show how independent variables affect the dependent variable. Game theory partially bridges this gap by indicating that the framework of individual decisions is made within the context of a set of rules that govern human interaction. I have contended that tax compliance is an assurance game in which compliance is contingent on fairness, reciprocity, adaptation, and socialization; in sum, it correlates with politically and socially defined categories. These are facilitators of cooperation, as well as some of the indispensable mechanisms that contextualize the structure of individual payoffs.

As a coordination game, the assurance type requires a focal point or a guarantor of cooperation. Throughout this book, I have emphasized that the state has a paramount role to play as the guarantor of cooperation. Here, I have described the mechanism by which effective enforcement mobilizes more widespread compliance. Contingent compliance played as an assurance game requires a state capable not only of enforcing the rules but also of creating a contractual relation between itself and taxpayers that engenders a virtuous lasting effect.

A good Law is that, which is Needfull, for the Good of the People,
and withal Perspicuous. . . . Unnecessary Lawes are not good Lawes;
but trapps for Mony.

— THOMAS HOBBES, *Leviathan*

It is safe to say that nearly everyone would love to avoid the cost of taxation while enjoying the benefits of public goods. Nobody likes to pay taxes. Yet some societies are more successful than others in eliciting semi-voluntary compliance from citizens. In these social orders, citizens abide by the rules because they perceive their contributions to be meaningful and because the decision to consent overrides the temptation to free ride. Why some societies are more capable of fostering compliant tax environments than others is the question at the center of this book.

The importance of governments lies in their ability to foster horizontal fairness. States that collect taxes only through the power of the stick are doomed to fail, whereas those that foster compliance environments stand a better chance of succeeding. My project has been to study compliance with tax laws by focusing on the legal and cultural environments in which citizens operate. The analysis of tax climates provides some explanations for tastes and preferences instrumental to explaining compliance behavior.

My arguments are valid for three main reasons. First, I provide several independent types of evidence to show that social norms, culture, and governmental enforcement account for different degrees of tax compliance. Second, I explain the emergence of compliance and evasion as an evolutionary process wherein the aggregate decisions of agents reach multiple equilibria that tend to be stable and self-sustained. I rely for this explanation on a set of causal mechanisms that are conducive to a given equilibrium, and I show that compliance equilibria are path-dependent. In this sense, my argument follows the logic of analytical narratives (Bates et al. 1998). Third, I stress the importance of norms and culture in taxation, despite the fact that rigorous statistical analysis of their effects is sometimes unattainable. Had Max Weber been asked to submit rigorous statistical causation analysis of the effect of Calvinism in the development of capitalism, he probably would have failed. Of course, this book is no *Protestant Ethic and the Spirit of Capitalism,* but it follows the same path to support one of Weber's core arguments: "Not ideas, but interests—material and ideal—directly govern men's conduct. Yet very frequently, the 'world images' that have been created by 'ideas' have, like switchmen, determined the tracks along which action has been pushed by the dynamics of interests" (Weber 1946, 280) The noncompliance and compliance cultures that I have described in the preceding chapters create the tracks along which actions (tax evasion or tax compliance) are pushed by the dynamics of self-interest. People's beliefs and social imagery shape the mental constructs that they rely on to acquire information, and thus they shape the way that people process and evaluate tax alternatives while undertaking tax actions.

I propose a novel perspective on enforcement that depends on the nature of tax climates. Effective enforcement in a compliance equilibrium reduces the pool of noncompliers, strengthens social norms and horizontal enforcement, and fosters cultures of compliance. Successful enforcement rewards legalists and eliminates suckers. Countries that achieve substantive adherence to the law do so by claiming allegiance to the trusted values of the collective and by making sure that free riding is seriously curtailed. But given that enforcement is endogenous to the type of equilibrium, the effectiveness of enforcement diminishes in societies where citizens' initial dispositions to comply are weak. Dictatorships are not the best systems to promote compliance because they unravel voice and horizontal cooperation. In modern states, democracies are better suited to foster conditional cooperation because these regimes better promote the rule of law.

These arguments are helpful for explaining how conditional cooperation in taxation works. Perhaps we need to rethink the Eurocentric argument that social traps are overcome through the extension of social rights, the promotion of exchange equity, and the technical competence of the tax administration. Although I do not wish to undervalue the importance of citizenship, my claim is that a state capable of punishing free riders is key to the success of contingent compliance. Effective states are those that not only mobilize their citizens for public endeavors but also guarantee horizontal fairness and some measure of equality. The scale of tasks determines initial success, thus setting in motion, or accelerating, the mechanisms that either facilitate or hinder voluntary cooperation.

In this final chapter, I review the central conclusions of this study and discuss the practical implications of the argument. The first section begins with a succinct review of the evidence of different chapters, the second section briefly summarizes the main conclusions of this research, and the final section presents seven guiding policy recommendations.

A BRIEF REVIEW OF THE EVIDENCE

In this book, I have presented a data-driven account of the differences in tax compliance in Argentina and Chile. I have argued that making such a comparison is important for at least three reasons: First, despite many similarities, these countries represent typical cases of distinct compliance equilibria. Second, such a comparison enables a closer examination of correlates and causes that might solve the puzzle of successful enforcement. Third, this comparison has important implications for the study of policies, the state, and the rule of law in the region. I discussed these issues at length in the introduction and chapter 1.

In chapter 2, I described the dependent variable, tax compliance. Using different methods, I showed that divergences in tax compliance between Chile and Argentina are noticeable over several decades. Even though measures of tax compliance concentrate on the VAT, I provided data to suggest that similar trends are found for other taxes as well. I also presented comparative data that clearly places Chile among the more tax compliant nations of the world and Argentina at the intermediate-to-less-compliant level.

In chapters 3, 4, and 5, I examined the classic deterrence argument as it applies to taxation, and I argued that general deterrence is somewhat effective in compliance environments and very ineffective in other tax climates. Using a wide range of data sources, I argued that the straightforward proposition of certainty and severity of punishment for tax evasion is insufficient to explain how individual tax decisions are made. In chapter 3, I demonstrated that while the administrative capacities and professionalism of the tax agencies in Chile and Argentina are comparable, taxpayers in Chile believe that noncompliance can be more easily detected than do their Argentine counterparts.

Chapter 4 focuses on the effectiveness of general deterrence in encouraging tax compliance. The survey and administrative data shows that taxpayers in Chile perceive that escaping punishment for tax noncompliance is difficult, whereas Argentines believe that impunity is relatively high. I contended that the success of the Chilean state lies in its ability to engender law-abiding behavior through an effective administration of its sanctioning power. This is possible, however, because the pool of cheaters is smaller in Chile and the scale of the problem is manageable for courts, prosecutors, and other agencies.

In chapter 5, I analyzed tax-return data to elucidate the extent to which the imposition of sanctions on individuals who break the law enhances their tax compliance. The results of this investigation of the operation of specific deterrence are conclusive: cheaters keep cheating after enforcement actions have been taken against them, whereas moderate compliers are deterred from noncompliance by audits and other enforcement measures. I argued in this chapter that the effect of enforcement is rather indirect: it serves the purpose of general deterrence, but its usefulness is very limited for individual deterrence. This conclusion has important implications for enforcement strategies according to the type of equilibrium. The goal of enforcement should always be to reduce the pool of cheaters to allow voluntary compliance and conditional cooperation to survive.

The final two chapters move to integrate an understanding of how norms operate in tax compliance decision making with the previous chapters' observations regarding enforcement. In chapter 6, I analyzed survey data to study the problems of information, trust, and reciprocity in taxation. Using similar surveys conducted in the two different countries, I examined the claim that culture matters in compliance decisions. I concluded that both social solidarity and the culture of law abidance in Chile are superior to those in Argentina; I also argued that in Chile social solidarity and the culture of law abidance promote taxpayers' sense of the fairness of the system and their normative motivations to comply with the rules of the collective. Culture clearly matters in taxation as a viable information source for rational decision making.

Chapter 7 inquires into some of the mechanisms that taxpayers use to make strategic decisions, resulting in valuable tools for optimization. I presented data from an experiment that I conducted with students in both countries, focusing on three of these mechanisms: contagion, reciprocity, and the lasting effect of enforcement. The evidence shows that these three mechanisms contribute to an explanation of how taxpayers learn and process the inputs from the perceived environment in which they live. These mechanisms also contribute to an explanation of why the two most salient equilibria in taxation tend to be stable.

EIGHT CONCLUDING REMARKS

First, compliance and noncompliance equilibria are adequate constructs to describe the level of tax compliance in different countries. They have better predictive power for this purpose than do substantive legal policies; they account for the initial dispositions of taxpayers to abide by rules and, given the marginal nature of changes in taxation behavior, better explain aggregate patterns and rates of compliance. Once an equilibrium is reached, changes to the nature of the equilibrium become costly to make and therefore are unlikely to occur.

Second, pure cost-benefit analysis gives a far from realistic explanation of individual behavior. Strict microeconomic analysis is limited because people adopt routine conducts that yield, on average, satisfactory outcomes as they accommodate their behavior to tax or legal climates. Therefore, it seems more useful to account for the institutional variation across climates that affect individual choices than to rely on Homo economicus as the starting analytical unit.

Third, taxpayers rely on shared beliefs, values, and dispositions to guess their best decision in a context of low information, and past experience is the best predictor of their future decisions. Hence, aggregate tax decisions create a path-dependent explanation for decision making in taxation, imposing severe costs for radical changes. Culture matters precisely because it reduces the incentives for changes in legal behavior.

Fourth, rational imitation and socialization are the two mechanisms that best explain tax behavior. In an environment of severely limited information (like the one in which people make decisions about tax compliance), individuals evaluate the behavior of others to guide them as they make guesses about the safest strategic decisions they can make in their particular environment. Cheaters cheat to a great extent because they see other cheaters succeeding, and legalists comply because they observe behavior in equilibrium that enables them to not feel exploited.

Fifth, social norms are instrumental to explaining compliance behavior, but their role in a large-N setting is to promote an environment among players wherein people can trust others, expect reciprocity, and believe that they will receive fair treatment. Environments that promote such norms reinforce positive beliefs, values, and attitudes toward the law.

Sixth, there are two types of enforcement that are crucial to upholding compliance equilibria: vertical (governmental) enforcement and horizontal (peer) enforcement. The most important role of vertical enforcement is to ensure that compliers do not become suckers, whereas horizontal enforcement reinforces the adoption of values and beliefs. The mobilization of horizontal enforcement is more likely under compliance equilibria because it is less costly and better rewarded by the collective.

Seventh, strategies of enforcement are effective to the extent that they account for the compliance distribution and the individual cost of law abidance. Effective enforcement strategies are those that mobilize resources to achieve an initial compliance equilibrium (when the cost of new norms is likely to be initially resisted) and then gradual enforcement (when norms are widely embraced). The goal of norm-emergence enforcement is to generate initial widespread compliance, whereas the goal of norm-maintenance enforcement is to encapsulate cheaters and signal legalists that governments are honoring their part of the contract.

Eighth, and finally, the severe problems of size and reward in the provision of public goods for large-scale collective actions can only be resolved through conditional cooperation that coordinates enforcement (both horizontal and vertical) to reach a compliance-culture equilibrium. The institutionalization of legal behavior induces citizens to generate a threshold of resources that enable the provision of reasonable public goods, reinforcing values, beliefs, and satisfaction for community members. Conversely, noncompliance equilibria do not produce the necessary resources for the successful provision of public goods, reinforcing the sense of those forced to contribute that they are being treated like suckers.

POLICY GUIDELINES

With these conclusions in mind, I present several guiding ideas to be taken into account in policy formulation. The first and most obvious principle is that effective policies must account for the distribution of compliance among the population. Replication of policy prescriptions is futile if the initial compliance scenario between countries differs.

Second, the goal of enforcement is to reach wide compliance with norms—or, in other words, to enable such norms to operate in "automatic pilot" mode. Policies requiring continuous, stringent enforcement face insurmountable monitoring costs; further, they work to create an unstable equilibrium that might unravel the legitimacy of the norm.

Third, the provision of a TA with excellent technical and bureaucratic capacities is insufficient to reverse a noncompliance equilibrium, and the value of the incremental contribution of such a TA to eliciting compliance should not be overestimated. Therefore, to guarantee a threshold of compliance, widely defied rules should be reevaluated, and norm entrepreneurs (i.e., legislators and governments) will be better off reducing the expectations of legal solutions. For example, simple taxes that are easily collected and place smaller burdens on taxpayers are preferable to progressive taxation simply because the latter do not usually function as progressive in reality—rather, in a noncompliance equilibrium, they are a sure way to create large numbers of suckers and cheaters. In short, state capacities should not be developed without reference to the environment wherein these capacities operate.

Fourth, it is crucial to take individual incentives and contextual environments into account if new policies are to work. Although this is a straightforward statement, most legal provisions are introduced under conditions adverse to the solution of collective problems. For example, new taxes are usually levied when it is fiscally necessary for the state to increase revenues, often in times of economic recession. Taxpayers will be more reluctant to comply under such economic conditions, however, creating an adverse equilibrium for the new tax that will undermine compliance. In short, legislation of a type that encounters active resistance (such as the introduction of tax hikes or changes in hiring practices, immigration policies, or drug trafficking and consumption laws) will achieve more success if introduced when individual incentives can be aligned with favorable contextual-compliance environments. Political logic, however, usually operates in the opposite direction.

Fifth, norm-emerging enforcement strategies should be used for actively resisted laws in strong noncompliance equilibria. Such strategies should be used to implement simple laws that are easy to administer and that make it relatively easy to detect violations, and the strategies should produce severe punishment for noncompliers. At the enactment stage, legislators must have assurances that coordination problems between enforcement agencies and courts will be solved and that the probability that sanctions will be imposed is very high. Legislation must overcome the routine reluctance of enforcement agents to severely punish noncompliance. Cheaters will be deterred when the certainty of punishment is very high. Compliance equilibria can only emerge when impunity is low.

Sixth, norm-maintenance enforcement strategies should be geared for widely accepted norms with the goal of reducing the probabilities of contagion. Punishment may be less severe, but the likelihood of its imposition should remain high. Norm maintenance allows for the existence of complex laws, in which case stronger enforcement always focuses on the new provisions of given rules. Sanctions in such a context have a more symbolic function, reinforcing compliers' attitudes, and therefore punishment should be selective and mostly used for signaling purposes.

Seventh, and perhaps most important, states should legislate only what can be enforced. A noncompliance equilibrium will further deteriorate when mounting deficits of implementation undermine new laws; the defiance of new norms unravels citizens' initial disposition to comply. The perverse path-dependency of noncompliance can only be mitigated with minimal and strictly necessary rules, the reasonably successful enforcement of which will promote wider adherence to the norm, as well as equity, fairness, and the establishment of trust. This process, in turn, will further enhance horizontal enforcement. Paraphrasing Hobbes, unenforceable laws are not good laws but rather traps for money, as well as for corruption, unfairness, and mistrust. In turn, few necessary and enforceable norms might foster the rule of law, which becomes the pinnacle of compliance environments. The rule of law is the equilibrium wherein rights are generally delivered, fair laws are widely obeyed, and legal norms are likely to be implemented.

Data on Argentine and Chilean tax compliance is limited. Most research on tax evasion is based on aggregate information that measures evasion indirectly using macroeconomic indicators. As a result, it is virtually impossible to assess the direct effect of different policies and enforcement mechanisms on compliance. The exchanges and interactions between citizenship and tax contribution have not been widely studied and remain largely speculative.

This book presents, to the best of my knowledge, the first systematic information collected on individual-based tax-related issues for Argentina and Chile. This work constitutes an empirical assessment of relevant questions regarding the taxpayers' subjective perceptions on a range of tax-related problems, as well as the first factual study of enforcement effects on individual decision making on taxes.

In this appendix I describe the different data sets collected for this research. I will first discuss the general characteristics of data needed for analyzing individual and social compliance and review state-of-the-art methods in Western countries. Then I will present the three main types of data that I assembled: surveys, individual tax-return information, and experimental design.

DATA FOR COMPLIANCE ANALYSIS

The study of tax compliance represents a classic case of causality problems in social science. There are a wide variety of methodologies useful for validating or discovering causal relationships among tax policy and compliance, enforcement and individual decisions, and so forth. Finding the appropriate method, however, remains the central research question in this area of research. During the last twenty years, many studies attempted to understand the determinants of tax compliance. They were based on three different types of data, each of which has several limitations that constrain the analysis.

(a) *Aggregate data from audits.* Official data collected through audits and the TCMP (tax compliance measurement) program in the United States has served as the basis for myriad microeconomic studies that sought to understand the determinant of individual tax-abidance decisions. The main problem lies in the specifications of the dependent variable (noncompliance). Most studies use the result of an audit as a proxy for tax compliance. But this dependent variable is very unstable because it is based on auditors' judgments and very fragmented information, which does not necessarily measure the original individual tax decision (see Long 1992). In other words, tax evasion is a tax-conscious decision, but to assume that noncompliance is also a rational and conscious choice is a simplistic conclusion. There are many examples that violate this assumption (Kinsey 1987). Most noncompliance in the United States stems from clerical errors, judgments and interpretations of the tax code, and honest mistakes, none of which corresponds with the willful act implied in tax evasion. In short, official data is generally reliable, but serious questions about the validity of research remain, particularly regarding accurate measures of tax evasion.

(b) *Self-reports.* Surveys should also be analyzed with extreme care. Problems are usually related to reliability—that is, whether self-reports are accurate and reliable estimates of actual behavior. Validity problems in the tax domain are also abundant. Despite efforts to enhance anonymity and confidentiality in responses, the survey-methodology literature (Webley et al. 1991, 33–35) has found that deviant acts such as tax evasion are usually distorted, often because of the respondent's desire to gain approval (impression management). Results could be more accurate if answers were checked against respondents' records (whenever possible). Surveys cannot provide accurate estimates of tax evasion; they are better understood as estimators of subjective risk and individual perceptions than as measures of actual noncompliance.

(c) *Experimental designs.* Mostly used by social psychologists and in microeconomics, the data gathered in laboratory-type settings attempts to unravel the cognitive mechanisms and decision-making processes on which taxpayers rely for some tax-evasion choices. This data also has serious limitations. No matter how complex the experimental design, it rarely reproduces the complexities of the tax code and the different players acting in the tax decision-making process (the role of tax advisers, family, partners, the firm's position in the market, etc.). In other words, the "tax world" is extremely complex and hardly reproducible in experimental settings.

In sum, the array of methods used to collect empirical evidence in the tax field should be analyzed within the appropriate context. It is often suggested that a combined set of data be used (Andreoni, Erard, and Feinstein 1998). I rely on a compound analysis of different sources to provide more reliable answers to specific questions. To analyze individual perceptions and opinions, I relied on self-reports; for studying enforcement and compliance, I have collected official data; and to inquire on cognitive and other mechanisms for tax choices, I used laboratory-type experiments.

THE SURVEYS

Between 1997 and 1998, I conducted or supervised four different surveys in Argentina (1 to 4), and in 2002 I conducted a survey in Chile (survey 6). In addition, SII provided me with the database of a 1998 survey conducted in Chile by Mori (survey 5). For Argentina I mostly focus on findings from surveys 1 and 4, and occasionally from surveys 2 and 3; for Chile I rely on surveys 5 and 6 for chapter 6, and survey 6 for other chapters.

Survey 1: Taxpayer compliance. I designed and directed this survey. It had 112 questions, mostly closed-ended, on a wide range of tax-related topics. Several questions followed surveys conducted in the United States, and the rest were specifically designed for Argentina. The sample consisted of 549 taxpayers randomly selected from the TA registry, following a pre-designed methodology to assure representation of different segments of taxpayers. Respondents were mainly selected from the Greater Buenos Aires district, but 15 percent of the sample came from rural areas. Half the sample was aged forty to fifty-six, and a third of the sample was below forty years old.

Respondents were also selected from four broadly defined industries: (a) agriculture, (b) housing and construction, (c) commerce (including wholesalers and retailers), and (d) services (in particular, insurance, advertisement, and computer consultants). The fieldwork was carried out by a well-known Argentine polling company (Mora y Araujo, Noguera y Asociados), and was supervised by the research department of AFIP.

The interviews were arranged ahead of time and lasted thirty to forty-five minutes. The rejection rate was 52 percent (this high rate was expected due to the sensitivity of tax issues). Respondents were not told about being selected from AFIP registry. The World Bank funded the program, which was specified in the initial statement of the questionnaire.

Survey 2: Tax officials. After the above survey was completed, the TA asked me to measure perceptions and opinions of regional tax directors on the same issues. Therefore, the same survey was conducted on 150 regional directors of operations, directors of audit departments, and audit supervisors. Questionnaires were mailed with a letter assuring anonymity. AFIP research department was in charge of the administration. It is unclear how effective and reliable responses were, but this survey provides an overview of opinions held by tax officials.

Survey 3: Customs administration. In late 1998, the directorate of AFIP requested a small survey, similar to number 2, for customs officers. The survey included similar questions, adapted to foreign-trade operations. There were eighty-five personal interviews with directors of operations at several customs points. The administration of the survey was done by regular staff of the research department.

Survey 4: Audited taxpayers. Administered in November and December 1997 on a random sample of 550 taxpayers, this survey constitutes a second phase of the taxpayer-compliance survey (number 1). It had seventy-five closed-ended questions. Sixty-five percent of the survey replicated questions of the former questionnaire, and 35 percent was new. This survey targeted audited taxpayers (400), along with a control group of non-audited taxpayers (150), and its main goal was to evaluate the effect of audits on compliance. The first selection of the audited subsample was drawn from a pool of taxpayers audited within the last two years (a population of over thirty thousand). To assure sample representation of the population, it followed a selection process similar to that of survey 1, excluding the industry filter. The 150 non-audited taxpayers were also drawn using similar criteria as in survey 1. The rejection rate for this survey was 42 percent. The majority of respondents were from the Buenos Aires metropolitan area (85 percent), and the rest were from the interior. Eight-three percent of the sample were male and 66 percent were between thirty and forty-nine years old.

Survey 5: Estudios Mori Chile. In 1998, SII conducted a large survey of taxpayers randomly selected from the TA registrar above a certain threshold of tax payment (assuring the inclusion of medium and large taxpayers). It consisted of more than one hundred closed-ended questions on issues related to risk perception, service satisfaction, tax fairness, and so forth. The survey was designed and conducted by Mori.

Survey 6: Taxpayers Chile. In order to compare results from surveys 1 and 4 in Argentina, a similar survey was administered in Chile. The sample of 528 taxpayers was drawn from the SII registrar based on VAT payments above a minimum threshold to guarantee a proportion of medium and large taxpayers. Sixty percent of the sample were from Greater Santiago, 20 percent from the Antofagasta region (north), and 20 percent from the Concepción region (center-south). The questionnaire replicated questions from survey 4 in Argentina in addition to some questions from survey 1. Adaptation of colloquial local language and different monetary values were introduced. The rejection rate was 51 percent, similar to the rate in Argentina. There were two pools of samples: one of recently audited taxpayers, and one that had not been audited within the last two years. Sixty percent of the sample had been recently audited. Fieldwork was done by the polling company Veas y Asociados. The Ford Foundation provided support for the survey.

INDIVIDUAL RECORDS

I assembled data that includes three sets of samples randomly selected from Argentina's tax agency and two from Chile's tax administration. They were all collected under specific guidelines assuring the anonymity of taxpayers, and all results were reported to authorities. With this data I studied three different enforcement contacts:

1. *Audits.* These represent the most extensive and in-depth analyses of taxpayer behavior (Argentina and Chile).

2. *Temporary business closures.* This measure is used to sanction taxpayers "caught" violating formal requirements (usually evading taxes by not issuing invoices and thus misreporting real sales; Argentina and Chile).

3. *Fiscal cash registers.* In 1997 and 1998, retailers were obliged to use specially designed cash registers whose internal memory could not be violated or altered; therefore, specially trained tax-administration inspectors could verify all registered sales (Argentina).

Audits

Argentina. For the audited taxpayers, I used a randomly selected sample of all cases discharged in October and November 1997. Large taxpayers (primarily big corporations) were excluded, as were cases with incomplete information. The analysis is based on 1,086 audits, which represent 85 percent of the entire population. The two-month selection was made randomly. In addition, a control group of 1,200 non-audited taxpayers was randomly selected by computerized matching information of the audited cases. Therefore, each case has a parallel non-audited match as a control.

Given that audits usually last for a period of 120 days, I collected tax-return information on these taxpayers for the periods prior to the official notification of audits (December 1996–May 1997) and after the audits were closed (December 1997–May 1998). This data include the itemized information of two different tax returns: income tax (filed yearly) and VAT (filed monthly). In addition, each taxpayer's record was completed by the audit discharge report, including the auditor's assessments of true liabilities plus any funds or additional assessments that he or she might have found.

Chile. Similar data was collected, although the periods varied. Audit data included tax-return information for three years (1998–2000) and for taxpayers audited in 1999. This information allowed extended periods of time for testing comparisons between pre- and post-audit periods. The total audited sample of 680 included all cases discharged in August and September of 1999. The matching sample of 763 non-audited taxpayers was drawn using similar criteria as in Argentina.

Temporary Business Closures

Argentina. The sample consists of 689 cases, all of whom were effectively shut down for a few days between March and July 1998. Another randomly selected control group of 425 non-sanctioned taxpayers was added, following criteria that resembled the characteristics of the sanctioned group described in the audit section. All sanctioned cases for the above-mentioned period were included in the sample, which should be representative of all closed businesses. The data assembled is similar to the audit data—that is, each case includes tax returns for a period prior to and following enforcement, in addition to available information about the imposed sanction.

Chile. The sample here is larger, 4,594 sanctioned and 4,548 non-sanctioned taxpayers. It should be noted that only 40 percent of the businesses sanctioned were effectively closed (see chaps. 4 and 5). The sanctioned sample included all cases of the second semester of 1999, and the tax-return information is for the years 1998–2000. Cases with incomplete information were excluded from the analysis. The non-sanctioned sample was selected using similar matching information to previous cases.

Fiscal Cash Registers

Only Argentina. Because tax-return information for the fifty thousand taxpayers who installed cash registers by July 1998 was incomplete, I restricted the analysis to a sample of the eleven thousand retailers for whom the tax agency had internal access to complete tax data online. In each case, VAT tax-return data was compiled for at least a year prior to the installation of the register and for a year afterward. In addition, some information about the type of machine, type of petition, and number of registers was also added. Because this enforcement required only sales and purchases information (see chap. 5), no income-tax data was requested.

The AFIP and SII information departments processed all the individual official data. For every data set, I established the specification for sample selection, which required the use of specially written computer programs. For all samples, there was random manual cross-checking of cases to ensure that accurate information was drawn from the central database. In this way, information was validated.

EXPERIMENTAL DESIGN

The analysis of data of chapter 7 is partially drawn from an experiment conducted in 2002 at Universidad de Chile in Santiago and Universidad Torcuato di Tella in Buenos Aires. On a voluntary basis, undergraduate students were invited to participate in an experiment (which included monetary incentives) where they had to make decisions of paying taxes on given incomes for twenty-seven "rounds" (see chap. 7 for further explanation of the experiment). In Chile, 134 students participated, and in Argentina 132 participated. The computer program used was specially designed for this goal, and administration was conducted under strictly similar criteria in both countries. The experiment lasted two days in each country, and every student-subject "played" the game for approximately thirty minutes. A survey with closed-ended questions followed the game. The support for designing and conducting the game (including student-performance "earnings") was funded by a grant from the Hewlett Foundation.

This appendix develops some of the logic of tax compliance using elements of game theory. I do not pretend to fully develop a formal tax game. There is a large literature on cooperation and coordination games that can be used to account for this collective-action problem (Hardin 1982; Kreps 1990; Taylor 1995; Skyrms 1996; Fehr and Schmidt 1999; Bicchieri 1997; Axelrod 2004). My goal is to provide a modest contribution designed for the non-specialized reader to help clarify some of the concepts that I use throughout this book; the argument can be followed using simple logic, without the need for algebra.

THE BASIC FORM

For the purpose of demonstration, let us assume a 2 × 2 game wherein players can decide to pay taxes (P) or cheat on them (CH). The proceeds of tax collections are converted into public goods (PG). Four outcomes are possible:

(A) The player cheats and gets PG. This player is a free rider.
(B) The player does not cheat and gets PG. This player is a legalist.
(C) The player cheats and does not get PG. This creates a situation of anarchy.
(D) The player does not cheat and does not get PG. This player is a sucker.

For a single, egoistic player, alternative A is always the best and D is the worst.

Let us also assume that for a public good to be meaningful, both players must pay their taxes. When only a single player pays, the quality of the goods is so poor that no player perceives the benefits.

Now consider the following plausible situation. The subjective value of PG is significantly lower than the cost of paying for them—that is, the cost of taxes exceeds the perceived benefits of PG. In that situation, A > C > B > D, and the payoff matrix is as follows:

		Player 2	
		Cooperate	Defect
Player 1	Cooperate	BB	DA
	Defect	AD	CC

Here, player 1 is row and player 2 is column. The payoff on the left is for player 1, the payoff on the right is for player 2.

It is easy to derive the conclusion that the dominant strategy is mutual defection (both cheat), because no player has the incentive to change course unilaterally, and such an outcome results in equilibrium. Conversely, if the value of PG is considerably higher, then A > B > C > D and the payoff matrix remains the same, but the dominant strategy will now be cooperation. In a simple one-shot game, then, cooperation is attained when the subjective value of the public goods in question is sufficiently high that taxpayers will bear the cost of taxation.

This is illustrated in the following table. Suppose that the nominal cost of paying taxes for each taxpayer is always 3 (the first value in the top row). Suppose also that the value or gain of the public good is different for each game (the second value in the first row). The following table then describes the payoff that each player receives from a one-shot Prisoner's Dilemma (PD) type of game. (Notice, for example, that for A the payoff means the value of the good plus the amount that he does not pay in cheating—3 + 1, 3 + 2, 3 + 3, 3 + 4. For B, the payoff is the actual value of the good, because the cost of contribution is not included in the payoffs—that is, it is a net loss.)

	3-1	3-2	3-3	3-4
A	4	5	6	7
B	1	2	3	4
C	3	3	3	3
D	0	0	0	0

As the subjective value of the public good increases, strategy B becomes the second-best. (Remember that A will always be the best but is an inferior outcome under PD. D is always the worst, and C is constant.) This is intuitively a move in the right direction because the higher the value of PG, the higher the incentives to cooperate. Ultimately, once a critical value of the good is reached, it pays to move from defection to cooperation, because, according to the basic matrix, cooperative strategies yield higher social returns. In sum, as the value of PG increases, it becomes possible to move from a CC equilibrium to a BB equilibrium, which is a superior outcome.[1]

This example, however, shows that for cooperation strategies to be dominant in a one-shot game, the value of PG must be higher than the cost of taxpaying. But taxation is not symmetrical: some taxpayers will pay more, others less. This partly explains why larger taxpayers have naturally higher tendencies to avoid taxation: they rarely receive PG comparable to their actual contributions. Moreover, where only the value of PG is being considered, the free-rider strategy will always dominate, because total revenues less transaction and administration costs produce less PG compared to the total revenues.

In addition to the value of PG, two other factors influence the tax compliance equilibrium: the discount rate of taxpayers regarding future interactions, and the role of negative selective incentives in the form of sanctions for cheating. For the former, it is crucial to transcend the one-shot game and move to repetitive games, in which taxpayers assign value to payoffs that they will receive in subsequent interactions. For the second, the effect of deterrence and the state should be analyzed.

But before analyzing this crucial and more complex set of games, let us examine the possibilities of cooperation without third-party or state intervention in the one-shot environment. Chicken and assurance games are two good depictions of this situation.

SPONTANEOUS COOPERATION

Although a single taxpayer will prefer to defect if there are enough taxpayers who do cooperate, tax compliance is not a chicken game, because it is unreasonable to believe that a single taxpayer or a small group can contribute enough to provide for the public good. Under the logic of chicken games, there is a strong motivation for players to pre-commit to force others to cooperate. But the basic assumption is that those who contribute regard their contribution as essential for the provision of the public good; without that contribution, cooperators will be worse off, regardless of other players' decisions. Taxpayers who cheat on their taxes

1. For example, when the provision of public security is perceived as qualitative, most people adopt a disposition to pay taxes to support it.

are probably better off for not contributing unless, of course, everybody else also cheats on their taxes. This condition makes any chicken-type arrangement for tax compliance very unstable, because the rush to pre-commit to noncompliance cannot secure the cooperation of others once a critical mass of defectors is reached. This violates the basic principle of chicken games.

If the subjective value of the public good is very low with respect to the value of the private good, then the optimal response to the contributions of others is not to contribute (the free-ride paradigm). But what happens when the subjective, perceived value of the public good rises? There are two possible responses. First, if others contribute enough the best strategy will be a pure chicken type—that is, to not cooperate so long as everyone else does cooperate, but contribute to the provision of PG if others do not. The other possibility is a mixed assurance/chicken strategy, where a player cooperates to the extent that others cooperate based on the value of the public good. This is the basic framework of the tax compliance game.

In order for the tax compliance game to be played as an assurance game, taxpayers must assign some value to the public good provided by their contributions (see Hardin 1982). This is why the equity of taxation is crucial. When the subjective value of the current public good approaches zero, the game will be played as a prisoner's dilemma. As the value of the good rises, conditions for cooperative games can be reached. Players' optimal strategies are determined by their perceptions about the contributions of others, as well as of the value of the good itself.

N-PERSON ITERATED TAX COMPLIANCE GAMES

Because the value of PG rarely exceeds the total cost of contributing to it, under one-shot games the likely outcome will always be PD. Taxation, however, is a ritual performed at least once a year (for income tax) and sometimes monthly (for VAT). Therefore, tax compliance should be considered an iterated game.

In repetitive games, a player's move can be made conditional to other players' earlier choices (Axelrod 1984, 2002). Cooperation can be contingent on the cooperation of others, yielding tit for tat and other coordination games. I have shown that for *unconditional* cooperation to emerge, the value of PG must be very high, but for *conditional* cooperation to emerge, in the absence of a third-party enforcer, players must regard the future of cooperation very highly. For example, if a taxpayer values the education of her children highly, she might contribute today to support the construction of a solid public education system that will serve her dependents in the future. Conversely, if she does not trust the state to provide reliable goods, she might cheat on her taxes, because she does not expect to receive valuable public goods in the future in exchange for her tax payments. N-person conditional-cooperation games are in equilibrium if they satisfy every player's discount-factor rate (see Taylor 1995, chap. 4).

Although satisfying players' discount-factor rate is a necessary condition for cooperation games to reach equilibrium, it is not sufficient. If this taxpayer believes that other taxpayers do not care for the public school system and that they are not ready to contribute for it, her own regard for the future will not really matter. The state's collection of the necessary revenues for future goods is contingent on all players' current contributions (or at least the contributions of most of them). In short, cooperation is attained if the majority of taxpayers have similar discount rates—or, in other words, if they live in societies that share similar values, norms, and so on. For tax cooperation to be stable, taxpayers must share a threshold of common goals, have some cohesiveness, and value common future endeavors. These are necessary and sufficient conditions for cooperation, but these conditions do not predict the actual outcome of games.

In iterated games, individual players' cooperation is conditional on other players' previous moves. Hence, when everybody pays taxes, a single defector might trigger defections in subsequent rounds. The extent of noncooperation will depend on the nature of the social contract; as a rule, however, universal defection will be triggered when taxpayers notice other people cheating, and thus the provision of PG deteriorates. Cheaters do not disclose their defection so that they may continue to exploit the contributions of other players (among other reasons).

Public individual defection inhibits future universal cooperation. In an environment of conditional cooperation, a single defector has a large discount rate, so the immediate gain of free riding outweighs the lower payoffs of future universal defection. Tax cheaters in noncompliance equilibria value the immediate rent of present defection much higher than the value of future cooperation. This has disastrous consequences, because it not only inhibits the current provision of public goods but also, and perhaps more important, undermines the conditions for future cooperation. Universal defection shapes preferences and higher discount rates, whereas universal cooperation elicits the individual consideration of the future.

· When taxpayers consent to taxation, they are interested in all others doing so as well. Cooperation benefits from what Hardin (1982) calls double incentives for each player, where on top of their own motivations to cooperate, players also have an interest in ensuring that others cooperate. This makes the emergence of a tax compliance game as a coordination game possible (see also Alm and McKee 2000). Social sanctions among legalists emerge to institutionalize wider compliance.

EQUILIBRIUM AND LIKE-MINDEDNESS IN TAXATION

Equilibrium is the outcome of a players' strategy where no one can obtain a larger payoff by changing strategy, as long as the other players' strategy remains the same. That creates the expectation that there is no better strategy to take, and therefore it generates incentives for players to keep playing the game in the same way that they have in previous iterations. Therefore, when everybody expects a particular outcome, this outcome will most likely be an equilibrium. If a game has only one equilibrium, that will be the outcome. For example, if everybody expects others to cheat, there will be a noncompliance equilibrium. But if there are multiple simultaneous equilibria and one is preferred by all players over the others, then no player will expect others to choose an inferior outcome, and therefore each player will choose the best strategy, resulting in equilibrium. For instance, if a taxpayer believes that others will cooperate and pay taxes, that taxpayer will also pay, resulting in a compliance equilibrium. But what happens when a fraction of players expect one equilibrium and others expect another equilibrium? In such a case, no equilibrium will be reached.

In chapter 7, I demonstrated with experimental data how taxpayers bow to cooperative and noncooperative strategies. They comply more when they perceive others to be cooperating. Although there are several ways of formally demonstrating why people decide to cooperate instead of defecting, consider the following simple strategy: Suppose that people are randomly paired, and one decides to cooperate (C) and the other decides to defect (D). They will evolve into a defection PD equilibrium. In the real world, however, this is hardly the situation because people do not interact randomly, but rather with relatives, neighbors, and the like. Let us assume that a cooperator is paired with another cooperator. These individuals will continue to cooperate. The more C-type people there are in the community, the higher the probability that they will be matched with other cooperators. In short, the higher the correlation of like-minded people within a population, the more that people are likely to reach an equilibrium. (Strong correlations lead to the fixation of dominant strategies.) This conclusion is consistent with Jeffrey's (1965) concept of ratifiability, which postulates that people decide based on weighted average probabilities of acts (i.e., conditionally) that can be verified in subsequent acts and then adjusted. Taxpayers will comply better if they believe that others are like-minded and that such beliefs can be verified later on: the more legalists in a society, the higher the possibilities of cooperation; the more cheaters, the higher the possibilities of universal defection. Some of the evidence of the experiment described in chapter 7 corroborates this assertion.

CONDITIONAL COOPERATORS AND COERCED COOPERATORS

What happens when within a community there are some voluntary (non-coerced) conditional cooperators and some players who can only be coerced into cooperation. Let us examine a two-person game in which player 1 is a conditional cooperator and player 2 a coerced cooperator:

		Player 2	
		Cooperate	Defect
Player 1	Cooperate	XM	ZN
	Defect	YO	WL

For player 1, $Y > X > W > Z$, and for player 2, $N > M > L > O$. Given these preferences, the most likely outcome will be WL (DD). Player 1 knows that player 2 cooperates only to the extent that he or she is coerced, and therefore player 1 knows that player 2's dominant strategy is always L (D). Hence, player 1 will also play W (D). In short, unless deterrence is so effective as to warrant cooperation from otherwise-natural defectors, the equilibrium will be universal defection (the makeup of PD). More important, when a critical mass of coercion-only cooperation is reached, noncompliance becomes the expected general behavior, and thus the taxpayers' preferred strategy. Reversal into natural consenting behavior becomes very difficult, as it is a poor decision for each individual taxpayer to make.

FAIRNESS, JUSTICE, AND COMPLIANCE

Noncompliance can be a strongly stable equilibrium, but it can also be a very inefficient one.[2] Suppose that the fixed payoff of a tax game totals 1.[3] A player matched in a pair has to decide what share of the total payoff he will demand. If both demand more than 0.5, the payoff is loss. If both demand less than 0.5, both get their respective requested share. Any outcome that totals 1 will be a Nash equilibrium, whereas any outcome that totals less than 1 will be suboptimal.

What will the players' strategies be if both play simultaneously without previous information? If both share the same desire to get a piece of the payoff, then they will have to estimate the other player's strategy in order to optimize their own decision. If A chooses to demand 0.75, any demand above 0.25 of player B will be disastrous and any demand below .25 will satisfy A's demand. But even a modest demand of 0.26 by player B will be detrimental for him as well, given A's strategy. As will be shown below, in the absence of the state, fairness and justice emerge in this case as a valuable device to resolve this collective-action problem. Both players most likely will settle spontaneously on 0.5 and receive the amount that they ask for. This will turn out to be an efficient and very stable equilibrium. As most of the literature emphasizes, the prospect of the evolution of justice increases among like-minded individuals.

But what happens when, in a given population, half the taxpayers are of the type A, who want 0.75 (pay less, get more), and half of the type B, who demand 0.25 (pay more, get less)? If any taxpayer A is matched with any taxpayer B, then there is an optimal solution, but when an A type is matched with another A, both lose. (Remember, anything beyond 1 is total loss.) Conversely, if a B is matched with another B, both get 0.25, which is suboptimal. Given a population made up half of As and half of Bs, the average individual payoff is 0.25. More important, when the proportion of A rises within the population, the probability of A matching another A increases, and hence the average payoff diminishes. Conversely, if the proportion of A shrinks, then the average payoff

2. I am drawing from Skyrms 1996.
3. For the sake of simplicity, let us assume that a payoff means a combination of contribution (negative) and public good (positive). In this sense, the expectation of, say, 0.5 implies a combination for a taxpayer in which she pays taxes and receives public goods for the value of 0.5. The more she pays and the less she receives, the lower the payoff will be; the less she pays and the more she gets in PG, the higher the payoff.

increases. In short, when players' demands and strategies converge with justice and fairness, the average payoff increases.

Notice that justice evolves to the extent that most taxpayers settle on 0.5 because everybody is better off with this outcome. (It is easy to demonstrate that under this scenario the average individual payoff is 0.5, and that no other collective strategy yields higher returns.) But when some free riders deviate from this strategy, the average payoff decreases. The more free riders there are, the lower the payoffs and the less just and fair the outcome. This is intuitively in the right direction. What is remarkable is that even when the A-type strategy gets closer to 1 (say 0.9) and the B type closer to 0 (say 0.1), the total social output decreases but the incentive to deviate from this inefficient outcome does not spontaneously arise (because, after all, everybody gets what they want). The endogenous necessary condition for the natural solution of this collective-action problem is for players to embrace some shared criteria of fairness. Any other solution requires either the finite division of the total output or the coerced solution provided by an exogenous agent (the state).

As I claim in chapter 1, the initial balance matters a great deal. Because strict fairness and strict unfairness tend to be equilibria, it is very hard to spontaneously reverse course. As shown in the simulation of the next appendix, the onset of tax compliance games determines whether they will tend toward equilibria.

Chapter 1 developed the argument that legal culture affects tax compliance and that the effect of enforcement is constrained by the costs, incentives, and compliance distribution of the population. Moreover, I have stressed that enforcement can affect compliance to the extent that it nurtures a virtuous equilibrium, but in order to reach such a stage, enforcement has to be geared toward guaranteeing the conditional cooperation of taxpayers. Proving the coevolution of enforcement and compliance culture, however, requires time-series data, and that is hard to get: I use a longitudinal design to analyze the effect of enforcement on future compliance (chap. 5) and an experiment wherein I show how early enforcement affects later variations in compliance (chap. 7). In addition, I develop in this appendix a simulation game designed to show how enforcement and compliance culture affect each other over time.

Tax compliance is by nature an iterated game. People make successive moves according to the payoffs of previous rounds. Taxpayers file taxes regularly, they learn about other taxpayers' audit experiences, and they rely on professional advice and the lessons of their personal tax history. Thus, although the exact probability of audit remains unknown to them, taxpayers have some idea about the chances of being selected for auditing and about the level of sanctions that would be imposed on them if they were caught cheating.

Though the simulations that follow are far from comprehensive, they attempt to show the role of enforcement under different scenarios, as well as its impact on compliance. Although the model focuses on taxes, the general principles can be applied to almost every other norm.

ASSUMPTIONS

The most basic assumption is that people are rational and pursue the maximization of their own benefits. Cultural explanations are not given but rather are the result of players' rational behavior. The second assumption is that, all things being equal, the outcome of previous rounds affects the behavior of players in future rounds. As mentioned, individual tax decisions are repetitive. In iterated games, players decide to comply or to cheat based on previous experience. The following are rational taxpayers' decisions given their immediate payoffs from previous audit or non-audit experience. Let A stand for "audited in previous round," C for "compliant," NA for "not audited in previous round," and NC for "noncompliant." Therefore:

(1) If A and C in t_1, then C in t_2.
(2) If A and NC in t_1, then C in t_2.
(3) If NA and NC in t_1, then NC in t_2.
(4) If NA and C in t_1, then X in t_2.

In other words, it is reasonable to assume that the outcome of previous audits will likely determine future compliance behavior.[1] If a taxpayer has cheated and was audited, she will report accurately in the following round (2), whereas if she was audited and complied, she will continue to comply (1). Conversely, if she cheated and was not audited (3), she got away with a higher payoff and there is no reason to believe that she will not continue to cheat.[2] These three cases are, therefore, straightforward and predictable. The presence of the outcome X in the fourth case indicates that the question of how the taxpayer will behave in subsequent rounds remains open (4).

Because tax administrations audit a small fraction of taxpayers, the probability of selection for auditing is low, but the effect of audits on compliance decisions is cumulative for the next three or more rounds. Given that the outcomes of (1), (2), and (3) are predictable, the only question is how a complier who has not been audited will decide (4). Leaving risk constant and assuming that change from compliance to noncompliance is only determined by probability of selection,[3] a higher audit rate

1. This is not always the case. If an audit of a tax evader is poorly performed, it creates incentives for this taxpayer to continue cheating. For the purpose of this simulation, let us assume that audits are done well and deter taxpayers from cheating in future rounds.

2. There are some instances where a tax evader can retract from cheating and shift to compliance, particularly for those who cheat under severe circumstances and have a deep sense of guilt. Again, for the purpose of this simulation, let us assume that there are no people like these in this category.

3. I assume that such a probability is determined by the audit rate. Taxpayers learn that more audits lead to a higher probability of selection.

will reduce the number of compliers tempted to cheat. On the other hand, because the effect of audits is cumulative for only a certain amount of rounds, audited taxpayers might ultimately change to noncompliance.

In this case, I propose a complex yet reasonable criterion regarding the probabilities of compliance or noncompliance: A non-audited person who complied at t_1 will shift to noncompliance at t_2 based on a combination of external and internal factors. The latter are determined by the incentives that the person has to breach the norm that she has abided by in the past. For instance, a taxpayer who owns a profitable business and has paid all the taxes might later reverse into noncompliance if economic conditions change for the worse and paying taxes leads to losses in her business; such an economic shift might tempt the taxpayer to explore noncompliance in order to stay in business. Let us call this internal factor (I).

The external factor (cultural) is determined by the way that taxpayers perceive the environment. If a person feels that cheating will not be detected, then that person might suddenly change behaviors. Usually this is what happens when new information alters a previous individual equilibrium. But the main reason for a person to change to noncompliance on the basis of cultural factors is that he finds out that many other people cheat and get away with it. This discovery raises feelings of being exploited, which might lead to noncooperative behavior. Thus, the more that people cheat, the more likely it is that honest taxpayers will be tempted to escape compliance. Let us call this the contagious effect (C).

For practical reasons, I propose to measure the likelihood of shifting from compliance into noncompliance as the product of these two factors. The incentives (internal) factor is a number between 0 and 1 that measures a subjective dimension of commitment to the norm. The contagious (external) factor is the probability of shifting on the basis of knowing other cheaters. Therefore, in a world of 80 percent cheaters, the probability that a given taxpayer will know other cheaters will be 80 percent. For the sake of simplicity, let us assume that in a world of X percent cheaters, the contagious factor will be that X percentage. Therefore, shifting from compliance to noncompliance is determined by I*C. For example, if I is 0.5 and the percentage of cheaters is 30 percent, compliers who will remain in that category will be 85 percent of that population, while 15 percent will shift to noncompliance (50 percent * 0.3 = 15 percent). Of course, the more cheaters there are or the higher the internal incentive to break the rule, the more people will cease to adhere to the norm.[4]

---

4. Formal shifts are detailed at the end of this appendix.

Let us assume additionally the following reasonable points:

- There are two large groups, compliers and cheaters. Compliers report 90 percent of their legal taxes due (I assume that nobody pays all their taxes), and cheaters vary their compliance rate. I assume that on the first round, one-third of noncompliers cheat 25 percent of their tax dues, one-third 50 percent, and one-third 75 percent.
- People will tend to increase their level of cheating if they are not caught. Some of the cheaters of 25 percent at t_1 will be tempted to cheat 50 percent at t_2. Only a fraction of taxpayers move into higher "brackets" of tax evasion.
- Audits and other enforcement mechanisms are effectively conducted, and there is also a weighted random selection of cases for audits (although both assumptions are not entirely accurate in the real world).[5]
- The total number of taxpayers selected for enforcement is 5 percent.[6] We will call the entire range of in-depth enforcement measures "audits."
- Audits in a given round will affect compliance for three successive rounds.
- Taxpayers will test limits and shift from low noncompliance to higher noncompliance as determined by the pool of compliers. Twenty-five percent in each category will increase their level of noncompliance (e.g., from 50 to 75 percent).
- Two types of simulations are presented. The first (A) is based on different random selections of cases for audit. The second (B) is based on a more weighted selection of cases, where the probability of selection is generally twice as large when the cheating is 75 percent compared to 25 percent (see the section on "Formal Shifts" at the end of this appendix for details). The first (A) simulation assumes a poor tax administration, and the second (B) assumes a good tax administration.
- Each simulation has three starting scenarios. The first (figs. C.A1 and B) is a world of 50 percent compliers and 50 percent cheaters,

5. In the real tax world, however, tax administrations and other agencies enforce the law by randomly selecting cases for audit on the basis of information provided in the tax returns and its comparison with other taxpayers.

6. In-depth audits rarely exceed 1 percent of total tax returns. A TA, however, not only conducts in-depth audits but also performs a wide range of surveillance and controls that effectively contact a much larger number of active taxpayers. Five percent is a reasonable rate of taxpayers who have been enforced in some way by a TA for a given year.

Fig. C.1A Simulative Evolution of Tax Compliance with Random Selection of Enforcement, Initial Distribution 50/50

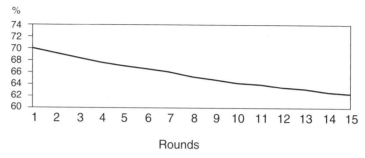

Rounds

Fig. C.1B Simulative Evolution of Tax Compliance with Weighted Selection of Enforcement, Initial Distribution 50/50

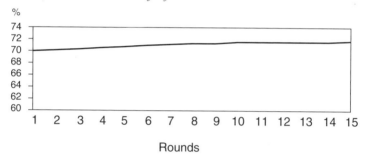

Rounds

the second (figs. C.2A and B) has a starting universe of 80 percent compliers and 20 percent tax evaders (a compliance environment), and the third (figs. C.3A and B) begins with 20 percent tax compliers and 80 percent tax evaders (a noncompliance environment).

- The value of I is 0.3 and fixed for all simulations presented. This is hardly the case in the real world, but for the purpose of this exercise I decided to leave it constant to allow for a better comparison between compliers and cheaters. Opportunities to cheat, risk-aversion levels, and so on greatly affect incentives. Economic cycles are crucial in shaping incentives; when taxpayers face adverse economic conditions, (I) increases. Nonetheless, I decided to leave (I) fixed in this simulation, although many possibilities allow for testing this parameter as a variable.

- For the purpose of this simulation, I assume that every taxpayer has to pay one dollar in taxes for the period. Therefore, the distribution of different taxpayers at different levels of compliance yields a total tax compliance rate for that population.

Fig. C.2A Simulative Evolution of Tax Compliance with Random Selection of
Enforcement, Initial Distribution 80/20

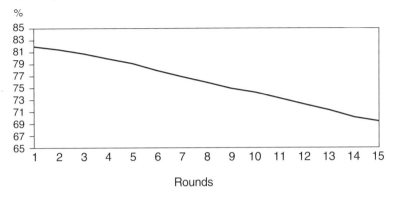

Rounds

Fig. C.2B Simulative Evolution of Tax Compliance with Weighted Selection of
Enforcement, Initial Distribution 80/20

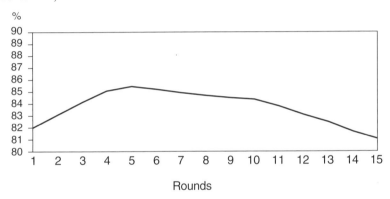

Rounds

Figures C.1A and B, C.2A and B, and C.3A and B present the results of
these simulations expressed in the total compliance rate for the group for
fifteen rounds (years). Figures A denote a poor administration and figures
B a good tax administration.

This simulation yields several results. First, the audit rate is important
in developing individual perceptions of the risk of being audited, but it is
usually marginal, simply because most taxpayers cannot be audited.

Second, and more important, the selection of cases matters more than
the audit rate. Selecting cases according to the perceived severity of cheating yields much higher tax compliance rates because people who engage
in large-scale tax evasion perceive the threat of audit as more meaningful. A good selection of cases (figs. B) yields higher tax compliance rates
compared to a random selection (figs. A).

Fig. c.3A Simulative Evolution of Tax Compliance with Random Selection of Enforcement, Initial Distribution 20/80

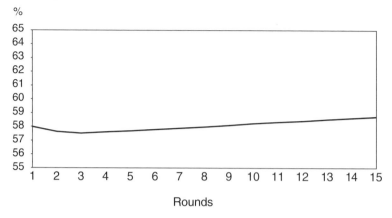

Fig. c.3B Simulative Evolution of Tax Compliance with Weighted Selection of Enforcement, Initial Distribution 20/80

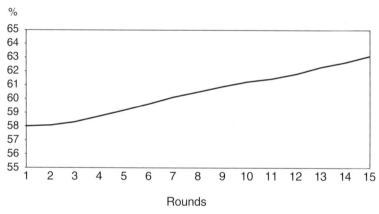

Third, good administrations (those that select cases more effectively because they have good information systems) are capable of getting reasonable results, even in very adverse conditions (fig. c.3B). Poor administration has, in the long run, a deteriorating effect on compliance (fig. c.2A). This result supports my theories about the necessary mix of culture and administration. A good administration can tilt the balance into a compliance equilibrium, but doing so will require many rounds. Poor administrations will undermine compliance equilibria because the pool of cheaters will expand and contagion will further weaken enforcement.

Fourth, good administrations yield a distribution of taxpayers who cheat moderately (in the real world, these are taxpayers who overstate some deductions or understate a small fraction of income), but this distribution generally includes only a small number of large tax evaders. Poor administrations, on the other hand, generate a considerable number of large tax evaders (compare fig. C.1B to fig. C.1A, fig. C.2B to fig. C.2A, and fig. C.3B to fig. C.3A).[7] If we assume that each round equals a tax year, then it will take a good administration working with a poor compliance environment about fifteen years of strong enforcement to reach the level of more compliant societies that do not have a strong TA. (The case of Spain is a good illustration of this.)

Fifth, and most important, the distribution among compliers and cheaters at the onset matters a great deal. Higher noncompliance at the norm-emergence phase inhibits the establishment of a tax compliance environment. After many rounds, the highest compliance rate is still that for figure C.2B, which initially had the highest proportion of tax compliers. Moreover, the same initial distribution with a poor tax administration (fig. C.2A) still yields higher compliance rates at $t15$ than a tax-noncompliance society with an effective administration (fig. C.3B). If a society with good compliance and poor enforcement (fig. C.2A) is capable of developing even a slightly better TA, it will reach equilibrium between $t10$ and $t15$ at higher compliance rates than a poor compliance society with good enforcement (fig. C.3B). But a compliant society that initially has a poor tax administration (fig. C.2A) will deteriorate slowly but steadily and reach equilibrium at much lower levels of compliance. In other words, bad enforcement will not hold honest taxpayers in check for long. In this environment, however, moderate enforcement will yield very good compliance results. A high compliance environment does not require strong enforcement to achieve a sustainable compliance equilibrium, as moderate enforcement will suffice. Conversely, a noncompliance equilibrium requires very strong enforcement for an extended period of time to produce a compliance-friendly equilibrium. Only when that is attained can enforcement be moderate. Enforcement, however, should also be tied to the general health and the stability of the economy (which affects individual decisions).[8]

7. After fifteen rounds, the number of taxpayers who evaded 75 percent of their taxes under weak administration increased on average by 56 percent, whereas under good administration that number decreased by 89 percent. For a full discussion, see appendix in Bergman 2003.

8. This simulation takes into consideration very simple assumptions regarding the effect of enforcement on compliance from a micro perspective. Once macro events (recurring fiscal crises, recessions, etc.) are included, the cultural diffusion of noncompliance increases and the effect of successful enforcement dilutes. I thank James Mahon for this valuable comment.

This simulation provides strong proof that initial conditions affect compliance. The distribution of conformance or nonconformance to tax law within a society with a tradition of law abidance accounts largely for the degree of success of a new norm. This simple evolutionary simulation explains why culture affects tax compliance. On the other hand, such a model does not imply that noncompliance trends cannot be reversed. It is not very deterministic. After all, some countries with large-scale tax evasion have indeed changed, but such change required extremely effective institutions and very stringent enforcement for a sustained period of time. Good enforcement fosters legal culture in the long run. Under certain conditions, enforcement and a culture of compliance may coevolve.

SUMMARY

This model is based on simple assumptions regarding the rationality of taxpayers. In good-compliance climates, most taxpayers cheat a little but refrain from massive evasion; in tax environments of poor compliance, however, most taxpayers take larger risks. Enforcement can only somewhat contain the flow from compliance to evasion; it cannot by itself transform, in a short period of time, a noncompliant society into a compliant one.

This model suggests that although compliance with norms benefits from effective enforcement, it is more tied to the environment in which taxpayers operate. Under the assumption that nobody likes to pay taxes, there are still social settings where even poor enforcement does not have harmful consequences, at least in the short run. Poor enforcement of norms with high costs, however, will ultimately diminish general compliance. As costs of compliance rise, there is a need for better tax administrations. Because paying taxes is by definition very costly, the legitimacy of taxation can never be very high, and consequently the need for enforcement will be more important than is the case with other widely accepted norms. Not surprisingly, without good enforcement tax compliance will tend to decrease.

Compliance with taxes depends on many factors, such as favorable economic conditions and the nature of the tax system. Controlling for these and other factors, I argue that a culture of noncompliance can be slowly reversed by altering the weight of enforcement. Such enforcement must be widespread, effective, and costly for tax evaders. The simulation model allows us to predict that the same level of enforcement in Chile and Argentina yields different results because, at the onset, the distribution of compliance was significantly different. Holding constant other variables, for Argentina to be as successful as Chile would require Argentina to execute even better enforcement than Chile for a very extended period of time.

FORMAL SHIFTS

The following are the formal shifts of taxpayers in round x to round x + 1 according to the four possible categories of compliance (90, 75, 50, and 25 percent). These are only for taxpayers not audited in the previous round.

$$C1_{i+1} + cu1_i * na1_i$$

Where:

$C1_{i+1}$ = General pool of taxpayers who comply at 90 percent in period i + 1.

$cu1_i$ = Percentage of taxpayers who comply at 90 percent out of total taxpayers in period i.

$$C2_{i+1} + cu2_i * na2_i * 0.9$$

Where:

$C2_{i+1}$ = Taxpayers who comply at 75 percent in period i + 1.

$cu2_i$ = Percentage of noncompliance taxpayers (who comply at 75, 50, and 25 percent) out of total taxpayers in period i.

$na2_i$ = Taxpayers who complied at 75 percent, not audited in period i.

$$C3_{i+1} + na2_i * na3_i * 0.9$$

Where:

$C3_{i+1}$ = Taxpayers who comply at 50 percent in period i + 1.

$na2_i$ = Taxpayers who complied at 50 percent, not audited in period i.

$$C4_{i+1} + na3_i * 0.1 + na3_i$$

Where:

$C4_{i+1}$ = Taxpayers who comply at 25 percent in period i + 1.

$na3_i$ = Taxpayers who complied at 25 percent, not audited in period i.

Many countries in Latin America have enacted good practices and policy recommendations (laws) but have failed to strengthen the most critical institution to execute them (the state), thereby undermining the conditions for compliance equilibria (the rule of law). In this appendix, I briefly discuss these topics, which are central to the problem of tax compliance. I argue that there is an underlining theme in general compliance: in countries where the rule of law is strong, the level of tax compliance tends to be high; in countries where violations to the rule of law are widespread, tax evasion is rampant. More than a simple correlation, I claim that there is a causal link between tax compliance and the strength of the rule of law.

During the last decades, scholars have shown an increasing interest in the study of the rule of law in Latin America (Nino 1992; Domingo and Sieder 2001; Barros 2002; Ungar 2002; Brinks 2007; Hilbink 2007). Most studies focus on the modernization of the judicial system—an important, yet limited, perspective on the problem, as the rule of law transcends the courts. It is far from a tautology to say that the rule of law is the rule of rules, an equilibrium reached by players who accept governance by rules, regardless of their effects. The rule of law should be studied as a social equilibrium that enhances general welfare.[1]

The rule of law has been modeled as a set of interactions between rulers and citizens, where the former decide to abide by the constraints of legal standards because citizens are capable of punishing governments by overthrowing them.[2] To overcome the manipulative character of rulers,

1. It is not Pareto, because not everybody is better off in such an equilibrium.
2. Several studies on this topic fail to distinguish clearly between democracy and the rule of law (Shapiro 1994 North and Weingast 1989; Maravall and Przeworski 2003). In Weingast's 1997 study, the difference appears blurred, as he uses the terms interchangeably. Przeworski (2003) and Ferejohn and Pasquino (2003) focus more on democracy than on the rule of law. This literature is more concerned with rule than with law, emphasizing restrictions on and costs to rulers rather than studying the nature of such constraints. The

constitutions and other focal points serve as coordination devices to mobilize the citizenry to resist the transgression of rights (Weingast 1997),
and civil organizations become non-coordinated, autonomous watch-
dogs to protect citizens (Smulovitz 2003). I propose an extension of these
models. I argue that the simple proposition that rulers have a wide range
of instruments to enhance the compliance of citizens (incentives, coercion,
etc.) is very complex and must be incorporated into a model that shifts
the focal solution from a coordination game to an assurance-type game.
Moreover, the role of bureaucracy introduces a nested principal-agent
game within a broader coordination game. In a context of restricted information, under the rule of law, rulers have to operate with bureaucratic
semi-veto power: the more autonomous the bureaucracy is, the smaller
the maneuvering range of rulers and the larger the constraints on them.
Rulers, as principals, cannot bypass agents to transgress citizens' rights.
Bureaucrats, as agents, have their own set of interests, which might col-
lide with those of principals and citizens. The rule of law encompasses
more than rulers' willingness to abide by constraining rules; it also includes the delegation of ruling to a stable bureaucracy. This Weberian
perspective has been lost in the recent literature. The rule of law entails
that in addition to the rulers, citizens also choose to comply, not out of
fear of the rulers' wrath but because the enforcement of rules is perceived
as plausible. Citizens undertake costly actions by abiding by laws voluntarily, and hence the self-enforcing nature of compliance does not apply
only to rulers. A salient attribute of the rule of law is its capability to
curtail free riding.

The most important feature of the rule of law is the state. An interesting semantic comparison is in order: whereas the Anglo-Saxon tradition
calls it "the rule of law," the Continental tradition uses a slightly different term, "the state of law" (*Rechtsstaat* in German, *État de droit* in
French, and *Estado de Derecho* in Spanish).[3] The state is as important as
the law in the Continental tradition. The *Estado de Derecho* means that
the whole set of institutions and organizations embodied in the state are
positioned to serve the law. In Latin America, the problem is not the law
but the state. As Centeno (2002) writes, the weakness of states remains

---

basic question is why rulers agree to abide by rules that limit their discretionary power (see
also Holmes 2003). In a nutshell, rulers will obey the rules because their time horizon is
broad, allowing them to discount current losses for future gains. As I said, the main issue
here is democracy and limited government, not the rule of law. I maintain that the rule of
law is as much about enforcement as it is about ruling.

3. The Spanish term "imperio de la ley" is much closer to the English "rule of law."

the core component of the "Latin American puzzle."[4] State building has become crucial (Evans 1997; Fukuyama 2004; O'Donnell 1999). "Bringing the state back in" has become an academic as well as a political challenge. Creating a set of effective institutions to meet political and social goals is one of the most prominent and difficult endeavors that the polity faces. Stronger states are those that do not depend on rulers to make everyday decisions. The institutions and organizations that embody the state are the guarantors of a stable and dominant equilibrium. Transgressions are curtailed because their costs are perceived as severe, and their costs are severe because somebody is capable of enforcing them.

The rule of law is the state of law (as opposed to Louis XIV's maxim, l'état, c'est moi). States capable of functioning under the self-imposed restrictions of the law, and yet able to penalize transgressors, can foster virtuous circles of compliance. The perceived threat of regular enforcement among citizens elicits better conformity with rules than does the threat of the severe wrath of rulers. The former are stable, the latter occasional. When laws become predictable, more citizens are better off abiding by rules if everybody else complies. In short, the rule of law meets the basic conditions of coordination games, wherein players create the power to enforce agreed-on bargains (see Hardin 1995, chap. 2). Such coordination is based on individuals' interest in promoting this equilibrium as long as others do so.

Following Olson (2000) and Barzel (2002), I assume that rulers want to keep ruling and that citizens want to minimize the cost of being ruled. But rather than begin with a complex bargaining process between the bandit (the ruler) and the subjects (the citizens), my starting point for good taxation is the ability of the ruler to convey to the ruled that it is in *their best interest* to be taxed. There are multiple reasons for the subjects to accept this proposition: it might be that the ruler is perceived as brutal and effective, that the ruler shares with the subjects part of the theft by converting it into valuable public goods, that the ruler sets up a system of theft that allows subjects to prosper compared to other systems, and so forth. Usually, the ruled agree to accept taxation for a number of reasons, all of which depend on a basic fact: in the absence of the ruler's strong initial threat of punishing noncompliance, the subjects will not comply. Afterward, brute force alone will not generate conformity unless

4. After explaining the failure to develop strong states, he writes: "In Latin America, political institutions suited for a city-state were given empires to rule. We should not be surprised that they failed to do so" (164).

the ruler is capable of signaling readiness to share some of the profits. Only then do subjects accept the ruler as legitimate.

This is a basic theory of government, but not of the rule of law. Rulers need law when brute force is insufficient to raise taxes, and subjects need law to limit the ruler's extraction capacity. At one point, rulers and subjects realize that both parties profit from self-restraint—that all other alternatives are unstable. This is an efficient equilibrium resulting from a trade-off between the dictator's desire for size and the citizens' preference for prosperity (Alesina and Spolaore 2003). When rulers and subjects look forward to the future, laws become valuable because they enhance performance. Free riders, however, might torpedo this tenuous equilibrium: rulers can break promises, or subjects can invite other bandits to take over the realm. In order to overcome these threats, law can become stable if rulers are capable of fostering two basic conditions: they must have the capacity to limit free riding and punish cheaters, and they must convince their subjects that the current deal is better than other alternatives. The ruler must convince her subjects that she is more benevolent than others are, but also that any attempt to free ride will be severely punished. The stick must precede the carrot, but the carrot should be present.

The initial equilibrium creates a virtuous circle because new generations learn that the ruler is very powerful, that free riders might get caught and punished, and that the current deal has enough incentives for subjects to profit to make it worthwhile to cooperate. Both parties are subject to the basic predicament of a binding coordination game (Hardin 1995, 1999) where the collective-action capacities of the ruled successfully establish the principles of the rule of law (Barzel 2002). If the ruler suddenly decides that she needs more taxes and tries to levy them, some subjects will be tempted to cheat. If the ruler cannot act swiftly to curtail free riding, more subjects will learn that they will be better off cheating, and the previous equilibrium will rapidly become unstable. Conversely, if the ruler can reduce taxes without diminishing the quality of public goods, fewer subjects will be tempted to escape from the agreement. Therefore, rulers should be interested in developing administrative agencies that can independently enforce the law. The passage from a principal-agent problem into an assurance game signals the beginning of the rule of law.[5]

Subjects' agreement to pay is contingent on their receiving the quality of life and protection from other bandits that taxes generate. Bandits

---

5. I thank Carlos Rosenkrantz for this valuable comment.

(rulers) offer protection in exchange for taxes. But what happens when such protection fails? What are the consequences when a bandit who solicited the support of subjects to prevent other thieves from taking over fails to deliver the promised public goods? Again, the previous equilibrium is shaken, some subjects will free ride, and, if they succeed, many more will follow, making tax evasion an epidemic. A stable equilibrium will deteriorate into an unstable one, and people will give up on the rule of law because the players are not keeping their bargains.

Taxes must allow citizens to prosper, but at the same time the ruler's threat must be credible. The rule of law results from a bargain that creates strong incentives for both rulers and subjects to abide by their agreement. This system has two major differences from other forms of government and taxation: constraints on rulers are embodied in laws that tend to be general, and rulers' enforcement agencies are autonomous from their will. The more rulers are constrained by the principles of taxation previously established with the subjects by means of bargaining, and the more they refrain from personal or party intervention in enforcement, the more their subjects will find taxation legitimate and be willing to comply. Under the rule of law, nations reach tax compliance equilibrium if they have two variables in place: a set of rational tax policies that allow most citizens to play by the rules and prosper, and the establishment of strong, autonomous enforcement organizations that serve the law directly and the ruler only indirectly.

As Guillermo O'Donnell (1999) has rightly stated, the "(un)rule of law" is one of the most crucial explanations for Latin American underdevelopment. Up to this point, however, no guiding theory has been advanced that explains why Latin American countries have been unable to develop a strong rule of law. I contend that in order to foster a genuine *Estado de Derecho*, one must address problems of administrative enforcement, political organization, and social equity.

The basic conceptualization of the modern rule of law rests on two fundamental principles: predictability and fairness. Predictability has been the cornerstone of positivist *Rechtsstaat*. This tradition stresses reliance on the legal process rather on the individual will. Although there is no dependence on the moral or the substantive nature of laws, as in Anglo-Saxon tradition, *Rechtsstaat* nonetheless protects against arbitrariness through due process and the administrative state.[6] Nowadays, however, the rule of law cannot prosper without also promoting substantive and

6. The source of Weberian pessimism lies precisely in the lack of virtue of this rather mechanic concept of legal domination.

procedural fairness. Legitimacy is undermined if most people do not feel genuinely included in the legal order. Thus, the rule of law callzs for predictability as well as for some measures of substantive fairness. Protection of expanding rights becomes as important as the regularity of the legal process.[7]

The extensive literature on the tension between predictability and fairness has neglected the predicament of one on the other (Rosenfeld 2003). I contend that in the twentieth century, most Latin American nations failed to develop a stable rule of law because rulers, in order to gain approval, promoted rights well beyond their material capacity to ensure the predictability of these legal norms. In other words, law prevailed over states. The populist pursuit of fairness prevailed over the solid establishment of predictability. Historically, states that have successfully fostered the stable rule of law have proceeded in the opposite direction: first they developed the institutional capacities to achieve attainable goals, and only then did they expand rights. For example, the United States established a rule of law in the midst of slavery; justice and fairness issues were redressed two centuries later. In spite of the recent apartheid, the prognosis for the rule of law in South Africa is more positive than in Brazil. South Africa and many other nations developed institutions capable of protecting property rights, the cornerstone of both the *Rechtsstaat* and economic growth.[8]

Predictability and fairness have two necessary conditions: enforcement and welfare. To make rules predictable, states need to develop the instruments to deliver judicial protection of rights (basically property, contract, and penal law). Rules must be reasonably enforceable, and the threat of the stationary bandit must be credible. When unenforceable rules are seriously challenged, the preservation of the legal order calls for the annulment of legal provisions. For example, the Eighteenth Amendment of the U.S. Constitution (inspired by the moralist temperance movement) was abolished in the 1930s because the laws based on it were not being upheld, thereby undermining basic governmental capabilities.

Affluent societies are better equipped than poor societies to promote justice through law. Universal education, public health, and other social

---

7. Drawing from the Argentine experience, institutional weakness as the result of actors' behaviors that are constrained by the type of initial equilibrium they live in, and how this creates expectations of stability and the willingness to invest in institutions (283–88). This argument is parallel to mine. Although there are no clear references to how bureaucracies and enforcement agencies operate within a rule of law scenario, they do point to the importance of studying actors' strategic behaviors within the given equilibrium.

8. A similar conclusion can be derived from Lieberman 2003.

and economic rights are successfully promoted through law when social orders have achieved a threshold of welfare. Developed countries created welfare states in the 1950s and 1960s only after the rule of law had been solidly grounded. Conversely, most populist states in Latin America incurred high social expenditures in an attempt to create similar welfare states without a firm base of fiscal health. Chile, again, was the exception: a centralized and efficient state based on the rule of law had been solidly established before any serious redistribution of wealth was promoted (Hojman 2002). Even under Pinochet, when no meaningful justice issues were addressed, a legal framework zealously guarded property rights and protection. Fairness issues began to be moderately addressed by the Concertación government through minimalist, deliverable laws.[9]

What lessons can be drawn from this discussion? Rulers and citizens can reach a stable legal equilibrium when institutional legal capacities (particularly property rights, moderate security protection, and some political constitutional safeguards) are solidly grounded. These orders are positioned to generate economic growth that can be distributed through law. This enhances the state's legitimacy, fostering a virtuous circle of legality and a self-sustained legal equilibrium. In other words, predictability must precede fairness, and enforcement must precede welfare. But welfare elicits justice and improves legitimacy, a stable path of legal development.

Most Latin American nations developed in the opposite direction. In order to address fairness, growing states over-legislated, without the institutional capabilities to reasonably enforce the laws that they passed.[10] To compensate for this incapacity, these states enacted more rules to fix previous deficiencies. They continued to lack the institutional devices to enforce the laws, however, and continued to be deficient in the provision of welfare.[11] More and more laws became less and less enforceable, creating

9. See also Barros 2002 for an in-depth account of the constitutional makeup of the military junta in Chile. The main difference from my argument is that Pinochet and the junta operated within a well-constituted state capable of generating initial compliance; Argentina in the same period was also governed by a military junta, which promoted rules that were transgressed by the same players who enacted them.

10. No state can completely enforce its laws. There is always some degree of lawlessness. The legal provisions of rules of law have a "wider coverage" compared to discretionary populist and anomic states.

11. Fukuyama (2004) makes the same argument, but he does not explain the mechanisms that led to the failure to establish solid institutions. He suggests that a normative approach should be taken into consideration (66), and that "context-specific" conditions are relevant to explain why the import of "best practices" from successful cases usually failed in developing countries (chap. 2).

a vicious cycle of more laws with fewer people willing to obey them. To break this impasse, it is necessary to reduce rather than expand legislation; instead of shrinking, however, Latin American states have generally enacted more unenforceable laws, thereby fostering more illegality. States became more anomic rather than more legalist (see Nino 1992). Consequently, public disenchantment has expanded over the last decades. States are increasingly incapable of enforcing laws as they attempt to reverse their deficiencies with the same failing tools. Many have reached an endogenous, circular impasse. Instead of concentrating on establishing a small number of enforceable taxes, larger-scale tax evasion has led to the creation of more and more complex taxes that quickly become less enforceable, augmenting tax evasion and further diminishing the legitimacy of taxation. This has fed a genuine culture of tax evasion.

I have claimed that the culture of compliance largely results from taxpayers' interaction with the legal environment and their internalization of the perceived costs of compliance. Legal culture matters because it facilitates conditions of coordination and aligns incentives for cooperation. Political entities capable of fostering the rule of law stand a better chance of creating more widespread law abidance, including tax compliance. In this scenario, cheating on taxes becomes a problem of scale and a coordination game. In anomic states, governments fight a "war on tax evasion," usually yielding a prisoner's dilemma outcome. Yet under the rule of law, states need only to curtail free riding—a much simpler task.

REFERENCES

AFIP (Administración Federal de Ingresos Públicos). 1998. *Estadísticas tributarias*. Dirección de Estudios: Buenos Aires.

———. 2002. *Estadísticas tributarias*. Dirección de Estudios: Buenos Aires.

———. 2006. "Estimación del Incumplimiento en el IVA 2005." Buenos Aires: AFIP. Available at http://www.afip.gov.ar/institucional/estudios/archivos/Incumplimiento_iva_2006.pdf.

Akelroff, G., J. Yellen, and M. Katz. 1996. "An Analysis of Out-of-Wedlock Childbearing in the United States." *Quarterly Journal of Economics* 111: 277–317.

Akers, R. 1977. *Deviant Behavior: A Social Learning Approach*. 2nd ed. Belmont, Calif.: Wadsworth.

Alesina, V., and E. Spolaore. 2003. *The Size of Nations*. Cambridge, Mass.: MIT Press.

Allingham, M., and A. Sandmo. 1972. "Income Tax Evasion: A Theoretical Analysis." *Journal of Public Economics* 1:323–38.

Alm, J. 2000. "Tax Compliance and Administration." In *Handbook on Taxation*, ed. W. Hildreth and J. Richardson. New York: Marcel Dekker.

Alm, J., and W. Beck. 1993. "Tax Amnesties and Compliance in the Long Run: A Time Series Analysis." *National Tax Journal* 46:53–59.

Alm, J., B. Erard, and J. Feinstein. 1996. "The Relationship Between Federal and State Income Tax Audits." In *Empirical Foundations of Household Taxation*, ed. M. Fedelstein and J. Poterba. Chicago: University of Chicago Press.

Alm, J., B. Jackson, and M. McKee. 1992. "Deterrence and Beyond: Toward a Kinder, Gentler IRS." In *Why People Pay Taxes: Tax Compliance and Enforcement*, ed. J. Slemrod. Ann Arbor: University of Michigan Press.

Alm, J., and J. Martinez-Vazquez. 2003. *Institution, Paradigms, and Tax Evasion in Developing and Transition Countries*. In *Public Finance in Developing and Transition Countries*, ed. J. Martinez-Vazquez and J. Alm. Cheltenham: Edgar Elgar.

Alm, J., and M. McKee. 2000. "Tax Compliance as a Coordination Game." Paper presented at the Southern Economic Association, University of Mississippi, in Jackson.

Alm, J., M. McKee, and W. Beck. 1990. "Amazing Grace: Tax Amnesties and Compliance." *National Tax Journal* 43:23–37.

Alm, J., I. Sanchez, and A. de Juan. 1995. "Economic and Noneconomic Factors in Tax Compliance." *Kyklos* 48:3–18.

Andreoni, J., B. Erard, and J. Feinstein. 1998. "Tax Compliance." *Journal of Economic Literature* 35:818–60.

Angell, A. 2006. "Democratic Governance in Chile." Manuscript. St. Antony's College.

Arellano, J., and M. Marfán. 1987. "25 Años de Política Fiscal en Chile." *Colección Estudios CIEPLAN* 21:129–62.

Arenas de Mesa, A., and F. Bertranau. 1997. "Learning from Social Security Reforms: Two Different Cases, Chile and Argentina." *World Development* 25:329–48.

Argañaraz, N. 2004. *La Verdadera Presion Tributaria Argentina.* Buenos Aires: Asociación Empresaria Argentina. Avaialable at http://www.ieral.org.

Axelrod, R. 1984. *The Evolution of Cooperation.* New York: Basic Books.

———. 2004. *La Complejidad de la cooperación.* Buenos Aires: Fondo de Cultura Economica.

Bakija, J., and J. Slemrod. 2004. *Taxing Ourselves: A Citizen's Guide to the Debate over Taxes.* 3rd ed. Cambridge, Mass: MIT Press.

Banerjee, A. 1992. "A Simple Model of Herd Behavior." *The Quarterly Journal of Economics* 107:797–817.

Bardach, E., and R. Kagan. 1982. *Going by the Book: The Problem of Regulatory Unreasonableness.* Philadelphia: Temple University Press.

Barra, P., and M. Jorrat. 1999. *Estimación de la Evasión Tributaria en Chile.* Santiago: Departamento de Estudios, Servicio de Impuestos Internos (SII).

Barros, R. 2002. *Constitutionalism and Dictatorship: Pinochet, the Junta, and the 1980 Constitution.* New York: Cambridge University Press.

Barzel, Y. 2002. *A Theory of the State: Economic Rights, Legal Rights, and the Scope of the State.* Cambridge: Cambridge University Press.

Bates, R. 1989. "A Political Scientist Looks at Tax Reform." In *Tax Reform in Developing Countries,* ed. M. Gillis. Durham: Duke University Press.

Bates, R., A. Grief, M. Levi, J. Rosenthal, and B. Weingast. 1998. *Analytic Narratives.* Princeton: Princeton University Press.

Becker, G. 1968. "Crime and Punishment: An Economic Approach." *Journal of Political Economy* 76:169–217.

———. 1991. "A Note on Restaurant Pricing and Other Examples of Social Influence on Prices." *Journal of Political Economy* 99.

Bendix, R. 1978. *Kings or People: Power and the Mandate to Rule.* Berkeley and Los Angeles: University of California Press.

Bergman, M. 1998. "Criminal Law and Tax Compliance." *International Journal of the Sociology of Law* 26:55–74.

———. 2001. "On Trust, Deterrence, and Compliance: The Sociology of Tax Evasion in Argentina." Ph.D. diss., University of California, San Diego.

———. 2003. "Compliance with Norms: The Case of Tax Evasion in Latin America." Documentos de Trabajo 5, CIDE.

———. 2009. "Confianza y Derecho." In *La Confianza y el Derecho en América Latina.* Mexico City: Fondo de Cultura Económica.

Beron, K., H. Tauchen, and A. Witte. 1992. "The Effects of Audits and Socioeconomic Variables on Compliance." In *Why People Pay Taxes: Tax Compliance and Enforcement,* ed. J. Slemrod. Ann Arbor: University of Michigan Press.

Bicchieri, C. 1997. "Learning to Cooperate." In *The Dynamics of Norms,* ed. C. Bicchieri, R. Jeffrey, and B. Skyrms. London: Cambridge University Press.

Bird, R. 1992a. "Tax Reform in Latin America: A Review of Some Recent Experience." *Latin American Research Review* 27:7–36.

———. 1992b. *Tax Policy and Economic Development.* Baltimore: Johns Hopkins University Press.

Bird, R., J. Martinez-Vazquez, and B. Torgler. 2006. "The Property Tax in a New Environment: Lessons from Tax Reform Efforts in Transition Economies." In *The Challenges of Tax Reform in a Global Economy,* ed. J. Alm, J. Martinez-Vazquez, and M. Rider. New York: Springer.

Bird, R., and O. Oldman, eds. 1990. *Taxation in Developing Countries.* 4th ed. Baltimore: Johns Hopkins University Press.

Bird, R., and F. Villancourt. 1998. "Fiscal Decentralization in Developing Countries: An Overview." In *Fiscal Decentralization in Developing Countries,* ed. R. Bird and F. Villancourt. Cambridge: Cambridge University Press.

Blumstein, A., and J. Cohen. 1987. "Characterizing Criminal Careers." *Science* 237:985–91.

Bocco, A. 1999. "Administración Tributaria y Reforma Institucional en la Argentina: Diagnóstico y propuesta de reforma de la AFIP-DGI." Mimeo.

Bocco, A., C. Golonbeck, G. Repetto, A. Rojze, and C. Scrica. 1997. *Regresividad tributaria y distribución del ingreso.* Buenos Aires: Unicef Losada.

Bourdieu, P. 1990. *Sociología y Cultura.* Mexico: Grijalbo.

Braithwaite, J. 1984. *Corporate Crime in the Pharmaceutical Industry.* Boston: Routledge.

———. 1989. *Crime, Shame, and Reintegration.* Cambridge: Cambridge University Press.

Braithwaite, J., and G. Geis. 1982. "On Theory and Action for Corporate Crime Control." *Crime and Delinquency* 28:292–314.

Brennan, G., and J. Buchanan. 1980. *The Power to Tax: Analytical Foundations of a Fiscal Constitution.* Cambridge: Cambridge University Press.

———. 1981. *Monopoly in Money and Inflation: The Case for a Constitution to Discipline Government.* London: Institute of Economic Affairs.

Brinks, D. 2007. *The Judicial Response to Police Killings in Latin America.* New York: Cambridge University Press.

Brinton, M., and V. Nee. 1998. "Introduction." In *The New Institutionalism in Sociology,* ed. M. Brinton and V. Nee. New York: Russell Sage Foundation.

Calello, E. 1992. "Amnistía Fiscal Versus Cumplimiento Tributario." *Revista de Administración Tributaria.* Panama: C.I.A.T., 105–14.

Carroll, J. 1992. "How Taxpayers Think About Their Taxes: Frames and Values." In *Why People Pay Taxes: Tax Compliance and Enforcement,* ed. J. Slemrod. Ann Arbor: University of Michigan Press.

Cassanegra de Jantscher, M. 1990. "Inflation Adjustment in Chile." In *Taxation in Developing Countries,* ed. R. Bird and O. Oldman. 4th ed. Baltimore: Johns Hopkins University Press.

Centeno, M. 2002. *Blood and Debt: War and the Nation-State in Latin America.* University Park: Pennsylvania State University Press.

Chong, D. 1999. *Rational Lives: Norms and Values in Politics and Society.* Chicago: University of Chicago Press.

Cialdini, Robert B. 1984. *Influence: How and Why People Agree to Things.* New York: Morrow.

———. 1989. "Social Motivations to Comply: Norms, Values, and Principles." In *Taxpayer Compliance*, vol. 2, *Social Science Perspectives*, ed. J. Roth and J. Scholz. Philadelphia: University of Pennsylvania Press.

Clotfelter, C. 1983. "Tax Evasion and Tax Rates: An Analysis of Individual Returns." *Review of Economics and Statistics* 65:363–73.

Coleman, J. 1988. "Social Capital in the Creation of Human Capital." *American Journal of Sociology* 94:S95–S120.

———. 1990. *Foundations of Social Theory.* Cambridge, Mass.: Harvard University Press.

Coleman, S. 1996. *The Minnesota Income Tax Compliance Experiment: State Tax Results.* St. Paul: Minnesota Department of Revenues.

Cook, D. 1989. *Rich Law, Poor Law: Different Responses to Tax and Supplementary Benefit Fraud.* Philadelphia: Open University Press.

Control de Gestion. 1998. *Internal Documents.* Buenos Aires: AFIP.

Cowell, F. 1990. *Cheating the Government: The Economics of Tax Evasion.* Cambridge, Mass.: MIT Press.

Croall, H. 1992. *White Collar Crime.* Philadelphia: Open University Press.

Das-Gupta, A., and D. Mookherjee. 1998. *Incentives and Institutional Reform in Tax Administration: An Analysis of Developing Country Experience.* Delhi: Oxford University Press.

Davis, J., G. Hecht, and J. Perkins. 2003. "Social Behavior, Enforcement and Tax Compliance Dynamics." *The Accounting Review* 78:39–69.

Davis, D., and C. Holt. 1993. *Experimental Economics.* Princeton: Princeton University Press.

DGI (Dirección General Impositiva). 1996. "Jornadas: Reunión de equipo Económico para el Estudio de la Evasión." *Internal Documents.* AFIP: Buenos Aires.

Domingo P., and R. Sieder. 2001. "Conclusions." In *Rule of Law in Latin America: The International Promotion of Judicial Reform*, ed. P. Domingo and R. Sieder. London: Institute of Latin American Studies.

Dubin, J. 2004. "Criminal Investigation Enforcement Activities and Taxpayer Noncompliance." In *Statistics of Income.* Washington, D.C.: IRS.

Dubin, J., M. Graetz, and L. Wilde. 1990. "The Effect of Audit Rates on the Federal Individual Income Tax, 1977–1986." *National Tax Journal* 43:395–409.

Dubin, J., and L. Wilde. 1988. "An Empirical Analysis of Federal Income Tax Auditing and Compliance." *National Tax Journal* 41:61–74.

Durán, V., and J. C. Gómez Sabaini. 1995. "Lecciones Sobre Reformas Fiscales en Argentina: 1990–1993." Serie Política Fiscal 68, CEPAL.

Durand, F., and R. Thorp. 1998. "Reforming the State: A Study of the Peruvian Tax Reform." *Oxford Developmental Studies* 26:133–51.

Eaton, K. 2002. *Politicians and Economic Reform in New Democracies: Argentina and the Philippines in the 1990s.* University Park: Pennsylvania State University Press.

———. 2004a. "The Link Between Political and Fiscal Decentralization in South America." In *Decentralization and Democracy in Latin America*, ed. A. Montero and D. Samuels. Notre Dame: University of Notre Dame Press.

————. 2004b. *Politics Beyond the Capital: The Design of Subnational Institutions in South America*. Stanford: Stanford University Press.

ECLAC. 1998. *The Fiscal Covenant: Strengths, Weaknesses, Challenges*. Santiago: ECLAC.

Edwards, S. 1995. *Crísis y Reforma en América Latina*. Buenos Aires: Emecé.

Eisenstadt, S. 1966. *Modernization, Protest, and Change*. Englewood Cliffs, N.J.: Prentice Hall.

Elizondo, C., and Perez de Acha, L. M. 2006. "Separación de Poderes y Garantías Individuales: La Suprema Corte y los Derechos de los Contribuyentes." *Cuestiones Constitucionales* 14:91–130.

Elster, J. 1983. *Sour Grapes*. New York: Cambridge University Press.

————. 1989. *The Cement of Society: A Study of Social Order*. New York: Cambridge University Press.

————. 1999. *Alchemies of the Mind*. Cambridge: Cambridge University Press.

Erard, B. 1992. "The Influence of Tax Audits on Reporting Behavior." In *Why People Pay Taxes: Tax Compliance and Enforcement*, ed. J. Slemrod. Ann Arbor: University of Michigan Press.

Erard, B., and J. Feinstein. 1994. "The Role of Moral Sentiments and Audit Perceptions in Tax Compliance." *Public Finances* 49:S70–S89.

Etcheberry, J. 1993. "Métodos para la Medición de la Evasión Tributaria y para la Medicion del Comportamiento de los Contribuyentes." Paper presented at the CIAT Conference, November 1–5, in Venice.

Evans, P. 1997. "The Eclipse of the State? Reflections on Stateness in an Era of Globalization." *World Politics* 50:62–87.

Fehr, E., and K. Schmidt. 1999. "A Theory of Fairness, Competition, and Cooperation." *Quarterly Journal of Economics* 114:817–68.

Fennell, C., and L. Fennell. 2003. "Fear and Greed in Tax Policy: A Qualitative Research Agenda." *Washington University Journal of Law and Policy* 13:79–138.

Ferejohn, J., and P. Pasquino. 2003. "Rule of Democracy and Rule of Law." In *Democracy and the Rule of Law*, ed. J. Maravall and A. Przeworski. New York: Cambridge University Press.

FIEL. 1991. *El Sistema Impositivo Argentino*. Buenos Aires: Manantial.

————. 1998. *La Reforma Tributaria en la Argentina*. Buenos Aires: FIEL.

————. 2004. *La Presión Tributaria Sobre el Sector Formal de la Economía*. Buenos Aires: Editorial Manantial.

————. 2006. *La Presión Tributaria Sobre el Sector Formal de la Economía*. Buenos Aires: FIEL.

French Davis, R. 1973. *Politicas Economicas en Chile: 1952–1970*. Santiago: CIEPLAN.

Frey, B. 1997. *Not Just for the Money*. Cheltenham: Edward Elgar.

Frey, B., and L. Feld. 2002. "Deterrence and Morale in Taxation: An Empirical Analysis." Working Paper 760, CESifo.

Friedman, J. 1991. *Estudio de la Evasión en el IVA*. Santiago: Universidad de Chile.

Friedman, L. 1975. *The Legal System: A Social Science Perspective*. New York: Russell Sage Foundation.

————. 1985. *Total Justice*. New York: Russell Sage Foundation.

Fukuyama, F. 2004. *State-Building: Governance and World Order in the Twenty-First Century*. Ithaca: Cornell University Press.

Galligan, D., and M. Kurkchiyan. 2003. *Law and Informal Practices: The Post-Communist Experience*. Oxford: Oxford University Press.

Gambetta, D. 1988. "Mafia: The Price of Distrust." In *Trust: Making and Breaking Cooperative Relations*, ed. Diego Gambetta. Oxford: Blackwell.

Gillis, M. 1989. "Tax Reform: Lessons from Postwar Experience in Developing Nations." in *Tax Reform in Developing Countries*, ed. M. Gillis. Durham: Duke University Press.

Gottfredson, M., and T. Hirschi. 1990. *A General Theory of Crime*. Stanford: Stanford University Press.

Gouldner, A. 1960. "The Norm of Reciprocity: A Preliminary Statement." *American Sociological Review* 25:161–79.

Graetz, M., J. Reinganum, and L. Wilde. 1986. "The Tax Compliance Game: Towards an Interactive Theory of Law Enforcement." *Journal of Law, Economics, and Organization* 2:1–32.

Granovetter, M. 1978. "Threshold Models of Collective Behavior." *American Journal of Sociology* 83:1420–43.

Grasmick, H., and W. Scott. 1982. "Tax Evasion and Mechanisms of Social Control: A Comparison with Grand and Petty Theft." *Journal of Economic Psychology* 2:213–30.

Grasmick, H., and R. Bursik Jr. 1990. "Conscience, Significant Others, and Rational Choice: Extending the Deterrence Model." *Law and Society Review* 24:837–61.

Grasmick, H., R. Bursik Jr., and K. Kinsey. 1991. "Shame and Embarrassment as Deterrents to Noncompliance with the Law: The Case of an Antilittering Campaign." *Environment and Behavior* 23:233–51.

Guthrie, C. 2003. "Prospect Theory, Risk Preference, and the Law." *Northwestern University Law Review* 97:1115–1163.

Gutman, P. 1977. "The Subterranean Economy." *Journal of Financial Analysis* (November–December): 26–34.

Harberger, A. 1987. *Modern Developments in Public Finance*. Oxford: Blackwell.

Hardin, R. 1982. *Collective Action*. Baltimore: Johns Hopkins University Press.

———. 1995. *One for All: The Logic of Group Conflict*. Princeton: Princeton University Press.

———. 1999. *Liberalism, Constitutionalism, and Democracy*. New York: Oxford University Press.

———. 2001. *Trust and Trustworthiness*. New York: Russell Sage Foundation.

Harris Inc. 1987. *1987 Taxpayer Attitude Survey*. Washington, D.C.: IRS.

Hedstrom, P. 1998. "Rational Imitation." In *Social Mechanisms*, ed. P. Hedstrom and R. Swedberg. New York: Cambridge University Press.

Hedstrom, P., and R. Swedberg. 1998. "Social Mechanisms: An Introductory Essay." In *Social Mechanisms*, ed. P. Hedstrom and R. Swedberg. New York: Cambridge University Press.

Heredia, B. 2006. *Contested State: The Politics of Trade Liberalization in Mexico*. Ann Arbor: University of Michigan Press.

Hilbink, L. 2007. *Judges Beyond Politics in Democracy and Dictatorships*. New York: Cambridge University Press.

Hobbes, T. 1990. *Leviathan*. Cambridge: Cambridge University Press.

Hojman, D. 2002. "The Political Economy of Chile's Fast Economic Growth: An Olsonian Interpretation." *Public Choice* 111:155–78.

IMF (International Monetary Fund). 1996. *Government Finance Statistics Yearbook*. Washington, D.C.: IMF.

———. 2001. *Financial Statistics Yearbook*. Washington, D.C.: IMF.

INDEC (Instituto Nacional de Estadísticas y Censos). 1997. *Encuesta Permanente de Hogares*. Buenos Aires: INDEC.

IRS (Internal Revenue Service). 1992. *Statistics Income Bulletin*. Washington, D.C.: IRS.

Jeffrey, R. 1965. *The Logic of Decision*. New York: McGraw-Hill.

Johnston, D. 2007. "Agents Say Fast Audits Hurt I.R.S." *New York Times*, January 12, business section.

Jones, M., P. Sanguinetti, and M. Tommasi. 2000. "Politics, Institutions, and Fiscal Performance in a Federal System: An Analysis of the Argentine Provinces." *Journal of Development Economics* 61:305–33.

Jorrat, M. 1996. *Evaluación de la Capacidad Recaudatoria del Sistema Tributario y de la Evasión Tributaria*. Documento preparado para la Conferencia Técnica del CIAT, Viterbo, Italia, October 1996. Available at http://www.sii.cl/aprenda_sobre_impuestos/estudios/tributarios15.htm.

Kagan, R. 1989. "On the Visibility of Income Tax Law Violation." In *Taxpayer Compliance*, vol. 2, *Social Science Perspectives*, ed. J. Roth and J. Scholz. Philadelphia: University of Pennsylvania Press.

Kahan, D. 2000. "Gentle Nudges vs. Hard Shoves: Solving the Sticky Norms Problem." *University of Chicago Law Review* 67:607–46.

———. 2001. "Trust, Collective Action, and Law." *Boston University Law Review* 81:333–47.

Kahneman, D., P. Slovic, and A. Tversky. 1982. *Judgment Under Uncertainty: Heuristics and Biases*. Cambridge: Cambridge University Press.

Kidder, R., and C. McEwen. 1989. "Taxpaying Behavior in Social Context: A Tentative Typology of Tax Compliance and Noncompliance." In *Taxpayer Compliance*, vol. 2, *Social Science Perspectives*, ed. J. Roth and J. Scholz. Philadelphia: University of Pennsylvania Press.

Kinsey, K. 1987. "Survey Data on Tax Compliance: A Compendium and Review." Working Paper 8716, American Bar Foundation.

———. 1988. "Theories and Models of Tax Cheating." Working Paper, American Bar Foundation.

———. 1992. "Deterrence and Alienation Effects of IRS Enforcements: An Analysis of Survey Data." In *Why People Pay Taxes: Tax Compliance and Enforcement*, ed. J. Slemrod. Ann Arbor: University of Michigan Press.

Kinsey, K., and H. Grasmick. 1993. "Did the Tax Reform Act of 1986 Improve Compliance? Three Studies of Pre- and Post-TRA Compliance Attitudes." *Law and Social Policy* 15:293–325.

Kinsey, K., H. Grasmick, and K. Smith. 1991. "Framing Justice: Taxpayer Evaluation of Personal Tax Burden." *Law and Society Review* 25:845–73.

Klepper, S., M. Mazur, and D. Nagin. 1988. "Expert Intermediaries and Legal Compliance: The Case of Tax Preparers." Working Paper, Carnegie Mellon University.

Klepper, S., and D. Nagin. 1989a. "The Deterrent Effect of Perceived Certainty and Severity of Punishment Revisited." *Criminology* 27:721–46.

———. 1989b. "Tax Compliance and Perceptions of Risks of Detection and Criminal Prosecution." *Law and Society Review* 23:209–40.

———. 1989c. "The Criminal Deterrence Literature: Implications for Research on Taxpayer Compliance." In *Taxpayer Compliance*, vol. 2, *Social Science Perspectives*, ed. J. Roth and J. Scholz. Philadelphia: University of Pennsylvania Press.

———. 1989d. "The Anatomy of Tax Evasion." *Journal of Law, Economics and Organization* 5:1–24.

Knight, J. 1992. *Institutions and Social Conflict*. New York: Cambridge University Press.

Kreps, D. 1990. *Game Theory and Economic Modeling*. Oxford: Oxford University Press.

Larrañaga, O. 1995. "Casos de Exito de la Política Fiscal en Chile: 1980–1993." Serie Política Fiscal 67, CEPAL.

Lederman, L. 2003. "The Interplay Between Norms and Enforcement in Tax Compliance." *Ohio State Law Journal* 64:1453–1514

Lempert, R. 1992. "Commentary." In *Why People Pay Taxes: Tax Compliance and Enforcement*, ed. J. Slemrod. Ann Arbor: University of Michigan Press.

Levi, M. 1988. *On Rule and Revenue*. Berkeley and Los Angeles: University of California Press.

———. 1997. *Consent, Dissent, and Patriotism*. Cambridge: Cambridge University Press.

Levitzky, S., and M. V. Murillo. 2005. "Introduction" and "Conclusion: Theorizing About Weak Institutions: Lessons from the Argentine Case." In *Argentine Democracy*, ed. S. Levitzky and M. V. Murillo. University Park: Pennsylvania State University Press.

Levy, M. 1987. *Regulating Fraud: White Collar Crime and the Criminal Process*. London: Tavistock.

Lieberman E. 2003. *Race and Regionalism in the Politics of Taxation in Brazil and South America*. New York: Cambridge University Press.

Long, S. 1981. "Estimating Criminal Tax Violations." *Tax Notes* 12:1325–26.

———. 1992. "Commentary." In *Why People Pay Taxes: Tax Compliance and Enforcement*, ed. J. Slemrod. Ann Arbor: University of Michigan Press.

Long, S., and J. Swingen. 1991. "Taxpayer Compliance: Setting New Agenda for Research." *Law and Society Review* 25:637–83.

Lopez-Alves, F. 2000. "The Transatlantic Bridge: Mirrors, Charles Tilly, and State Formation in the River Plate." In *The Other Mirror: Grand Theory Through the Lenses of Latin America*, ed. M. Centeno and F. Lopez-Alves. Princeton: Princeton University Press.

Mahon, J. 2004. "Causes of Tax Reform in Latin America, 1977–95." *Latin American Research Review* 39:3–30.

Mann, K. 1985. *Defending White Collar Crime: A Portrait of Attorneys at Work*. New Haven: Yale University Press.

Maravall, J., and A. Przeworski, ed. 2003. *Democracy and the Rule of Law*. New York: Cambridge University Press.

———. 2003. "Introduction." In *Democracy and the Rule of Law*, ed. J. Maravall and A. Przeworski. New York: Cambridge University Press.

Marcel, M. 1986. "Diez Años del IVA en Chile." *Colección Estudios CIEPLAN* 19:88–134.

March, J., and J. Olsen. 1989. *Rediscovering Institutions*. New York: The Free Press.

Mark, N. 2002. "Cultural Transmission, Disproportionate Prior Exposure, and the Evolution of Cooperation." *American Sociological Review* 67:3232–344.

Martinez-Vazquez, J., and M. Rider. 1995. *Multiple Models of Tax Evasion: Theory and Evidence*. Working Paper, Department of Economics, Georgia State University.

———. 2003. "Institutions, Paradigms, and Tax Evasion in Developing and Transition Countries." *Public Finance in Developing and Transition Countries*, ed. J. Martinez-Vazquez and J. Alm. Cheltenham: Edward Elgar.

Mason, R., and L. Calvin. 1984. "Public Confidence and Admitted Tax Evasion." *National Tax Journal* 37:489–96.

Mason, R., and K. Kinsey. 1996. *Less Taxes, More Services: Negativity Biases in Tax Exchange Evaluations*. Working Paper 9514, American Bar Foundation.

Mazur, M., and D. Nagin. 1987. "Tax Preparers and Tax Compliance: A Theoretical and Empirical Analysis." Unpublished paper. School of Urban and Public Affairs, Carnegie Mellon University.

McBarnet, D. 1991. "Whiter than White Collar Crime: Tax, Fraud Insurance, and the Management of Stigma." *British Journal of Sociology* 42:3232–344.

Merry, S. 1990. *Getting Justice and Getting Even: Legal Consciousness Among Working-Class Americans*. Chicago: University of Chicago Press.

Merton, R. 1957. *Social Theory and Social Structure. Glencoe, Ill.: Free Press*.

Ministerio de Economía de la República Argentina. 1999. *Estado de la Recaudación*. Buenos Aires: Ministerio de Economía de la República Argentina.

Minnesota Survey of Taxpayers. 1996. Mimeo.

Mora y Araujo, Noguera y Asociados. 1994. "El Régimen Impositivo en la Argentina. Informe de Líderes de Opinión." Unpublished.

Mori, E. 1998. *Investigacion del Comportamiento de los Contribuyentes frente a la Obligacion Tributaria*. Santiago: s11.

Murrell, P. 2001. *Assessing the Value of Law in Transition Economies*. Ann Arbor: University of Michigan Press.

Newman, D. 1958. "White Collar Crime: An Overview and Analysis." *Law and Contemporary Problems* 23:228–32.

Nino, C. 1992. *Un País al Margen de la Ley*. Buenos Aires: Emecé.

North, D. 1990. *Institutions, Institutional Change, and Economic Performance*. New York: Cambridge University Press.

———. 2005. "Introduction." In *Understanding the Process of Economic Change*. Princeton: Princeton University Press.

North, D., and B. Weingast. 1989. "Constitutions and Commitment: The Evolution of Institutions Governing Public Choice in Seventeenth-Century England." *The Journal of Economic History* 49:809–32.

O'Donnell, G. 1999. "Polyarchies and the (Un)Rule of Law in Latin America." In *The (Un)Rule of Law and the Underprivileged in Latin America*, ed. J. Méndez, G. O'Donnell, and P. Pinheiro. Notre Dame: University of Notre Dame Press.

Olson, M. 1965. *The Logic of Collective Action: Public Goods and the Theory of Groups*. New Haven: Yale University Press.

———. 2000. *Power and Prosperity: Outgrowing Communist and Capitalist Dictatorship*. New York: Basic Books.

Ostrom, E. 1990. *Governing the Commons: The Evolution of Institutions in Collective Action.* New York: Cambridge University Press.

———. 2000. "Collective Action and the Evolution of Social Norms." *Journal of Economic Perspectives* 14:137–58.

Oszlak, O. 1982 *La Formación del Estado Argentino.* Buenos Aires: Editorial de Belgrano.

Parsons, T. 1977. *The Evolution of Societies.* Englewood Cliffs, N.J.: Prentice Hall.

Paternoster, R. 1987. "The Deterrent Effect of the Perceived Certainty of Punishment: A Review of the Evidence and Issues." *Justice Quarterly* 4:101–46.

Paternoster, R., L. E. Saltzman, T. Chiricos, and G. Waldo. 1982. "Causal Ordering in Deterrence Research: An Examination of the Perception-Behavior Relationship." In *Deterrence Reconsidered: Methodological Innovations,* ed. J. Hagan. Beverly Hills: Sage.

Paternoster, R., and S. Simpson. 1996. "Sanctions Threats and Appeals to Morality: Testing a Rational Choice Model of Corporate Crime." *Law and Society Review* 30:549–84.

Plumley, A. 1992. "Commentary." In *Why People Pay Taxes: Tax Compliance and Enforcement,* ed. J. Slemrod. Ann Arbor: University of Michigan Press.

———. 2002. "The Impact of IRS on Voluntary Compliance: Preliminary Empirical Results." Paper presented at the National Tax Association Conference, November 12–14, in Orlando.

Posner, E. 2000. *Law and Social Norms.* Cambridge, Mass.: Harvard University Press.

Poterba, J., and J. von Hagen. 1999. "Introduction." In *Institutions and Fiscal Performance,* ed. J. Poterba and J. von Hagen. Chicago: University of Chicago Press.

Przeworski, A. 2003. "Why Do Political Parties Obey the Results of Elections?" In *Democracy and the Rule of Law,* ed. J. Maravall and A. Przeworski. New York: Cambridge University Press.

Putnam, R. 1993. *Making Democracy Work: Civic Tradition in Modern Italy.* Princeton: Princeton University Press.

Reskin, B. 2003. "Including Mechanism in Our Models of Ascriptive Inequality." *American Sociological Review* 68:1–21.

Rose Ackerman, S. 1999. *Corruption and Government: Causes, Consequences, and Reform.* New York: Cambridge University Press.

Rosenfeld, M. 2003. "The Rule of Law, Predictability, Fairness, and Trust: A Critical Appraisal." Paper delivered at the Conference on Law and Trust, October, in Mexico City.

Roth, J., J. Scholz, and A. Witte, eds. 1989. *Taxpayer Compliance: An Agenda for Research.* Philadelphia: University of Pennsylvania Press.

Rothstein, B. 2005. *Social Traps and the Problem of Trust.* New York: Cambridge University Press.

SARC/SELECCIO. 1998. "Indicadores de Gestión." *Internal Documents.* Buenos Aires: AFIP.

Scholz, J. 1998. "Does Trust Enhance Compliance? An Adaptative Intelligence Model of Taxpaying." Mimeo. State University of New York, Stony Brook.

———. 2003. "Contractual Compliance and the Federal Income Tax System." *Washington University Journal of Law and Policy* 13:139–203.

Scholz, J., and M. Lubell. 1998. "Trust and Taxpaying: Testing the Heuristic Approach to Collective Action." *American Journal of Political Science* 42: 398–417.

Scholz, J., and N. Pinney. 1995. "Duty, Fear, and Tax Compliance: The Heuristic Basis of Citizenship Behavior." *American Journal of Political Science* 39: 490–512.

Schwartz, R., and S. Orleans. 1967. "On Legal Sanctions." *University of Chicago Law Review* 34:274–300.

Serra, P. 1991. "Estimación de la Evasión en el Impuesto al Valor Agregado." Serie Documentos de Trabajo 5, Universidad de Chile.

Shapiro, I., ed. 1994. *The Rule of Law.* New York: New York University Press.

SII (Servicio de Impuestos Internos). 1996. *Indicadores de Gestion.* Santiago: Subdirección Jurídica.

———. 1999. *La Administración Tributaria en los Años Noventa.* Santiago: Subdirección de Estudios.

———. 2001a. *Indicadores de Gestión.* Santiago: Subdirección Jurídica.

———. 2001b. *La Justicia Tributaria en Chile.* Documento elaborado por la Subdirección Jurídica y la Subdirección de Estudios Servicio de Impuestos Internos. Santiago: Subdireccion de Estudios.

———. 2007. *Ingresos Tributarios Anuales, 1993–2007.* Available at http://www.sii.cl/aprenda_sobre_impuestos/estudios/estadistribu/ingresos_tributarios.htm.

Silvani, C. 1995. *Perspectivas de la Administración Tributaria.* Washington, D.C.: IMF.

Silvani, C., and J. Brondolo. 1993. *Medición en el Cumplimiento en el IVA y Análisis de sus Determinantes.* Paper presented at the CIAT Conference, November 1–5, in Venice.

Simon, H. 1999. "The Potlatch Between Economics and Political Science." In *Competition and Cooperation: Conversations with Nobelists About Economics and Political Science,* ed. J. Alt, M. Levi, and E. Ostrom, eds. New York: Russell Sage Foundation.

Skocpol, T. 1979. *States and Social Revolutions: A Comparative Analysis of France, Russia, and China.* Cambridge: Cambridge University Press.

Skyrms, B. 1996. *The Evolution of the Social Contract.* New York: Cambridge University Press.

Smith, K. 1992. "Reciprocity and Fairness: Positive Incentives for Tax Compliance." In *Why People Pay Taxes: Tax Compliance and Enforcement,* ed. J. Slemrod. Ann Arbor: University of Michigan Press.

Smulovitz, C. 2003. "How Can the Rule of Law Rule? Cost Imposition Through Decentralization Mechanisms." In *Democracy and the Rule of Law,* ed. J. Maravall and A. Przeworski. New York: Cambridge University Press.

Stalans, L., K. Kinsey, and K. Smith. 1991. "Listening to Different Voices: Formation of Sanction Beliefs and Taxpaying Norms." *Journal of Applied Social Psychology* 21:119–38.

Steenbergen, M., K. McGraw, and J. Scholz. 1992. "Taxpayer Adaptation to the 1986 Tax Reform Act: Do New Tax Laws Affect the Way Taxpayers Think About Taxes?" In *Why People Pay Taxes: Tax Compliance and Enforcement,* ed. J. Slemrod. Ann Arbor: University of Michigan Press.

Steinmo, S. 1993. *Taxation and Democracy: Swedish, British, and American Approaches to Financing the Modern State.* New Haven: Yale University Press.

Stigler, G. 1970. *The Organization of Industry.* Homewood, Ill.: R. D. Irwin.

Sunstein, C. 2001. *Designing Democracy: What Constitutions Do.* New York: Oxford University Press.

Sutherland, E. 1949. *White Collar Crime: The Uncut Version.* New York: Dryden Press.

Tait, A. 1988. *Value-Added Tax: International Practice and Problems.* Washington, D.C.: IMF.

Tanzi, V., ed. 1982. *The Underground Economy in the United States and Abroad.* Lexington, Mass.: Heath.

Tanzi, V., and P. Shome. 1993. "Tax Evasion: Causes, Estimation, Methods, and Penalties: A Focus on Latin America." Serie Política Fiscal 38, CEPAL.

Tauchen, H., and A. Witte. 1986. "Economic Models of How Audits Policies Affect Voluntary Tax Compliance." In *Proceedings of the Seventy-eighth Conference of the National Tax Association–Tax Institute of America.* Columbus, Ohio: National Tax Association.

Taylor, M. 1982. *Community, Anarchy, and Liberty.* New York: Cambridge University Press.

———. 1995. *The Possibility of Cooperation.* New York: Cambridge University Press.

Tilly, C. 1975. *The Formation of National States in Western Europe.* Princeton: Princeton University Press.

———. 1980. *Sanctions and Social Deviance.* New York: Praeger.

———. 1990. *Coercion, Capital, and European States, A.D. 990–1990.* Cambridge, Mass.: Blackwell.

———. 1992. *European Revolutions, 1492–1992.* Oxford: Blackwell.

Tittle, C., and C. Rowe. 1973. "Moral Appeal, Sanction Threat, and Deviance: An Experimental Test." *Social Problems* 20:488–98.

Triest, R., and S. Shefrin. 1992. "Can Brute Deterrence Backfire? Perceptions and Attitudes in Taxpayer Compliance." In *Why People Pay Taxes: Tax Compliance and Enforcement,* ed. J. Slemrod. Ann Arbor: University of Michigan Press.

Trujillo, J. 1998. "La Experiencia Chilena en el Combate a la Evasión." Documento preparado para el Instituto Latinoamericano y del Caribe de Planificación Económica y Social. Available at http://www.sii.cl.

Tversky, A., and D. Kahneman. 1974. "Judgment Under Uncertainty: Heuristics and Biases." *Science* 185:1124–31.

———. 1981. "The Framing of Decisions and the Psychology of Choice." *Science* 211:453–58.

Tyler, T. 1990. *Why People Obey the Law.* New Haven: Yale University Press.

———, ed. 2007. *Legitimacy and Criminal Justice: International Perspectives.* New York: Russell Sage Foundation.

Ullman-Margalit, E. 1977. *The Emergence of Norms.* New York: Oxford University Press.

Ungar, M. 2002. *Elusive Reform: Democracy and the Rule of Law in Latin America.* Boulder, Colo.: L. Rienner.

Unión Panamericana. 1966. *Estudios Sobre la Recaudación Tributaria de América Latina*. New York: Naciones Unidas.

Valenzuela, S. 1998. "La Constitución de 1980 y el Inicio de la Redemocratización en Chile." In *Crisis de Representatividad y Sistemas de Partidos Políticos*, ed. Torcuato di Tella. Buenos Aires: Grupo Editor Latinoamericano.

Waisman, C. 1987. *The Reversal of Development in Argentina*. Princeton: Princeton University Press.

Weber, M. 1946. "The Social Psychology of the World Religion." In *From Max Weber: Essays in Sociology*, trans. and ed. H. Gerth and C. W. Mills. New York: Oxford University Press.

Webley, P., H. Robben, H. Elffers, and D. Hessing. 1991. *Tax Evasion: An Experimental Approach*. New York: Cambridge University Press.

Weingast, B. 1997. "Political Foundations of Democracy and the Rule of Law." *APSR* 91:245–63.

Weisburd, D., S. Wheeler, E. Waring, and N. Bode. 1991. *Crimes of the Middle Class: White Collar Offenders in the Federal Courts*. New Haven: Yale University Press.

Wenzel, M. 2001. "Misperceptions of Social Norms About Tax Compliance: A Field Experiment." Working Paper 8, Australian Taxation Office, Center for Tax System Integrity.

Westat Inc. 1980. *Self-Reported Tax Compliance: A Pilot Survey Report: Prepared for the Internal Revenue Service*. Rockville, Md.: Westat Inc.

Wheeler, S., K. Mann, and A. Sarat. 1988. *Sitting in Judgment: The Sentencing of White-Collar Criminals*. New Haven: Yale University Press.

Witte, A., and D. Woodbury. 1985. "The Effects of Tax Laws and Tax Administration on Tax Compliance: The Case of the U.S. Individual Income Tax." *National Tax Journal* 38:1–14.

Yankelovich, Skelly, and White Inc. 1984. *Taxpayer Attitude Study: Final Report: Public Opinion Survey Prepared for the Public Affairs Division, Internal Revenue Service*. New York: IRS.